THEORY AND PRACTICE FOR WRITING TUTORS

FIRST EDITION

Ethan Krase
Winona State University

Dr. J. Paul Johnson
Winona State University

PEARSON
Prentice
Hall

Upper Saddle River, New Jersey 07458

10 9 8 7 6 5 4 3 2 1

ISBN 10: 0-20-562071-X
ISBN 13: 978-0-20-562071-5

TABLE OF CONTENTS

Preface

Theory and Practice for Writing Tutors is the cumulative result of many years of training new tutors of writing, having evolved out of hundreds of dialogues, readings, and tutorials. The writing center we have both directed has been the locus of most of these conversations, although many too have been motivated by our own teaching and scholarship. Our purpose in writing this book has been to provide new tutors of writing with a thorough preparation to their work. Given that writing tutors might be asked, at any moment, to assist nearly any writer, at almost any level of experience or expertise, with almost any kind of dilemma in the process of completing practically any kind of task, we know that the job can be complex. And more than anything else, this book has evolved out of a desire to prepare new tutors for the variety of situations they may encounter.

Therefore, *Theory and Practice for Writing Tutors* addresses that variety in each of its chapters. It does so in ways, we hope, that will allow new tutors to apply a consistent set of sound tutorial strategies, all grounded in the scholarship of rhetoric and composition, to any scenario they might encounter. The book provides not only general advice for the interpersonal communications new tutors will need in their work, but also specific strategies for addressing the very kinds of questions that writers frequently ask: *How do I get started on this project? How do I develop this argument? How can I make my argument stronger? Are these sentences clear? Why can't I make this make sense? Do I need a comma here?* A tutor's responses to each must be deliberate, and successful tutorial dialogue is dependent upon a sound knowledge of invention strategies, argument structure, and prose style and correctness.

While it may be used in any course or situation aimed at training tutors of writing, *Theory and Practice for Writing Tutors* does not presume prerequisite knowledge of its readers. We assume that most readers will have at least some experience in introductory composition courses, but the book is designed to provide thoughtful instruction for readers from the introductory undergraduate to the graduate level. In the main chapters of the text, we speak directly to our primary audience: the new tutor of writing, one who has just begun, or is soon to begin, assisting others with their writing projects. We aim to provide these readers with knowledge of relevant scholarship, an array of good practices, and multiple opportunities to consider how their developing knowledge can be put to use in different scenarios.

The book consists of seven chapters, each guiding its readers through the processes of meeting and helping writers. For each, we provide strategies for working with writers, dialogues that demonstrate sound practice, and scenarios for further reflection. Chapter one introduces readers to the theory and practice of tutoring, with an overview of the history of the writing center and of the contemporary theories that inform practice there. Chapters two and three explore the dynamics of interpersonal and rhetorical situations that comprise tutoring sessions, both of them providing heuristic approaches to engaging dialogue. Chapters four and five suggest strategies for developing ideas and arguments, respectively, while chapters six and seven address matters of prose style and grammatical correctness. In each of these chapters, we have aimed to provide sound strategy, based on respected scholarship, that will apply well to a variety of situations.

Each chapter concludes with suggestions for related reading. These selected entries are those we recommend as most crucial to the topic of each chapter. Instructors or supervisors may wish to assign some, or most, of these as a part of the training. We've provided complete bibliographic entries so that they can be located through library periodical or catalog circulation, electronic databases, or inter-library loan services. Full citations for each of the texts mentioned in the chapters appear in the list of References.

Because writing tutors often work with students writing on a wide variety of subject matters, our chapters feature a wide range of disciplinary examples. Just as the students who frequent our writing center come to us from courses in nursing, health science, literature, art, composition, philosophy, physics, economics, and other fields, so too do those in our sample dialogues, with tutorial dialogues that illustrate each of the strategies presented. Many of the strategies and scenarios attend explicitly to sessions with English-as-a-Second-Language

(ESL) writers, and others provide multiple opportunities to consider how the tutor can work successfully with students who are more or less experienced, reticent, resistant, and/or able.

With the dialogues that illustrate tutorial practices, we have strived to present examples of tutors who work with their writers successfully. It would have been possible—and in some respects much easier—to illustrate with these examples strategies chosen thoughtlessly or employed poorly. But, our aim in *Theory and Practice for Writing Tutors* is to demonstrate how a tutor can use theoretical knowledge grounded in scholarship to inform successful practice. In our dialogues, then, readers will see tutors making smart choices, employing successful strategies, and responding appropriately to their students' questions.

Each chapter also concludes with a number of case studies for further study, writing, and discussion. These case studies are designed to elicit discussion, promote critical thinking, and foster inductive learning. Long employed for educational purposes, especially in business and medical schools, cases have become increasingly commonplace in higher education, and for good reason. Simply put, cases allow us to relate the concepts we learn to carefully contextualized scenarios that reflect the complexities of real-life situations. Not only do they thus reflect the realities of the situations where tutoring occurs, they also emanate *from* them; nearly all of the cases presented in this book have their origins in our—and our tutors'—own history. As humans are natural storytellers, cases have the virtue of appealing to both the novice and the experienced. New tutors can use the cases as a means of testing out their developing understanding of tutorial dynamics and strategies; the experienced tutor, mentor, or director can relate the case to similar situations and experiences.

New tutors using this book can be assigned to respond in writing to the cases, either by continuing the scenario in written narrative form or by providing a transcript of the extended exchange; or, alternatively, they may be asked to prepare to discuss each case in training or classroom sessions. We have designed the cases to provoke discussion, illustrate strategies, challenge ethics, and test critical thinking abilities. They typically focus specifically on concepts and strategies illustrated in each chapter, and they, thus, increase incrementally in their complexity. Students may, finally, be encouraged to write or present their own cases for discussion with their colleagues.

In discussion of any of these dialogues or case studies, one pedagogical approach to employ is a variation on *What If? What if* the writer had said something else here? *What if* the tutor responded differently? *What if* the writer had been enrolled in Anatomy and Physiology rather than Philosophy, had been a non-native speaker, had been a senior instead of a freshman, or had said the grammar was perfect, not horrible? *What if* the paper had been submitted online or the discussion were taking place in a synchronous (or asynchronous) chat rather than face-to-face? *What if* the writer took exception to, or flatly rejected, the tutor's suggestion? Discussion of any of the dialogues or case studies can be complicated further in this way, thus, helping to prepare tutors for almost any eventuality.

Given this wide variety of dialogues and scenarios—focusing on different kinds of questions posed by different kinds of writers in different kinds of situations featuring different kinds of problems—this book is appropriate for use in nearly any kind of training course, session, seminar, or even self-paced individualized instruction. We have long offered a two-semester hour course for these purposes, but we know that many institutions offer a one-hour course and some a three-hour course; others, we know, build their tutor-training into a pre-semester orientation, weekly staff meetings, and/or assignment sequences. *Theory and Practice for Writing Tutors* is designed to accommodate any of these needs.

For those offering a one-hour course, the complete text can be assigned in full, but with less time spent on the individual cases concluding each chapter. A two-semester-hour course like ours might assign the entire text, a few of the suggested readings, and require students to work through more of the case studies both in class and in written assignments. (We additionally require of students some work with a grammar and usage handbook.) A three-semester-hour course—or one that spans across a full year—can assign the entirety of the text and a number of the suggested readings, many of which are available online through internet archives and full-text subscription databases, and still leave room for an independent research project.

But, even those who do not offer an institutionalized course in tutoring writing can employ *Theory and Practice for Writing Tutors*. A pre-semester orientation session could focus on the first three chapters, with the subsequent chapters assigned as the semester is underway. Those who provide weekly training sessions in the form of staff meetings could assign the individual chapters in advance of the meetings and address the case studies during the meetings themselves. Alternatively, written responses to the cases—in the form of dialogues themselves—could be required of students or presented by them in the meetings. We've found that in both our credit-bearing course and the weekly training sessions that preceded it, asking students to compose their own dialogues in response to the cases has been a consistently productive activity. Last, even when there is no regularized form of tutor-training, *Theory and Practice for Writing Tutors* can be assigned, simply, as a self-paced individualized instruction module, one that could be completed in as little as a half-semester or, at a slower pace, over the course of a full term or year.

Whatever the specifics, though, of each adopter's use of *Theory and Practice for Writing Tutors*, we are optimistic that it can be used in much the same way that we have: to introduce the new tutor of writing to a dynamic field of study and a rewarding educational enterprise. We hope, too, that our readers find it a helpful introduction to tutoring—and one that can inform the myriad paths their work with writers will take in the years to come.

Over the course of conducting the research and preparing the manuscript of *Theory and Practice for Writing Tutors*, we have come to appreciate the contributions of those who've helped us in one way or another:

- The dozens of graduate teaching assistants and undergraduate students who've completed English 324 or an earlier iteration of our training, all of whom have provided purposeful feedback and thought-provoking questions that allowed us to improve our work;

- In particular, former students Jessica McLain, Brigitte Demasi, Dawn Meier, and Bree Malone for contributing individual dialogues and scenarios;

- At Prentice Hall, executive editor Kevin Molloy, assistant editors Dave Nitti and Melissa Casciano, and editorial assistant Tracy Clough for their encouragement and able contributions, and our anonymous reviewers for their careful readings of our work-in-progress;

- University of Tennessee writing center director Kirsten Benson, one of Ethan's early mentors whose warmth, wisdom, and insight were foundational to his later writing center work;

- Former Winona State professors Ann Nichols and Mike Meeker, whose experience and expertise were invaluable to Paul in his formative years as a writing center director;

- Numerous supportive colleagues at Winona State who stepped in at key points to offer insight, resources, or encouragement; in particular, we are grateful for contributions from Holly Shi, Chris Buttram, Ditlev Larsen, and Will Hacker;

- Maybe most importantly, our families—Paul's wife Kay and daughters Madeleine and Veronica—who manage to combine grace, good humor, patience, and charm in a way that made the completion of this book possible; and Ethan's wife Jill and daughter Willa, who light the way each day, making all things achievable, including this book; and new baby Adelaide, who like her sister before her, waited just long enough.

J Paul Johnson and Ethan Krase

1.28.2007

CHAPTER ONE

THE THEORY AND PRACTICE OF TUTORING WRITING

CHAPTER ONE

THE THEORY AND PRACTICE OF TUTORING WRITING

With this book, we aim to introduce you to the rich array of dynamics, resources, and strategies for tutoring writing. We promote an approach to tutoring that we believe to be purposeful, knowledgeable, and, ultimately, *dialogic*—a descriptive adjective we will define and elaborate in detail as we proceed. Our readers, we assume, are those who are interested in tutoring writing—most likely in a writing or learning center, perhaps in support for a course or program, or even in a private arrangement—and who are using this book either as a required part of their training or as an adjunct to it. For many such individuals, tutoring writing is an important stage in the process of becoming a teacher of writing at the elementary, secondary, or even more likely at the postsecondary level. Therefore, most of the scenarios we describe are located in and around the curriculum of postsecondary institutions, and the strategies we advocate are those that have been developed, refined, and tested across years of scholarship in the field of rhetoric and composition studies.

As you will soon learn, one of the ironies of tutoring writing is that while it typically takes place in a quiet dialogue between two individuals mulling together over a work in progress, they are never really "alone," in a sense. The writer works in a context that includes the dynamics of the institution, considerations of genre, format and audience, and a developing understanding of both language and subject. The tutor, meanwhile, normally not only represents a service, program, or institution, but also works in an established tradition of scholarship, a domain of knowledge that can inform much of the work of the tutorial. Over the last century, and more especially its last decades, academic scholarship has increasingly attended to the work of the writing center and tutor. Today, a writing tutor can rely on the keen insights of scholars like Donald Murray, Peter Elbow, Lisa Ede, Andrea Lunsford, Kenneth Bruffee, Muriel Harris, Stephen North, Ilona Leki, Cristina Murphy, Joan Mullin, David Coogan, and Irene Clark. Their work and that of others provides writing tutors an understanding of how writers write. From this scholarship we understand today how writers generate, shape, and support arguments, how they interpret and respond to others, how they imagine and construct their audiences, how they negotiate linguistic boundaries and barriers, how they understand rules and conventions, and even how they punctuate and format their writing.

From our perspective, this scholarship may be a tutor's strongest asset, and as you develop your understanding of the field, you're certain to find your confidence and abilities growing. In a sense, doing so may be the ethical contract to which you're promised: to make use of the resources at hand to develop into the *best* tutor you can. At the same time, tutors (and prospective, or novice tutors) should realize that that they've arrived at this moment by virtue of some promise. If you've been presented an opportunity to tutor other writers, that opportunity is more than likely a result of someone's strong estimation of your abilities or potential. Perhaps you have recently completed a degree in English, writing, or a related field. Perhaps one of your professors has noted your own writing ability or your penchant for articulately explaining ideas and concepts. Perhaps your fondness for language and conversation is seeking an altruistic outlet. Perhaps you're embarking upon this course as a means of finding out if you really have—or can develop—"what it takes" to tutor writing well. Or, perhaps, all of these and more are true, to one extent or another. But whatever it is that brings you to this particular moment, it's likely the result of some ability or proclivity you or others have realized in you. Our advice is to take, and tap, that particular resource, and let it, along with the scholarship and strategies we suggest, shape you into a flexible, experienced, and effective tutor. Your colleagues in this endeavor—the writers you tutor, your peers, your supervisor or mentor—will also help shape the kind of tutor you become, and your daily conversations with them about the matters we raise in this book will be essential to your developing ability to tutor.

FOUNDATIONS AND ASSUMPTIONS

Our introduction to the theory and practice of tutoring writing is one that is rooted in the scholarship of the field and in our experience in and around writing centers. Tutoring writing is, as we have come to envision it, based upon four foundational principles.

Tutoring writing ...

1. ... is grounded in historical tradition and contemporary practice.
2. ... brings together individuals to collaborate through dialogue.
3. ... demands knowledge, vision, and ethics.
4. ... promotes and fosters better writing.

From these, the strategies and suggestions in subsequent chapters follow.

1. Tutoring writing ... is grounded in historical tradition and contemporary practice.

A strong tradition informs the tutoring of writing. What follows is a brief history of the writing tutorial and its governing practices. It is provided not as a self-sufficient overview of the field but as an invitation to its key threads and as an introduction to the more specific contents of the chapters that follow. A few of the works cited here are listed at the end of the chapter as suggestions for further reading, and they may be assigned for supplemental reading by your mentor, professor, or advisor.

While the very earliest incarnations of the writing center may be traced to the instruction of Plato in ancient Greece, a more immediate descendant is the "writing lab" or laboratory.

The notion of such a laboratory was first articulated in the "Dalton Laboratory Plan" that migrated to American education from England in the 1920s. The Dalton Plan aimed to extend the laboratory method of science instruction to other subjects—including writing— with classroom concepts applied in a laboratory of sorts, where both individualized and collaborative instruction were fostered by self-paced plans involving formative feedback (Douglas, 1924; Durkin, 1926; Sheridan, 1926). Though originally imagined as a revolutionary approach to education, one eventual result of the Dalton Plan's implementation was the "writing laboratory" that focused its attention on the remedial student (Moore, 1950). Such laboratories, often required of underprepared and at-risk students, later became known as "writing clinics," a telling coinage fostering a notion of instruction as treatment for an ill condition. As Carino (1992) notes, such metaphors as *lab* and *clinic* adroitly suggest the boundaries which defined these services. In an article that has become something of a watershed for writing center scholarship, "The Idea of a Writing Center," North (1984) concluded that that focus on remediation had regrettably delimited the work of these services to "the grammar and drill center, the fix-it shop, the first aid station" (p. 437).

North's 1984 article, though in one sense fatalistic, in another proved prophetic, as his "Idea of a Writing Center" helped mark a paradigm shift in the broader field of composition studies, where the focus had turned from "product" to "process." This shift, noted both in the research and in the classroom, had many effects, the most salient of which for the writing center were an invitation to look at the process of writing, to bring new attention to stages of invention, drafting, and revising—and to the function of critical readings inherent within these stages. One result was an unprecedented surge of scholarship examining generative heuristics (methods of invention), process protocols, and theoretical explanations of audience and genre—much of which remains vibrant, purposeful, and provocative today. A second is that the work of the *writing center* evolved in the very direction that North had hoped. As the research addressed the processes by which individual writers composed, so too did the writing center provide a means of individualized attention to those same exact processes. Tutors in these centers provided advice and direction for writers of all ability and at virtually any stage of the writing process—and almost always with their work focused more on the individual writer's progress than on generic instructions or abstractions. No longer a remedial service for at-risk students, and no longer labeled as a clinic where the diseased sought treatment, the writing *center* was more aptly named to claim its place at the literal center of higher learning, or, as North claimed, "a kind of physical locus for the idea and ideals of college or university or high school commitment to writing" (p. 446).

These new writing *centers* invited all writers (not just the struggling) to discuss all aspects of writing (not just its rudiments), and they sought for themselves an alignment with writing-across-the-curriculum and faculty development movements in the process. These centers have in recent years continued to evolve into more diverse iterations—sometimes, with multiple sites serving local needs in satellite locations, with discipline-specific branches attending to particular colleges and programs, and online services offering computer-mediated tutorials. Lunsford (1991) and Cooper (1994), describe some of the challenges writing centers have faced more recently as they have continued to broaden their scope, as do edited collections by Mullin and Wallace (1994) and Nelson and Everetz (2001), among others.

Yet no matter *where*, *how*, or *who* you find yourself tutoring, the basic dynamics of the tutorial—that extended conversation over an idea or position—remain in an essential way largely unchanged from Plato's dialogues with his students some 2,500 years ago. As a writing tutor, you will be largely on your own, "on call" so to speak, when your scheduled appointee or drop-in arrives, and you will, for the most part, work quickly to greet your writer, determine a course of action for the session, assess the work-in-progress, and guide your student through the course of the session. In most of these sessions, you'll attend to concerns illustrated by the writer's work: developing evidence for the argument in one session, polishing claims in the next, economizing or varying the sentence style in another. The collegial rapport developed over the course of a session is, our tutors report, both the essence and the delight of tutoring. And it is the dynamics of those tutorial dialogues that comprise the focus of this book.

2. *Tutoring writing ... brings together individuals to collaborate through dialogue.*

If tutoring writing is always a conversational exchange, then it is one that is absolutely *interpersonal* in nature. A good tutor will recognize how important effective interpersonal communication skills are to a successful session. Purposeful body language, listening skills, eye contact, linguistic markers—even appropriately professional attire, demeanor, and affect—all of these play crucial roles in tutorial sessions. They are all, we note, wholly within the tutor's ability to hone with experience. Furthermore, since tutorials can involve participants from very different cultural, educational, and linguistic backgrounds, writing tutors need to be sensitive to *difference* in its varying manifestations: between gender expectations, cultural norms, learning styles, class distinctions, power relationships, and language barriers. Tutors benefit from the experience of working with a wide variety of individuals—and from the challenges and rewards each unique opportunity provides.

That different writers learn, work, and develop differently may today seem to us rather obvious, but it is to the work of second-wave feminist theorists that we owe a major portion of this understanding. Carol Gilligan (1982) contrasted women's moral and psychological development with traditional paradigms of individualism and self-centeredness, and, in the epochal work *Women's Ways of Knowing*, Mary Belenky et al. (1986) articulated the concept of "connected knowing," an essentially feminine and feminist way of knowing dependent more upon experiences and relationships than on objective and isolated abstractions. The work of these and the many feminists who followed in composition studies articulated the importance of interactions between students and peers, of interpersonal dialogue, of negotiated meaning, and of communal experience. The one-to-one teaching of writing that takes place in tutorial conversations might thus well be synonymous with feminist pedagogy.

A second strand of scholarship that has helped tutors understand how different learners compose differently has come from the intersection of composition studies and applied linguistics. Referred to as English as a second language (ESL) or, more broadly, teaching English to speakers of other languages (TESOL), this field of linguistics has demonstrated that students writing in English as a second (or third, or fourth) language bring with them characteristics, expectations, and abilities that differ from those of students writing in their native languages (see Leki, 1992 for a thorough overview of these topics). Scholars of second language writing have explored the ways syntactic and rhetorical differences between other languages and English may present difficulties for ESL writers, a phenomenon referred to as "contrastive rhetoric" (see Connor, 1996 for a careful discussion). However, even as researchers have examined the ways differing cultural and rhetorical expectations can influence both ESL writing and the ways that others are likely to receive that writing, they have also cautioned that contrastive rhetoric by itself cannot explain all ESL writing difficulties (Carson, 1996; Leki, 1992). As Casanave (2002) suggests, learning to write in a second language is an undertaking that is always subject to social, cultural, rhetorical, political, and intellectual forces that can dramatically impact the way the writer approaches individual writing tasks. This thread of scholarship reminds us that ESL writers cannot be understood as intellectually deficient even when their texts evidence multiple usage errors or rhetorical difficulties. Rather, ESL writers are themselves unique individuals whose writing represents an attempt to navigate a discursive space whose practices and preferences are neither particularly intuitive nor explicit. Harris and Silva (1993) provide a thorough overview of the key concerns for tutors of second-language writers in an increasingly multicultural and diverse academy. Together with feminist theory, scholarship of L2 writing has helped writing tutors understand how they can work successfully with a variety of writers.

If we have learned better from applied linguistics and feminist theory how to understand the diverse learning processes writers bring to our tutorials, a more traditional strand of scholarship in rhetoric and composition has focused more broadly on collaborative learning. The fact that the very noun phrase *tutoring writing* implies a collaboration underscores the importance of *collaborative learning theory* to the work of the tutor. While collaborative learning theory has multiple origins in fields as disparate as education, social science, philosophy, psychology, and gender studies, in composition the work of Kenneth Bruffee (1973; 1984; 1986) best articulates the relationship of collaborative learning in writing as related to similar developments in these and other fields. For Bruffee, to teach writing involves demonstrating to students that "they know something only when they can explain it in writing to the satisfaction of the community of their knowledgeable peers" (1984, p.652). Thus collaboration of author, guide, and audience demonstrates a social engagement in intellectual pursuits, and it is made the center of students' educational development. Collaboration is not just merely "group work" but the very foundation of democratic, participatory society, and it is demonstrated often in writing as the effort of individuals to negotiate conflict, construct knowledge, build consensus, and achieve goals. A writing tutor at work, then, is always deeply engaged in and committed to this very kind of collaboration: the tutor questions, challenges, listens, and illustrates, all the while helping the writer to realize goals. This collaboration, requiring dialogue in order to fulfill its aim, presents another irony: though it is *writing* that provides the occasion, it is *speech* that fulfills its goals.

The thinking of Mikhail Bakhtin (1935), the Russian theorist whose broad range of work addressed language, ethics, aesthetics, culture, and literature, is important both to the development of collaborative learning theory in composition studies and to the understanding of tutoring writing we propose here. To suggest that tutoring is dialogic—as we do, early and often—is to emphasize not only that its work is conducted, literally, in dialogue. Rather, we see tutoring as *dialogic* in the sense that it is conducted in a broader, more philosophical, and continual dialogue with other authors, texts, and audiences. As such, the work of the tutorial is not aimed at merely *answering* or *correcting* (both of which would end dialogic exchange), but at *communicating*. For Bakhtin, all language (not just, certainly, the writing tutorial—a speech act he did not specifically address) is essentially *dialogic*: every utterance occurs in the context of what has been said and in anticipation of what might be said in turn. Participants in dialogue must hold themselves responsible for what they contribute and communicate. In this way, we see the work of the writing tutorial as essentially dialogic, both in its form (conversational exchange) and in its purpose (the ethical construction of knowledge). And it is this vision of the tutorial that informs the strategies and scenarios presented here.

Bakhtin's analysis is probably more focused on the context and purpose of speech acts than on the exact words that comprise them, but nonetheless, tutorials may be regarded as one kind of *speech act*, and thus subject to certain conventions. The sociolinguist Dell Hymes (1986) describes several kinds of "speech events" that feature their own set of rules or conventions to which willing participants adhere. A tutorial, a subset of a larger class of educational speech situations, features its own "rules or norms for the use of speech" (p. 56)—just as would a dinner table conversation, a therapy session, yard sale bartering, or formal debate. In recent decades, a number of researchers (Walker and Elias, 1987; MacDonald, 1991; Davis, et al., 1996) have turned considerable attention to the dynamics of tutorial conversations, examining the exchanges between the tutor and writer. Does the tutor dominate the conversation, issue directives, respond to questions? Does the writer process—or ignore—the tutor's comments? Does one interrupt the other? Wait patiently for a response? Indicate frustration, apathy, or ignorance? Praise or thank? In the training for tutors in our writing center, we have long required our apprentice tutors to observe sessions and then conduct a sociolinguistic analysis of the exchange. This self-reflective practice, they've reported consistently, is eye-opening.

3. *Tutoring writing ... demands knowledge, vision, and ethics.*

That tutoring writing is interpersonal, collaborative, and dialogic describes the dynamics of the exchange—the ways in which every tutorial will be necessarily different from the ones preceding and following it. At the same time, these dynamics are not, in and of themselves, the content of tutoring writing. All writing tutors need to build and develop a base of *knowledge* so that they have something concrete to offer their writers besides sparkling conversation. Writing tutors also need *vision* to be able to conduct and sequence effective tutorials: they need to be able to see what is working (and not) in the text, what the writer understands (and does not), and what must necessarily precede and follow in order to develop the writer's abilities. Third, a writing tutor must develop a strong code of *ethics* and be ready for the various challenges to fair play, academic integrity, and personal conduct that tutoring can raise.

The experience or inclination that has brought you to tutoring is, in all likelihood, a strong prospective source of knowledge about writing. Reading and writing both help develop that understanding, as does your coursework. But tutoring poses a greater challenge than does writing itself: a writer might choose correctly where to place a comma or how to order a sentence without stopping to articulate whatever rules or conventions govern the choice. And more frequently than not, experienced writers make such choices without conscious thought. Yet the writing tutor cannot simply rearrange punctuation or syntax without knowing and being able to explain and demonstrate those governing conventions. And, further, rather than simply make changes for the writer, the tutor must do so in a way that will allow the writer to come to an understanding of both the specific example and the governing principle. Simply articulating your own self-knowledge of a rule does not, by itself, suffice for teaching another to understand the same. Facets of rhetoric, logic, and grammar all are employed in writing tutorials, and to proceed without functional knowledge of each is to disadvantage yourself and your writer. As we proceed through the chapters of this book, we offer a number of concepts, examples, and resources for deepening your students' understanding of writing and its subsystems.

A second necessity for a writing tutor is what we call, liberally, *vision*. By this we mean the ability to *see* and *foresee*. As a tutor, you'll need to develop an ability to discern, quickly and accurately, from a writer's work-in-progress what direction your session might take. And you'll need to focus your attention on the clues that writers provide to their own abilities, skills, and/or problems. You'll need also to develop a sense of *foresight*. You may well need to determine quickly—within a matter of seconds, often—what kinds of questions you'll ask, examples you'll provide, directions you'll give, and resources you'll need, and the success of these can depend upon the thoughtful ordering and sequence in which they're undertaken. In a broader context, you may work with the same student on multiple occasions or on a regular schedule, in which case regularly sequenced work towards a specific goal can require you to develop plans for not just the next few minutes but the next few months.

Third, a writing tutor must develop, and hold to, a strong code of *ethics*, one that might well be challenged. If you are employed by your institution you are bound to contractual obligations that govern your work; even if you are tutoring for an unpaid internship or in a private arrangement, you will be subject to codes of academic honesty and integrity, aside from your own personal code of conduct. If you are at work in a school setting, your center may have its own mission statement or published code of expectations. Take these seriously. They were likely written with care—and with *you* in mind. They may provide guidance in difficult situations, and you can work with greater confidence if you know that your choices are ones your institution supports. At some point in your career, tutoring writing will challenge your code of ethics. You may witness writers plagiarizing published sources, purchasing prewritten papers, or pilfering others' ideas. Slightly less egregious challenges to your code of ethics may find you asked to "ghostwrite" parts of a student's paper, choose sides in a grading dispute, or endorse an offensive point of view espoused. In our experience, none of these is widespread, but any writing tutor may be confronted with such a possibility at any time. Throughout the chapters that follow, we discuss and examine some of the kinds of ethical dilemmas writing tutors face.

4. Tutoring writing ... promotes and fosters better writing.

Our other assumptions traced the history and traditions of tutoring writing, articulated the dynamics of tutorial situations and relationships, and presented some of the demands made on tutors by their work and their students. Every bit as important, though, are its *rewards*. Quite simply, tutoring writing serves a greater good by promoting and fostering better writing.

For the students who make good use of the tutoring available to them, the service is invaluable. They can get near-immediate feedback from qualified experts on work-in-progress, find a friendly ear for a vexing dilemma, or seek an answer to a nagging usage or documentation question. They can, in most instances we know of, do so without an appointment—and without spending a nickel. (Even a haircut, we note, requires an appointment these days, not to mention more than a nickel!) Their tutors are typically carefully selected, purposefully trained, thoughtfully supervised, and—in our experience—some of the most patient, helpful, and knowledgeable people around. More importantly, and more empirically verifiable, the research on tutoring writing speaks with considerable unanimity: tutoring is an effective model for improving skills, success, and attitudes, and other studies on tutoring (in general), the conferencing model, and peer response groups—all closely related to tutorial work—are equally encouraging.

If decades ago writing labs were perceived as a kind of educational penalty-box for committers of grammatical infractions, today's writing center instead openly invites all of its institution's writers, including and perhaps especially its very best, to work there on their writing. Many such centers sponsor workshops, speakers, contests, publications, and awards that further promote good writing in their community.

A second means by which tutoring writing promotes and fosters good writing is that writing tutors *themselves* improve. Tutors consistently report that their own tutoring—and the training, reading, and discussion that accompanies it—leads to improvement in their own writing. They develop stronger, more accurate vocabularies for rhetoric, logic, and grammar; they develop a greater array of strategies for development and argumentation; they develop an advanced and articulate understanding of systems for punctuation; they develop a heightened sensitivity to alternate possibilities in approaching a text. Harris (1988) demonstrates the various ways in which these improvements become manifest through tutoring. In short, tutors achieve a higher, more nuanced understanding of the possibilities each writing situation presents.

GETTING STARTED: ADVICE FOR NEW TUTORS

All tutors, then, have a lot to learn and a lot to gain, both for themselves and for their students. Our next chapters invite you into the specifics of tutorial situations and provide resources and strategies for the types of sessions you'll encounter. Before you get started with the next chapter—which invites you to examine the dynamics of particular tutorial sessions—we have three pieces of advice for new tutors: learn the culture, learn the expectations, and learn what tutoring writing is—and is not.

First, we suggest that you try to *learn the prevailing culture* of the place where you'll tutor. There is an identifiable culture at every tutorial site, though it may take some time to discern exactly what constitutes that culture. It's determined by many things: its origins, supervisors, publications, staff, clientele, location, and environs. Your first task when becoming a tutor is to familiarize yourself with this new culture, and this is a task you've probably already begun.

As you prepare to tutor, you should strive to learn about your service's origins and history, discerning what you can about how it has developed or changed over the years. Your immediate supervisor or another mentor may be able to lend some insight not only to its origins but to future goals or directions. You should read carefully what's written about the service in its (and its host institution's) publications, especially in its mission statement, but also in brochures, flyers, or other public announcements. (In particular, as a representative, you may frequently be asked questions that these kinds of documents are written to address.)

This is also an excellent time to start building relationships with your peers. In fact, the writing center we've directed places a keen emphasis in bringing together promising undergraduates, new graduate assistants, and experienced tutors in a community dedicated to the study and teaching of language and writing. It will help to learn about their experiences and aspirations: they may be colleagues and friends for a long time to come. (And it doesn't hurt to have their phone numbers or email addresses in case of an emergency, either.) If you are new to the institution where you tutor, you should also strive to learn about the students you'll be tutoring: whether they're enrolled in special academic programs, for instance, or dedicated to certain vocational goals or obligated to seek tutorial assistance. We advocate too spending a little extra time in the office or building where you'll be tutoring. Give yourself a chance to get familiar with its layout, resources, and technologies, so that when you need to take a phone message, respond to an email, or look up a citation format, you can do so without fuss.

Your second task as you prepare to tutor is to *learn what's expected of you*. You may be contracted to tutor a certain number of hours or students per week. But you will need to know what's expected of you during your "downtime," when no students are present (can you lounge about, or are there other tasks to fulfill?). And, more importantly, you'll need to find out exactly what's expected of you in your tutorial sessions themselves. There may be forms to complete—either on paper or online—or required preliminary or follow-up work besides the content of the tutorial itself. And there are likely privacy concerns or even laws that need to be respected in your work with students.

There may be other expectations as well. You may be, for instance, expected to maintain a certain grade point average or progress towards a degree in order to continue your position. You may undergo an observation or evaluation process designed to assess your tutoring. Some centers may have a dress code, explicit or implied, and some may have a published code of conduct. And there are almost always some additional expectations that come simply with being part of an organization—for instance, occasionally covering another's shift, participating in community service activities, or attending related cultural or social events. We don't advocate pestering your new supervisor with an endless litany of trivial questioning, but from publications and peers—and from the occasional thoughtful question of your supervisor—you can glean a clear sense of what will be expected of you in the months to come.

We conclude with a last caveat as you prepare to tutor. The remaining chapters of this book focus on strategies, concepts, and resources for tutoring writing one-to-one. But as you begin to meet your students and undertake your sessions, we feel compelled to dispel a few myths about tutoring writing, and your last undertaking is to *learn what tutoring is—and what it is not*.

As a writing tutor, your task will be to provide instruction and feedback to writers on their work-in-progress. In the process of doing so, you will often demonstrate conventions, illustrate principles with detailed examples, cite and explain rules, guide your writer through invention or research, and participate in the give-and-take of argument and evidence. But your work should not too closely resemble therapy, editing, proofreading, or classroom teaching, for the following reasons.

Tutoring writing is not therapy. There are superficial similarities between therapy and tutorial sessions, to be sure: both take place in private, focus on the client's needs, are essentially dialogic in nature, feature techniques for nondirective intervention, and aim ultimately at the client's eventual success and self-sufficiency. But a writing tutorial should not invite unnecessary information about a student's psychological or emotional state, and it should never attempt to address such directly. Your job, as a tutor, is to assist the writer with what the student needs to know or understand to *improve his or her writing*. And at times you may need to work to keep your tutorial focused on the matter at hand. But if your student volunteers information that suggests emotional or psychological turmoil, you will need to defer to an appropriate resource—a campus counseling center, for instance—before proceeding further.

Tutoring writing is not editing. Two people, one in a position of some authority and expertise, the other more novice and seeking advice, at work together on a text in need of revisions, is a scenario that can also resemble that of the traditional journalistic or literary editor. Yet while an editor is allowed, and even obligated, to change directly any and even all aspects of the text that can be improved, a writing tutor can almost never do so. A tutor's task is *not* simply to edit. Instead, tutors must respect the writer's ownership of the work-in-progress. The *writer* must be the one to choose and make changes, even if the tutor suggests and explains them—and the underlying principles, conventions, or rules that motivate those changes. To be able to do so, we note, is considerably more complex and time-consuming than simply making corrections, but ultimately a far more empowering course of action.

Tutoring writing is not proofreading. By proofreading, we mean the last-stage, surface-level review and correction of a text for clerical and mechanical errors. Some students, and even some faculty, as we've noted in our experience, mistake the tutoring service for a fix-it shop (see North, 1984), not unlike a while-you-wait digital photo kiosk or fast-food drive-through, where you expect a service to be delivered quickly and thoroughly. By and large, though, writing centers and other tutorial services do not provide this kind of commodity, despite how much certain students might desire it. The "service" a writing tutor provides is more elaborate than a glossy enlargement or king-size combo. As a writing tutor, you will need to resist such requests, explain patiently the kind of work you're expected to do, and wait to see if your student will agree to such. Certainly, proofreading jobs and tasks exist in our world, and they can be of considerable importance—but this kind of review and correction is not the job of the writing tutor.

Tutoring writing is not teaching. Well, tutoring *is* a kind of teaching, to be sure, but it is not a situation where you can expect to plan an hour's worth of "material," proceed directly through your lesson, and conclude as the bell rings. Tutoring differs in that you often don't know *who*, *what*, or *when* you'll be tutoring until you're doing it, requiring incredibly quick decision-making abilities. It is also, generally speaking, considerably more collaborative than most classroom teaching, with both participants contributing considerably to the negotiated content of the session. Furthermore, tutoring sessions tend to focus far more concretely on the writer's developing work and needs than on the teacher/tutor's agenda. And last, the tutorial depends less on the "mastery" of a given subject matter than on progress towards a mutually-agreed upon outcome. This last notion illustrates as well how tutoring writing is very different from subject-matter tutoring in a different discipline: a writing tutor is almost always focused on assisting a student with work-in-progress, where a subject-matter tutor in art history or biology may be devoted far more exclusively to explaining disciplinary concepts.

Neither editing, proofreading, therapy, nor teaching, tutoring writing is its own undertaking, one that, as we've demonstrated here, is steeped in a rich historical tradition, brings together individuals in context through dialogue, demands knowledge, vision, and ethics, and finally, promotes better writing. With a working knowledge of the culture and practices of your local context, and with a developing understanding of what tutoring writing is—and is not—we invite you to get started.

SUGGESTIONS FOR FURTHER READING

Bruffee, Kenneth. (1984). Collaborative learning and the 'conversation of mankind.' *College English 46*, 635-652.

Carino, Peter. (1992). What do we talk about when we talk about our metaphors: A cultural critique of clinic, lab, and center. *The Writing Center Journal 13*, 31-42.

Cooper, Marilyn. (1994). Really useful knowledge: A cultural studies agenda for writing centers. *The Writing Center Journal 14*, 97-111.

Harris, Muriel, and Tony Silva. (1993). Tutoring ESL students: Issues and options. *College Composition and Communication 44*(4), 525-537.

Hymes, Dell. (1986). Models of the interaction of language and social life. In John J. Gumperz and Dell Hymes (Eds.), *Directions in sociolinguistics: The ethnography of communication* (pp. 35-71). Oxford: Basil Blackwell.

Lunsford, Andrea. (1991). Collaboration, control, and the idea of a writing center. *The Writing Center Journal 12*, 3-10.

Moore, Robert H. (1950). The writing clinic and the writing laboratory. *College English 11*, 388-393.

Murphy, Christina. (1991). Writing centers in context: Responding to new educational theory. In Ray Wallace and Jeanne Simpson (Eds.), *The Writing Center: New Directions* (pp. 276-88). New York: Garland.

North, Stephen. (1984). The idea of a writing center. *College English 46*, 433-46.

North, Stephen. (1994). Revisiting "the idea of a writing center." *The Writing Center Journal 15*(1), 7-19.

CASE 1.1: AN UNEXPECTED WELCOME

Your first day of orientation and training to your new appointment working in your institution's writing center has been—so far—a successful one. You've met your colleagues and supervisor, spent some time where you'll be working, discussed the mission statement, and even heard some pep talks from the senior staff.

After the meetings conclude, you're lingering for a few minutes while you browse the bookshelves and finish your coffee. The telephone rings, just loud enough to surprise you into spilling a few drops of coffee onto the carpet. You could let the caller reach voicemail, you think, but instead you elect to answer.

The voice on the other end is formal, you think, perhaps just a bit overly so. "Good afternoon. My name is Professor Michaels, and I am new to the Biology department this year. I am trying to learn about the services the institution offers and wish to know more about your Writing Center. Do you have a minute to answer some of my questions?"

Somehow, you think, that coffee stain appears just a bit larger than it was only a few seconds ago. "Of course," you answer, introducing yourself, still eager to make a good first impression. "How can I help you?"

During the course of the conversation, Professor Michaels asks the following questions. Based on your understanding of your institution's mission statement, guides, materials, and accepted practices, determine how you would address his questions to the best of your ability.

- *Tell me about how this place works. Who works there, and what expertise or training do they have?*
- *Will your staff be able to assist with short laboratory and more formal scientific reports?*
- *I understand that many students at this institution are unable to write. How can you help them?*

- *Do you proofread and edit students' papers for them?*

- *I refuse to accept student papers with more than three grammatical errors in them. Can you ensure that they'll meet my standards?*

- *I'd like to require that all papers written for my class be proofread by the Writing Center. Will that be a problem?*

CASE 1.2: YOUR FIRST SESSION

Having just completed your first week of orientation—and the first chapter of the required reading for your seminar introducing the theory and practice of tutoring writing—you're feeling ready for your work to begin. But you and the other new tutors will need to wait until the official opening of the tutoring center, scheduled to take place just after the first week's open house concludes, one week from today.

After today's training session concludes, you take a minute to check e-mail before getting a head start on your other coursework, and in it, you find this message.

From: Jenny L.

Re: Remember me?

Hi, I hope you remember me—your friend Charlie's sister, Jenny. I'm a freshman at your school now. Charlie told me he hadn't talked to you for a year but heard you were doing so well you were going to be a tutor in the writing center this year. That's awesome. He said you always helped him with his writing in high school. Well, you know Charlie—he'd need it!

Maybe you can help me out a bit this year. Actually, I'm kind of nervous about college. You know the horror stories! Anyway, we all had to read this book over summer for our freshman seminar, and when we discussed in orientation, it sounded like fifteen kids had read fifteen different books! I thought I understood it until we started discussing it, anyway. And we have to have a paper ready on it in two weeks! Five pages, no sources allowed, and an "analytical thesis" with "textual references" and "parenthetical citations," whatever that means!

I kind of know what I want to write about for my paper but I'd like to get some real help as soon as I can. Are you guys open for business? Can I make an appointment or something? Please let me know what to do!

Based on your first weeks' reading and discussions, determine how you would address Jenny's questions and assist her with her paper to the best of your ability. It may help to select a specific book for her assignment and to extend the exchange from email to a face-to-face tutorial. Last, you may want to consider how you might respond to Jenny if, during your subsequent meeting, she volunteered any or all of the following:

- *I'm sorry I have no idea what to write! The other kids all seem like they know what they're doing.*

- *Now I really wish I'd read that book more closely. Do you think my professor will know if I don't understand it?*

- *Is it okay just to summarize what all the other students said?*

- *It seems like we just started the term and I'm already overwhelmed. Are all the writing assignments this hard?*

- *So what exactly IS an "analytical thesis," anyway? And what are we supposed to have for references?*

CASE 1.3: "CAN YOU EDIT THIS FOR ME?"

No sooner does the door open on the first day of business than does a student burst in with a simple question: "Can you edit this for me?" As you listen to Crystal's story, you learn that she is resubmitting a capstone project for her major, one which was not accepted by her advisor, in no small part because of its poor proofreading and editing. With her graduation delayed by a semester and an internship waiting on its completion, Crystal now feels in dire need. "This project is due at the end of the week," she says, "and if it's not written perfectly I'm not going to graduate at all." She sets down her laptop, opens up what must surely be at least a forty-page document, and pronounces: "As long as you can make sure it's written right, I think I'll be okay, though. How long will this take?"

Based on your first weeks' reading and discussions, determine how you would address Crystal's questions. Would you edit her paper? If not, what would you do to help her reach her goals?

CHAPTER TWO

SESSION DYNAMICS AND DIALOGUE

CHAPTER TWO

SESSION DYNAMICS AND DIALOGUE

Writing tutors can safely count on the fact that their work will always be subject to a wide range of variables. In addition to demographics like tutor and student age, ethnicity, class, and education, a host of other variables—the subject matter of the student's paper, the rhetorical context, the amount of time allotted, the length of the paper, the clarity of the student's understanding of the assignment, the student's ability and interest, and the way the tutor's and student's personalities mesh—all factor into how the tutorial will unfold. With so many variables in play, it is important to establish a constructive and stable direction as the tutorial begins. Building rapport with the student, engaging the dialogue, and defining the roles, the task, and the agenda—these will all ideally happen in the first few minutes. While trouble at the start of a tutorial in any of these areas does not guarantee failure (in fact, some very good tutorials sometimes come together from beginnings that look less than auspicious), it does hold true that a good start to a tutorial increases the likelihood of having productive dialogue throughout the session. In this chapter, we offer strategies that we have found tutors can use to make those first minutes—when the session dynamics are at their most variable and unpredictable—consistently and reliably purposeful.

BUILDING RAPPORT

At the core of all tutorial work is the relationship that the tutor and student establish with one another. When it's working well, this relationship is one where there are mutual feelings of respect, safety, and trust. However, as Christina Murphy (1989) points out in an essay entitled "Freud and the Writing Center: The Psychoanalytics of Tutoring Well," very often students enter tutoring contexts with fair measures of "anxiety, self-doubt, negative cognition, and procrastination that only intensify an already difficult situation" (p. 17). That these feelings are present for many student writers shouldn't be surprising, especially since, as anyone who has ever written anything of substance is well aware, producing effective prose is slow, labor-intensive, difficult work that regularly tests one's self-confidence. Pointing towards some of the psychic fallout the difficulty of writing can have on students, Murphy notes that students entering a tutorial may express thoughts like the following:

- *I know you're going to tear this paper to shreds, but here goes.*

- *I've never been able to write. This is hopeless.*

- *I know you can't help me, but I thought I'd try the writing center anyway.*

- *This teacher gives dumb assignments. If he'd just give me something I could write about, I know I'd do better.*

- *I've always made A's in English in high school, so I know I should be making A's in college, too.*

- *Can you help me with this paper? It's due at 2:00.*

Though certainly not all students make remarks betraying low self-esteem, defensiveness, or self-defeatism, it is not uncommon for thoughts like these to remain unvoiced. The question for new and developing tutors, then, concerns how to use the first few minutes of a tutorial to reduce stress, overcome doubt, and begin to engender the respect, safety, and trust that are necessary for improvement.

To illustrate some of the tutor's responsibilities during the opening minutes of a writing tutorial, think for a moment about what it's like to feel unwell as you walk into a doctor's office. Very likely you are hoping for a specific list of things to happen as you meet the doctor: you want to be welcomed and introduced, you want to feel like you have the doctor's undivided attention, you want the doctor to be professional, courteous, and intelligent, and you probably also want some sort of indication that whatever is ailing you is something the doctor knows how to handle. In a very real sense, you want to feel comfortable. What is especially noteworthy in this context is that it is the doctor who bears the responsibility for initiating your comfort.

Although, as Carino (1992) has suggested, the tutorial-as-medicine metaphor has its problems (after all, students are not "sick" writers that tutors can somehow "cure"), there are important similarities between what ideally occurs in the first few minutes in each setting. When a student comes in to a writing center, the onus is largely on the tutor to help that student feel comfortable so that productive work can follow. After all, for the majority of the students who visit writing centers, it is difficult to work well without first feeling welcomed into the space, listened to by the tutor, confident in the tutor's expertise, and assured that there is hope for improvement. While it is true that this process of supporting, knowing, and hearing students continues throughout a writing tutorial, when used effectively the opening minutes can lay the groundwork for effective tutoring.

To contextualize how tutors can build workable relationships with students, visualize for a moment a new student coming into a university writing center. The student walks in, and, unless she[1] is a frequent customer, she probably lingers near the doorway, waiting for the things that happen in a writing center to start happening. Maybe feeling slightly nervous or unsure of herself, when approached she says something about wanting to work with a tutor or, perhaps more likely, needing someone to check her paper. In a very real sense, the student

---

[1] Throughout this book we alternate back and forth between female and male pronouns rather than relying on somewhat unwieldy constructions like "he or she" and "him or her." Our decision to alternate pronoun usage stems from an interest in increasing the text's readability while also maintaining gender inclusivity.

has held up her end of things: she has entered the workspace and expressed a desire for help. It is up to the tutor to take the tutorial from this rather spare beginning to a place where the student can go about the complicated and difficult business of improving as a writer.

As an aside, we should mention here that in some sites there will be a receptionist who takes incoming students through a brief introduction and a short sign-in process. In many settings, however, introductions and paperwork fall under the responsibility of the individual tutor. Regardless of whether or not a receptionist makes the initial contact with the student, tutors still need to pay attention to how they approach the students with whom they work.

Returning now to that student lingering near the doorway, we should note that the tutor's approach does not have to be complicated. A fairly standard way to break the ice includes a smile, a greeting followed by a brief introduction, an invitation to have a seat, and a minute of small talk, usually about the course the student is taking. As tutors gain experience and comfort with their work, they usually develop a stable routine for how to approach students. The goal is simply to get introduced, release the bit of tension that often accompanies students as they bring their work to another person's eyes, and open up the dialogue that is at the core of skilled tutoring.

The following dialogue between Will (tutor) and Sue (student) shows an example of a tutor breaking the ice and building rapport with a student. As you read the dialogue, ask yourself what Will is trying to do with his contributions to the conversation.

Will: Hi, welcome to the writing center. How can I help you?

Sue: I was wondering if I could get someone to look at my paper?

Will: I'd be happy to take a look. My name is Will. Why don't we have a seat?

Sue: Sounds good. I'm Sue.

Will: Good to meet you. [as they're sitting down] So, what class is this paper for?

Sue: History 121.

Will: I remember my history class from few years ago. Interesting class. So, how's it going so far?

Sue: Not good.

Will:	What seems to be the trouble?
Sue:	There's a lot of homework and I'm behind.
Will:	Really?
Sue:	Yeah, I've got Dr. Lancaster. He's all right, but I'm having a hard time keeping everything straight, the names and dates.
Will:	I sometimes found that hard too.
Sue:	Yeah, and there's also tons of reading and a paper due every week.
Will:	Sounds like a lot of work.
Sue:	Yeah, I didn't do well on my first paper. History really isn't my thing.
Will:	What'd the professor say?
Sue:	He said I needed to explain my ideas more and to clean up my grammar, commas and stuff. Can you help with that?
Will:	I think we can definitely do something about these things. But first, why don't you tell me about the assignment you're working on.
Sue:	We're supposed to write 1000 words on the Cold War.
Will:	Did your professor give you an assignment sheet?
Sue:	Yeah, I've got it here somewhere. Just a sec. [*Retrieves assignment sheet*]

Now that Will and Sue are on their way, let's stop and think carefully about what happened in the first couple minutes. As part of the icebreaking, Will welcomes Sue and introduces himself. He invites her to sit (likely gesturing to the chair he'd like her to take) and asks about the class she is in and her work in it up to this point. He learns, among other things, that Sue is having a difficult time keeping up, that she was disappointed with her grade on her first paper, and that she understands herself to be struggling with elaboration and grammatical conventions.

Will establishes some common ground with Sue when he indicates that he too has taken a history course. It is also good that Will gets Sue talking a bit, inviting her to offer information about her work and, in the process, setting a tone where both of them will be taking an active verbal role in the tutorial. Will ends the period of introduction by asking Sue for an assignment sheet, signaling a movement into the specifics of the tutorial. Though Will should continue to improve his rapport with Sue as the tutorial progresses, in the opening minutes he has done what he can to alleviate Sue's anxiety and help make her comfortable and receptive to the teaching that is about to take place.

ENGAGING DIALOGUE

Because tutoring writing invariably revolves around the kind and quality of the relationship tutor and student co-create, it is well worth our time to pause and consider how verbal and physical interactions contribute to that relationship. Engaging another in dialogue is something of an art, to be sure, one that can be developed with careful listening skills, clear explanations and questioning strategies, and an awareness of appropriate body language and proxemics (the amount of physical space between two people as they communicate).

Listening Strategies. There is much you can do as a tutor to listen carefully—and to communicate to the student that you *are* listening carefully. You can, for instance, signal your receptiveness by leaning forward, ignoring distractions, communicating responsively (even with an occasional silent nod or *mm-hmmm*), and avoiding interrupting, even for the purposes of clarification. It helps to allow a short period of silence when your student has finished; doing so provides your student an opportunity for reflection, and it helps communicate that you value what's being said. As your student talks, take notice of how your student delivers his message: you might note expressions, hedges, disclaimers, and even nonverbal cues that provide insight. Then, when you do respond, you can try to do so in the context of the student's experience, as much as is possible. For some tutors, responding empathetically—with messages as simple as "Yes, I struggle with that, too," or "I know a lot of students say the same thing"—helps to show students they're not alone in their efforts.

Clear Questions and Explanations. Your goal in a session is to stimulate critical thinking and engage dialogue. Rather than spout rapid-fire handbook-style answers, you can foster better dialogue by encouraging students to answer their own questions and by repeating their answers back to them in your own words. When you ask questions of your students, try to make them brief but specific. Be especially cautious of overwhelming your student with too many questions. You may also find it useful to sequence your questions from simple to the more complex, moving from questions that require a simple answer towards those that are more open-ended, requiring fuller, more thoughtful responses. It helps, even when checking for student's understanding, to punctuate your questions clearly—"hitting the question mark," one of our tutors liked to say, and then waiting silently for a response, resisting the temptation to answer your own question. The explanations you give can also go a long way to foster engaged dialogue. If these sound condescending or seem circuitous, you'll see their negative results quickly. Try to make explanations clear and concise, and then provide an appropriate example or demonstration. Once you've done so, you can also ask students to provide some of their own. In general, whenever it seems possible, it works better to model a useful behavior than to give a long-winded explanation, and it may help to ask the student to perform a task that will help you assess her understanding of the concept. For instance, when demonstrating a grammatical rule or rhetorical convention, don't blather at length: instead, explain clearly, provide an example or two, then ask your student to do the same.

Proxemics. The seating arrangement can play a sizable role in tutor/student dynamics. In most settings, the tutor will be choosing between either sitting next to or across from the student. While we have seen both of these seating arrangements work well, it's useful to think carefully about their potential effect on the tutor/student interaction.

Unless it is handled quite carefully, sitting across from students can tend to create challenges. To see how, picture a Peanuts comic strip where Charlie Brown sits miserably across from Lucy as psychiatrist, leaning back as she dispenses advice. The doctor is in.

Lucy's posture, her positioning behind the table, the arch way she looks off into the distance as she interacts with Charlie Brown—these all send the message that she and Charlie Brown are not equals. Importantly, neither the potential soundness of Lucy's advice nor the goodness of her intentions really matter. By the hangdog look on Charlie Brown's face, we know that he feels poorly, is not listening carefully, and just wants his visit to the neighborhood psychiatrist to be over. That'll be five cents.

In the context of a writing tutorial, we might take a lesson from Lucy and Charlie Brown. For starters, it probably goes without saying that if tutors adopt Lucy's persona—brash, condescending, aloof—they aren't likely to build the sort of respect and trust that motivates sound tutoring. In terms of proxemics, the lesson may be a bit more subtle. When tutors sit across from students, the nonverbal message students may receive is that the tutor-as-doctor is "in." And furthermore, this message comes with some baggage: the tutor will need to counteract the idea that she has the answers. She may also need to work harder to convey that the student shoulders the responsibility for improvement. From a purely practical standpoint, because of their physical locations the tutor and student cannot look at the text together without craning their necks. While some tutors manage well the across-the-table set-up, it requires deft maneuvering on the part of the tutor. Not only must the tutor continually pass the student's paper back and forth across the table but she must also communicate that the student owns the paper and bears the responsibility for working towards a solution to his writing dilemmas. And, importantly, both of these become difficult at those times when the paper moves out of the student's hands so that the tutor can read and analyze it.

The other common option—tutor and student sitting side-by-side—can send a very different nonverbal message. Looking back to the dialogue between Will and Sue, if they sit next to one another a number of positive things can happen. For one, they can both easily look at the paper as they work through it. As Will addresses various aspects of the paper, he can point to specific passages he would like Sue to read aloud, ask questions about individual phrases or sentences, and more quickly pinpoint areas to attend to than he could if the two were passing the paper back and forth across the table.

Sue, as the author, never has the paper go out from under her eyes, reinforcing the idea that the paper is hers and that she bears the responsibility for improving it. It helps, then, that when seated next to her tutor she can easily re-read what she has written, point to passages she wants to ask about, pencil in corrections and revisions, and, either on her own or at Will's suggestion, write notes in the margins of things she would like to remember to do once she is on her own and revising the paper.

One of the other benefits of side-by-side seating is that it strengthens the nonverbal message that the tutor and student are working as equals well outside of the sort of hierarchy that the student might encounter if she were meeting her professor. Thus, the student can disagree with the tutor, offer insights and ideas that might be controversial, and ask questions that she may feel are ignorant or simple—things she would probably be less likely to do were she sitting down with the person who would be grading her work.

Body language. Although it is probably not necessary here to catalogue all of the body language that characterizes effective tutoring, a few words on the subject are warranted. Regardless of where the tutor and student sit, the nonverbal communication coming from the tutor ought to convey respect, attentiveness, and sincerity. Nodding as the student talks, making regular eye-contact, smiling, leaning forward slightly—all of these let the student know that the tutor is focused, ready, and interested in helping the student improve. If a student doesn't know that his tutor is focused, ready, and interested, there's little reason for him to maintain high levels of focus, readiness, and interest as the tutorial progresses.

Even as they monitor their own body language, tutors also need to be aware of the nonverbal signals students are sending. If, for example, a student is leaning back in the chair with his hands in his lap, the tutor may need to backtrack in the tutorial and try again to invite the student into a space where he feels ready to engage the text. When a student begins glancing at the clock, it may be time to ask her if she feels ready to tackle the paper on her own for a while. Perhaps a student becomes overly friendly, touching the tutor's arm or patting a knee, prompting the tutor to convey nonverbally that a line has been crossed, maybe just by shifting the chair over slightly or leaning away a bit. Writing tutorials are always a meeting of cognition and human interaction. Part of the tutor's job, then, is working to find the right tone for the interaction—one where both the student and the tutor are comfortable and feel respected as they get down to work. Both the verbal and the non-verbal signals that the tutor sends and receives contribute to the dialogue, and engaging your students in a focused, purposeful conversation about their work-in-progress will help you establish, monitor, and maintain a desirable tone.

.

DEFINING ROLES

Aside from building rapport and engaging dialogue the first minutes of any tutorial also define—intentionally or otherwise—how the roles are determined and how the tutorial will progress. At first glance, role definition might appear obvious: the tutor will assist the student. However, for this assistance to be lasting and meaningful, the tutor needs to help the student understand the sort of role each will play because the degree to which both tutor and student understand their roles goes a long way towards determining just how effectively they can work together.

Tutors need to understand three important points about their role upfront: 1) it is not the tutor's job to lecture to the student on what they know about writing; 2) it is not the tutor's job to edit student papers; and 3) it is not the tutor's job to tell students how to edit their papers. In fact, the latter is simply an inefficient version of the former.

Interestingly, lecturing, editing, and telling students how to edit can be quite tempting to tutors because these approaches sometimes feel like the right thing to do. In the opening paragraph of an article on what he refers to as "minimalist tutoring," Jeff Brooks (1991) addresses this temptation to edit student papers in what he refers to as "a writing center worst case scenario":

> A student comes in with a draft of a paper. It is reasonably well-written and is on a subject in which you have both expertise and interest. You point out the mechanical errors and suggest a number of improvements that could be made in the paper's organization; the student agrees and makes the changes. You supply some factual information that will strengthen the paper; the student incorporates it. You work hard, enjoy yourself, and when the student leaves, the paper is much improved. A week later, the student returns to the writing center to see you: "I got an A! Thanks for all your help!" (p. 1)

Brooks is right: this is a worst-case scenario, and the reason why is foundational to a tutor's understanding of his role. The problem in Brooks's scenario is that the only real lesson the student has learned is that the way to surmount writing difficulties is to give papers to a writing tutor. As Brooks put it, "when you 'improve' a student's paper, you haven't been a tutor at all; you've been an editor" (p. 2). And, if tutoring writing were synonymous with copyediting, there would be little reason for the student to even be present for a "tutorial"; like a dry cleaner's, a writing center could be little more than a place where students drop off their work, returning an hour later to pick it up.

Interestingly, the language that students and tutors use sometimes reinforces the notion that tutoring "equals" editing. When students come to writing centers, they may very much be hoping that a tutor will "fix" their paper. This desire to have a paper "fixed" by a tutor will sometimes be implicit—and sometimes explicit—in the language they use to interact with one another. In the following dialogue, the student, Dean, operates under the assumption that the tutor, Paige, will provide solutions to his problems.

Dean: Hi, I was wondering if I could get someone to go over my paper.
Paige: Sure thing. Why don't we have a seat?
Dean: I've never been here before, but my roommate said you guys could help me fix this [gesturing to paper].
Paige: I think we can probably help you improve it.
Dean: Good, because right now it's pretty hopeless. I'm about ready to give up and just turn it in.

Paige: Sounds like you're frustrated with it. Why don't you tell me about your assignment?

Dean: It's a reaction paper to a film we saw in my sociology class. It was that Michael Moore movie *Bowling for Columbine*. Have you seen it?

Paige: Yeah, I liked it.

Dean: Good. I hope you have better ideas about it than I do.

Paige: I'm sure you have some great ideas. Can you tell me more about the assignment? Or, better, do you have an assignment sheet?

Dean: Yep, it's right here.

Paige: [reading the assignment sheet] Okay, it says here that you need to discuss how the film challenges social norms. What do you think that means?

Dean: Well, I don't really know. I guess we're supposed to say what we think the point of the movie was? I was actually hoping you could explain it to me.

Paige: I can work with you on it. Why don't you just tell me what you've got so far?

Dean: Well, I've got two pages, but they're all messed up. I need help fixing the paragraphs so they flow better. I also need someone to check the grammar. Oh, and can you also make sure the citations are correct?

Note Dean's language, the way he references fixing and checking. From what he says it's apparent that in his mind bringing his paper into a writing center is akin to taking his car to the mechanic: just as a mechanic will diagnose and repair a leaky fuel line, so too will a tutor figure out why the paper does not "flow" and then offer a strategy for improvement. And, like a mechanic taking a quick look at an oil filter, as a bonus, the tutor will check the grammar and citations as well. Note too that Dean's language seems to remove him from the process, placing the burden of improving the paper onto his tutor.

It is not at all uncommon for students to think of tutors and tutorials as fix-its. But part of a tutor's job is to educate the student about how the tutorial will work, what it will feel like, and why it needs to be this way. Although Paige's contributions to the conversation point towards her understanding that Dean will need to take the initiative with his paper, before she proceeds any further she needs to help Dean understand what roles the two of them will play.

Before we get to how a tutor can do this for a student like Dean, it is important to be precise with regard to what the tutor's role should be. Stephen North (1984) argued that "In a writing center the object is to make sure that writers, and not necessarily their texts, are what get changed by instruction" (p. 438). Or, as North (1982) put it earlier in what has become one of the more oft-quoted sentences in composition scholarship: "our job is to produce better writers, not just better writing" (p. 439). Brooks (1991) concurs, contending that "a writing teacher or tutor cannot and should not expect to make student papers 'better'; that is neither our obligation, nor is it a realistic goal" (p. 2).

What both North and Brooks suggest, and we hope to reinforce, is that writing tutorials need to be about helping writers learn how to meet the demands of the specific writing challenges they face. For this to happen, the focus must extend beyond the individual paper to include the writer, helping him learn to think reflectively and recursively about his work and the various syntactic and rhetorical shapes it might productively take. In their best incarnations, then, writing tutorials are sites where tutor and student co-create a learning environment from which the student can begin to make inferences about how to more accurately and consistently meet the rhetorical demands of specific academic discourse communities. Hence, the focus must be on changing the writer so that he gains greater understanding of and control over the discursive practices of academic writing.

For these reasons, at the outset of each writing tutorial the tutor can be quite plain about what she will and will not do. We will return to Dean and Paige's interaction to see an example of how a tutor can define her own role and also the student's role so that the focus is more squarely on helping the student take ownership of his progress as a writer and less on simply getting a paper ready to submit.

> Dean: Oh, and can you also make sure the citations are correct?
>
> Paige: We can certainly work on citations. In fact, we can work on whatever you'd like us too. However, I should say first that I won't just edit your paper for you. It's your paper, and for that reason our time is best spent helping you understand some of the areas where you think it has problems and what options you have for addressing those problems.
>
> Dean: What do you mean?

Paige: Well, if we focus on teaching you how to make improvements—rather than me just doing it for you—then the next time you're writing you will have more ability to do these things yourself.

Dean: So, you're not going to fix my paper?

Paige: No, I'm not. If you're going to improve your writing, you will need to be the one who improves your paper. What I will do is ask questions that will help you think through some of the options you have and then make better decisions about your writing.

Dean: Okay, if you say so, I'll give it a try.

As part of the role-definition, the tutor must ensure that she and the student enter their work sharing the understanding that the student will be in control of the paper. The tutor's role is to frame the conversation in such a way as to allow the student to make better, clearer decisions about the writing, in the process drafting a paper that is more satisfactory. The tutor can also make a pitch for the long-term benefits of the tutorial: the student will begin to learn how to do some of the things that have perplexed him in the past, in the process moving closer to a point when meeting with a tutor would involve other, presumably more nuanced, sorts of writing issues.

ASSESSING THE TASK

Another of the tutor's major responsibilities at the outset of a writing tutorial is assessing the task—and in doing so, not only the task as it's been *represented* (by, say, the professor or some other person or agency), but also as it's been *understood* by the student. And the two (representation and understanding) do not always perfectly coincide. Though task assessment may sometimes be a simple matter, in actuality the rhetorical assessment required of tutors can be quite complex. For this reason, we provide a more comprehensive perspective on assessing rhetorical dynamics in chapter three. But before we study the dynamics of rhetorical situations more carefully, we suggest that in the first minutes of a tutorial you will need to discern answers to number of questions:

1) Rhetorically speaking, what is the student's understanding of the writing task?

2) Based on the information you can gather, what did the student's professor ask him to do?

3) Are the student's and professor's representations of the rhetorical task congruent with one another?

4) If they are, in his own words what exactly does the student understand the assignment to be asking him to do? Does this understanding feel sufficiently deep and specific?

5) If the student's understanding of the rhetorical situation is at odds with what the professor assigned, how can the tutorial bring the student's understanding into alignment with the professor's task?

Only after tutors have answers to these questions can the tutorial begin the other major area of task assessment: the student's actual paper. Here, the tutor needs to assess the paper's strengths and weaknesses and then offer some options for how the student might wish to spend the remainder of the tutorial. All told, that's quite a lot for tutors to do, and, if it's not done correctly, the tutor runs the risk of offering help that will result in a paper that fails to fulfill the requirements of the assignment.

Assessing student understanding of the assignment. The multi-level assessment can begin with the tutor simply asking the student about the assignment, something that is easy enough to work into the icebreaking period of the tutorial: "So, what are you working on here today?" usually suffices. When prompted by their tutors, some students will offer lucid articulations of their rhetorical task:

- *I have to write a descriptive essay that focuses on a significant event from my childhood and say how it is like or unlike how childhood is portrayed in Olive Ann Burns's book* Cold Sassy Tree.

- *It's an essay for my journalism class explaining how the letters to the editor in the* New York Times *and* USA Today *differ in terms of political slant, based on one week's worth of letters.*

- *I'm writing an essay that analyzes the political and philosophical differences between Mao Zedong and Chiang Kai-shek.*

While these are reasonably clear and specific representations of the task, sometimes students offer task representations that are less well defined:

- *We're supposed to write an informative essay about that book* Freakonomics.
- *It's a formal analysis of Percy Shelley's poem "Ozymandias."*
- *My professor wants us to do an essay on the book and movie versions of* Friday Night Lights.

There are also times when students are less able to articulate clearly and specifically what it is that they have been asked to do:

- *We're just supposed to say how we feel about this one essay we had to read.*
- *I'm not exactly sure what I'm supposed to do. I know we have to take a side on an issue and back it up with quotes.*
- *He just said to write five pages on the causes of global poverty.*
- *I don't know. I was hoping you could help me figure out what I'm supposed to do.*

Regardless of how the student answers the tutor's question about the assignment, whenever possible the tutor will want to cross-reference the student's verbal description with written instructions from the student's professor. For this reason, an absolute staple of the writing tutorial is the tutor's request for the student's professor's assignment sheet, a piece of paper on which the professor has articulated expectations for the writing project. There will certainly be times when students do not have assignment sheets with them or, unfortunately, when the professor has not supplied an assignment sheet or has supplied one that is itself vague and unclear. In these instances (and there will be some), in the immediate context the tutor's only real option is to use what the student can provide to try to flesh out a clearer, more specific articulation of the rhetorical task. If enough time permits, the tutor can suggest that the student request additional information about the assignment; in these cases, the tutor might help the student draw up a list of specific questions about the task that the student can use when consulting with the professor.

When a student does have an assignment sheet—and by publicizing the need for students to bring them to their tutorials writing centers can help ensure that this will happen regularly—the tutor should ask to see it. After reading what the professor has asked the student to write, the tutor can proceed directly into the tutorial in those cases where the student's verbal and professor's written descriptions are in comfortable accord with one another. It also does not hurt to ask a couple questions of the student to make sure that the student's understanding extends beyond a single cogent articulation.

More often, as in the case of the second group of quotes listed above, students will represent rhetorical tasks incompletely, shortening or simplifying the assignment into something that feels manageable. Here, the tutor's job is to help the student to move her understanding closer to the professor's actual assignment. Other times, students will have little idea of what they are supposed to do. Some admit this up front, others express anger at the professor about it ("No one knows what we're supposed to write!"), and still others are unaware of just how incompletely they understand the rhetorical situation. As with students who are able to only partially represent the task, the tutor's first job is to assist the student in defining the assignment's parameters. To show how a tutor can help a student understand the rhetorical situation, we'll return to our tutor Will and his student Sue, who left off with Sue retrieving her professor's assignment sheet:

Will: Why don't you tell me about the assignment you're working on.

Sue: We're supposed to write 1000 words on the Cold War.

Will: Did your professor give you an assignment sheet?

Sue: Yeah, I've got it here somewhere. Just a sec. [Retrieves assignment sheet]

Will: [after reading the assignment sheet] It says here that you're supposed to discuss the Cold War in terms of one of the following: economic, social, or ideological impact on the middle class. So, does that mean you choose one of these?

Sue: Yeah. We just choose one.

Will: What did you choose?

Sue: Ideological.

Will: What do you think your professor means by "discuss the Cold War in terms of ideological impact on the middle class"?

Sue: Well, I think he wants us to say how the Cold War affected people's thinking.

Will: Thinking about what?

Sue: Maybe about America?

Will: What do you mean?

Sue: Well, the Cold War and the way it was presented by the media made people scared all the time. There was so much paranoia.

Will: So, can you say how this is an ideological impact?

Sue: Hmmm, well it's about how people think, how they view the world.

Will: That's true, but what's the ideological impact there?

Sue: Well, before the Cold War really started, it seems that Americans were feeling pretty safe and secure. But, all that changed when the Cold War got going. People were starting to think that maybe America was going to go to war again, only not like the Korean War. It'd be much bigger. And that made the middle class—well, all Americans, but the middle class especially—really afraid because their memory of World War II was still fresh. So, their identity, who they thought they were as Americans changed as they became afraid of what lay ahead.

Will: That's interesting. So, if you're going to discuss the ideological impact—this alteration in thinking—what of what you just said do you need to include?

Sue: I need to say what the middle class was like before the Cold War and then say how they changed.

Will: I think you're right. Have you done that in your paper?

Sue: Well, I don't think I said much about how people were before the Cold War. I just talked about how it frightened people, and what they thought could happen. I'm going to need to add that part about what they were like before the Cold War really got going.

Will: Sounds like a smart addition. Do you have any questions about the assignment? Things that are unclear in your mind?

Sue: What does he mean by discuss? Is that the same as argue for? He said in class it was like an argument.

Will: I think what he means here is that it's supposed to be an academic argument, the sort of discussion you might imagine your professor having with other professors. So, if we think about it in terms of tone, or how it sounds, do you think this would really sound like an actual argument?

Sue: Well, probably not. It'd be a conversation where people had opinions but weren't stating them in an attempt to win an argument or anything.

Will: So, something more formal?

Sue: Yeah, more formal, like I'm having a reasoned discussion.

By slowing down with Sue and getting her to spend some time working to understand the rhetorical situation more precisely, Will helps Sue to confirm that she does know what the professor wants her to do, though in so doing he also helps her come to the conclusion that she has left out a significant part of the paper: her characterization of middle class ideology prior to the onset of the Cold War.

Sometimes tutors will have to work considerably harder to help students determine the rhetorical situation. Other times, tutors themselves will be unclear on what the student has been asked to do, even when professors do supply assignment sheets, a situation that can test and stress a tutor's ability to discern the professor's intentions and may require additional information from the professor.

Assessing the work-in-progress. Describing how writing tutors determine where to direct their efforts, Stephen North (1982) writes, "Tutorials must take their shape from where the writer 'is' in the composing process. The tutor's job is to find that place, then react accordingly (p. 435). Although some students come into writing tutorials with clear and fully articulated understandings of where they would like to focus their efforts, more often, as Muriel Harris (1995) writes, students "give the paper to the tutor, hoping the tutor can give names to their internal sense that something is needed" (p. 37). After talking with the student as part of the tutorial's icebreaking, the primary way for a tutor to know where the student "is" and what "is needed" is to read the student's work. Here, the tutor's assessment of the rhetorical situation crosses over from trying to determine both the task that the professor has given and how the student understands that task to trying to figure out how to approach rhetorically the paper itself.

Tutors must know upfront that they will very seldom address everything they possibly can in a student paper. Rather, tutors need to work with students to prioritize the areas that the student would like to focus on. As a general guideline, it is useful to help students address the areas that detract from the paper's effectiveness according to their severity. For example, imagine a student that brings in a paper that contains numerous distracting punctuation errors, inadequate transitions between paragraphs, occasional breakdowns in sentence-level clarity, and three paragraphs at the end that stray off topic. The student is eager to see that the paper improve in all respects. Though initially the amount of work that needs to happen may look overwhelming—punctuation, transitions, clarity, focus—the tutor can help the student prioritize so that they tackle the most serious problems first. In this case, if the paper gets away from the assignment in the final three paragraphs, then there is very little reason to take the student through exercises that will improve the sentence-level clarity, punctuation, and transitions until those final paragraphs are brought back toward a more workable focus. After all, a well-written paper with clear transitions is not all that effective if it gets off topic. Once the student has revised the essay so that it stays on topic from start to finish, he can return for a session focusing on improving the grammar, syntax, and transitions. (Specific strategies for these kinds of sessions are presented in chapters six and seven.)

NEGOTIATING AN AGENDA

As tutors and students negotiate the tutorial's agenda, the tutor needs to stay cognizant of the length of the tutorial. Some sessions might last only twenty or thirty minutes, while others might stretch out to an hour if the student has a longer paper (of, say, 15 or more pages) or a particularly lengthy list of concerns. But anything much longer than that can quickly become an exercise in diminishing returns, the tutorial growing too long for both the student and the tutor to keep a clean handle on everything that comes out of their shared work. For this reason, in many writing centers appointments are scheduled in finite blocks. Tutors can then go into each tutorial with the mindset that they and the student will do as much as they can in the time allotted, knowing that this means they may not attend to absolutely everything that needs attention. Thus, it is vital that tutors help students to prioritize an agenda for the tutorial. Of course, after completing a writing tutorial, students often schedule a follow-up appointment for a second session. This gives the student the necessary time to process information and integrate the teaching of the tutorial into his work before returning for additional help. In the following dialogue, Maurice (tutor) works with Padma (student) to negotiate an agenda for the tutorial.

Maurice: Hi, I'm Maurice. I'll be working with you today.

Padma:	I'm Padma.
Maurice:	I like that name. Where are you from?
Padma:	I was born in India, but we moved to the U.S. when I was seven. My dad took a job over here.
Maurice:	So, is English a second language for you?
Padma:	Kind of. I grew up speaking Hindi at home but English at school.
Maurice:	Well, it's good to meet you. Why don't we have a seat?
Maurice:	[as they're sitting down] So, what brings you to the writing center today?
Padma:	I've got a paper due tomorrow. My roommate read it last night and couldn't tell what my point was. So, I thought I'd come see if you guys could help.
Maurice:	I'm sure we can. What class is this for?
Padma:	English.
Maurice:	How's that been going for you?
Padma:	I think it's all right so far. My professor is a hard grader, but she's clear about what she wants, and I like what we're reading.
Maurice:	Is there anything other than your roommate's opinion that has you worried about this paper?
Padma:	Well, I'm not sure if I did what I was supposed to do for the assignment.
Maurice:	What was the assignment?
Padma:	We were supposed to write a literacy narrative.
Maurice:	That sounds interesting. Do you have an assignment sheet?
Padma:	I'm sorry, but I don't have one with me. Does that mean I have to leave? It's due tomorrow!
Maurice:	[reassuringly] No, of course not. But, before we go any further, can you just say more about how you understand the assignment? What you think it's asking you to do?
Padma:	Well, we're supposed to tell a key story from our literacy development and also analyze how it shaped us as a thinking, literate person.
Maurice:	Hmm, that's kind of cool. Can you say more about what you think this assignment is asking you to do?
Padma:	Well, I'm supposed to tell about something that happened in my past and how that has shaped who I am now as an incoming college freshman, my identity as a reader and writer.
Maurice:	Okay, I think I get it. Why don't you tell me about your paper?
Padma:	Well, I wrote about when I was in sixth grade and I came in second in my school's spelling bee even though everyone thought I was going to win because I had won when I was in fifth grade.
Maurice:	Why did you write about that?
Padma:	Well, I didn't think this at the time, but I think it was important because it gave me more determination to succeed and to work hard. I hadn't really prepared that hard for the spelling bee because I didn't think I had any real competition. I mean, I'm a pretty good speller, so once I won one time, I thought I'd probably win the next

time too. But, when I lost it showed me that I needed to always work hard, even at the things I was good at. And I think that's something that's still with me today as I start college.

Maurice: Okay, I think I understand the idea behind your literacy narrative. As I read your paper, is there anything you'd like me to pay special attention to?

Padma: Well, I need to know if it does or doesn't do what it's supposed to do. I'm also a little worried about whether or not I've given enough examples.

Maurice: [*taking notes while Padma has been speaking*] Okay, anything else?

Padma: Well, I know that right now the conclusion is weak and I'm not sure if I need a thesis or not.

Maurice: Okay.

Padma: And if you could check the grammar too that'd be good.

Maurice: All right—so we're looking at how closely the paper stays to the assignment, use of examples as support, the conclusion, potential thesis, and grammar. Why don't I read your paper to myself before we settle on exactly how we want to proceed with this list?

Maurice's next task is to judge where the paper is most in need of attention. He may have Padma lead him through it; he may read it silently while taking notes; or he may have Padma read it aloud to him. That choice will be governed by the length of the paper, the length of the scheduled session, and the prevailing practices where he tutors, and there are benefits (and drawbacks) to each approach. But the goal is to give the student an opportunity to re-enter her work with a critical eye. After reading through the paper, Maurice may very well conclude that one of the areas Padma has noted is indeed where the two need to begin their work, or perhaps there may be something that Padma did not name that demands their attention first. Another possibility is that Maurice will find several things that are in equal need of work and offer Padma a choice of where she would like to begin. As he reads, Maurice jots a few notes to himself so that he can remember what he thought about various aspects of the paper.

Maurice: [*after finishing Padma's paper*] Okay, I definitely like what you've got going here. The narrative is interesting to read and it really does give me a sense of who you are as you start your studies at the university.

Padma: Good, because I really wanted to try to explain that.

Maurice: In terms of where we might focus today, I think there are a couple areas. You mentioned that you were worried about a thesis statement.

Padma: Yes, do I need one? I don't have one right now.

Maurice: No, you don't have one, and that may be something you want to start with. And the other area that I think presents some difficulty is something you didn't mention. The part where you say who you are today almost feels stuck on, like an afterthought, or like it's somehow not connected to the spelling bee experience.

Padma: That's not good.

Maurice: Well, with work you can improve it. I also did notice some grammatical problems here and there, and as you suspected there were places where you can flesh out the examples in greater detail.

Padma: Wow, there's more to do than I thought.

Maurice: Well, yes, there is a lot to do, but based on what you've written, I'm pretty confident that you've got the ability.

Padma: Thanks, I hope so.

Maurice: As I look at the clock, I see we've got a little more than twenty minutes left. Where would you like us to start with your paper?

Padma: Well, as long as you think it sticks to the assignment, maybe it'd be good to start with the thesis since that's usually pretty important. And, once that's taken care of, we can work on that place where I move into explaining how the spelling bee effected who I am today.

Maurice: That makes sense because it will allow us to take the paper in the order in which it was written. Once we spend some time on the thesis, we'll move to the place where you transition from your past to your present. If there's leftover time, we can come back to the specific examples you use and grammar. How's that sound?

Padma: That sounds good.

Maurice: And if we don't finish all of that today, if you'd like you can schedule a follow-up appointment for this evening so someone can take another look after you've had a few hours to work on it.

Padma: Thanks, I'll probably do that.

From here, Maurice and Padma would move into the specifics of thesis articulation and development (see chapter five). However, what we might pay attention to is the way that Maurice involves Padma in setting the agenda for the tutorial. Once he has read the paper and made some notes to himself (an advisable move on his part because it prevents him from going into the paper unaware of the sorts of rhetorical, syntactical, and contextual issues that await), Maurice quickly reviews the rhetorical problems he observed in the paper and invites Padma to choose a starting place. In this way, he sends a clear message that Padma is in control of the paper and, by extension, that she is responsible for revising it as the tutorial proceeds. Were Maurice to simply set the agenda himself ("Well, Padma, after reading your paper, I think you need to work on X...") the underlying message is that Maurice is going to control what happens in the tutorial. However, given that Padma is the author of the paper,

Maurice needs to give her the space to say where she wants to direct her efforts. She may say that all she really wants help with is the grammar, something that Maurice has not suggested as a first step. If she does this, Maurice ought to try to help her see how this approach might not yield as desirable results as starting with larger-scale issues. Ultimately, however, Maurice needs to let Padma control her work, even if this means that she makes decisions that he himself would not have made.

Note, too, that in referencing the time remaining in the tutorial, Maurice creates space for concentrating on what can be done well in the allotted time, as opposed to promising to get to absolutely everything the paper needs. As Maurice suggests, Padma can, at her discretion, come back for a subsequent tutorial, presumably once she has spent time revising the paper according to the work that she is about to do with Maurice.

What is especially critical in assessing the paper and negotiating an agenda is that the tutor involve the student in the process as much as possible. While it is true that some students will be more adept than others at articulating where they would like to be helped, the tutor's approach remains consistent regardless of student ability level. If the student is to know that he is respected and taken seriously, he must have no doubt in his mind that the tutor views him as a writer with worthwhile ideas and opinions. For this to happen, the tutorial itself must be predicated on the student's control over and responsibility for both the text that he is writing as well as the tutorial in which he is currently working.

SUMMARY

This chapter opened with a catalog of the myriad variables that are always in play in writing tutorials. Although upon first glance these variables, when coupled with everything a tutor has to try to accomplish, appear overwhelming, tutors can take some comfort in knowing that writing tutorials can be grounded in a highly systematic approach. In virtually all writing tutorials, tutors will move along a fairly stable path from introductions and icebreaking into role definition, and from there to assessing the task and setting the agenda:

1. Building rapport
2. Engaging dialogue
3. Defining roles
4. Assessing the task
5. Negotiating an agenda

As tutors gain comfort in this very stable procedural movement, they can begin to slow down and perceive the ways that the interpersonal tutor/student relationship itself is evolving, in the process exercising their influence over the formation of a healthy, professional dialogue where both tutor and student know they are safe, respected, and involved in a meaningful educational endeavor.

SUGGESTIONS FOR FURTHER READING

Bishop, Wendy. (1988). Opening lines: Starting the tutoring session. *Writing Lab Newsletter* *13*(3), 1-4.

Bosker, Julie A. (2001). Peer tutoring and Gorgias: Acknowledging aggression in the writing center. *The Writing Center Journal 21*(2), 21-34.

Brooks, Jeff. (1991). Minimalist tutoring: Making the student do all the work. *The Writing Lab Newsletter, 15*(6), 1-4.

Devet, Bonnie. F. (2007). "Opening lines: starting the tutoring session." A synecdochic article from the Writing Lab canon. *Writing Lab Newsletter 31*(10), 12-13.

Harris, Muriel. (1995). Talking in the middle: Why writers need writing tutors. *College English 57*, 27-42.

Murphy, Christina. (1989). Freud in the writing center: The psychoanalytics of tutoring well. The *Writing Center Journal 10*(1), 13-18.

Shamoon, Linda K., and Deborah H. Burns (1995). A Critique of pure tutoring. *The Writing Center Journal 15(*2), 134-151.

CASE STUDY 2.1: ESTABLISHING RAPPORT AND SETTING GOALS

Now that you've begun your shifts, you are on duty when a new first-year student comes into the writing center for his scheduled tutorial appointment. The student, Nick, has brought with him both the assignment sheet from his professor as well as a draft of his essay's opening paragraph. Based on your understanding of the session dynamics presented in chapter two, determine how you would initiate a productive beginning to your session.

The assignment sheet from the student's Gender Studies professor:

Barbara Ehrenreich's *Nickel and Dimed: On (Not) Getting By in America* raises fundamental questions about the American Dream, a concept that traditionally refers to the idea that any person can succeed in this country if he or she is willing to work hard enough.

In an essay of three to four pages, discuss the validity of the American Dream, particularly the way it pertains to working women. To illustrate your opinion, draw from Ehrenreich's text, keeping in mind class discussions that have explored the ways that the book can be seen as both a challenge to, as well as a piece of support for the validity of the American Dream.

Here are some questions that might get your thinking started. Does the American Dream still exist in the early 21st century? If so, is it equally possible for both men and women to achieve it? Does the American Dream exclude anyone? What are the restrictions on the American Dream? Of course, these questions are merely to get you thinking. The essay you produce will likely range beyond these questions.

Your essay needs to be a formal, coherent, ordered, logical discussion of the issue. The essay should have a sound and clear thesis that it attempts to advance via citations and examples from Ehrenreich's text.

Nick's opening paragraph:

Nickel and Dimed is a very powerful book about whether the average American can work a minimum wage job and make enough money to survive. The author, Barbara Ehrenreich, is the focus of the book, taking on the task of becoming a minimum wage worker in corporate America. Overall, her research is very successful and convincing, and the book is very riveting for the reader. Ehrenreich's hard work and reliability make *Nickel and Dimed* a believable and moving book that shows the public the terrible plight of poor working women.

CASE STUDY 2.2: TROUBLESHOOTING THE OPENING MINUTES

Earlier in this chapter you read a dialogue between Paige (the tutor) and Dean (a student). This case study takes you back into their dialogue as it was presented previously. However, in the various options presented below we have altered Dean's response to Paige's comments. Each of the options will necessitate a reply from Paige. Based on what you have read about session dynamics and dialogue, how should Paige respond to Dean and direct the ensuing dialogue in a productive direction?

Option A

Dean: Hi, I was wondering if I could get someone to go over my paper.

Paige: Sure thing. Why don't we have a seat?

Dean: I've never been here before, but my roommate said you guys could help me fix this [*gesturing to paper*].

Paige: I think we can probably help you improve it.

Dean: Good, because right now it's pretty hopeless. I'm about ready to give up and just turn it in.

Paige: Sounds like you're frustrated with it. Why don't you tell me about your assignment?

Dean: It's a reaction paper to a film we saw in my sociology class. It was that Michael Moore movie *Bowling for Columbine*. Have you seen it?

Paige: Yeah, I liked it.

Dean: Good. I hope you have better ideas about it than I do.

Paige: I'm sure you have some great ideas. Can you tell me more about the assignment? Or, better, do you have an assignment sheet?

Dean: Yep, it's right here.

Paige: [*reading the assignment sheet*] Okay, it says here that you need to discuss how the film challenges social norms. What do you think that means?

Dean: How should I know? You're the tutor, can't you just tell me what it means?

Option B

Dean: Well, I've got two pages, but they're all messed up. I need help fixing the paragraphs so they flow better. I also need someone to check the grammar. Oh, and can you also make sure the citations are correct?

Paige: We can certainly work on citations. In fact, we can work on whatever you'd like us too. However, I should say first that I won't just edit your paper for you. It's your paper, and I think our time is best spent helping you understand some of the areas where you think it has problems and what options you have for addressing those problems.

Dean: What do you mean? Why can't you fix my paper for me? Aren't you a tutor? Isn't that what you do? I knew coming here was a waste of my time.

Option C

Dean: Hi, I was wondering if I could get someone to go over my paper.

Paige: Sure thing. Why don't we have a seat?

Dean: I've never been here before, but my roommate said you guys could help me fix this [*gesturing to paper*].

Paige: I think we can probably help you improve it.

Dean: Good, because right now it's pretty hopeless. I'm about ready to give up and just turn it in.

Paige: Sounds like you're frustrated with it. Why don't you tell me about your assignment?

Dean: Yeah, I guess I am frustrated! Do you know Dr. Sosa? No one in class has any idea what she's talking about! It's like she's in her own little world all the time. And the way she grades is so unfair. Do you think it's right that she expects us to write papers that have no more than four grammar errors? I mean, this is a sociology class, not English! What do you think of that!?

Option D

Dean: Hi, I was wondering if I could get someone to go over my paper.

Paige: Sure thing. Why don't we have a seat?

Dean: I've never been here before, but my roommate said you guys could help me fix this [*gesturing to paper*].

Paige: I think we can probably help you improve it.

Dean: Good, because right now it's pretty hopeless. I'm about ready to give up and just turn it in.

Paige: Sounds like you're frustrated with it. Why don't you tell me about your assignment?

Dean: It's a reaction paper to a film we saw in my sociology class. It was that Michael Moore movie *Bowling for Columbine*. Have you seen it?

Paige: Yeah, I liked it.

Dean: Really? That's amazing. I don't think I understood it entirely. I can tell you're smart. How about we talk about this over a cup of coffee?

Option E

Dean: Hi, I was wondering if I could get someone to go over my paper.

Paige: Sure thing. Why don't we have a seat?

Dean: I've never been here before, but my roommate said you guys could help me fix this [*gesturing to paper*].

Paige: I think we can probably help you improve it.

Dean: Good, because it's due in an hour.

CASE STUDY 2.3: ASSESSING THE TASK

Ashley, your 3:00 appointment, has brought in a fairly detailed assignment sheet to her tutorial. She is a business major who has taken numerous courses in her department, and this assignment requires her to research and analyze a failed product. Your opening exchange with her suggests to you that she is feeling overwhelmed.

Construct a dialogue demonstrating how you would use the assignment sheet to help Ashley understand what it is that she is being asked to do. You can assume that Ashley has some idea of the individual tasks that comprise the assignment but that overall she is quite uncertain about how she should approach the paper. Among the failed products on which Ashley has done some preliminary research are these three: R. J. Reynolds' 1988 "Premier" smokeless cigarettes, the 1993 "Earring Magic" Ken Doll, and Kellogg's 1999 "Cereal Mates."

Business 380: Business Communication

Report #2

The Situation

You have recently been hired as a research assistant to consultant Yevgeny Federov, who has just taken on a new project for a growing firm. One morning, Federov sends you this email:

> "Before my meeting next month, I want you to find out what went wrong with [select a failed product from the list distributed in class]: I need to know why it failed. Get back to me with an analysis two weeks from today. What happened and why?"

You have heard that Federov likes his reports succinct and to the point, with findings highlighted up front. He wants to get the gist of a report quickly, but he also needs numbers, charts, and visuals to make decisions. (He has also been known to blow a gasket upon finding errors of any sort!)

Your Task

Prepare your report for Federov. Make sure that it has two parts: (1) a brief chronological **narrative** presenting the failure of the product, and (2) an **analysis** of what went wrong.

Format
The final report should be about 1500 words long, with appropriate business document design, including headings and simple use of color and visuals.

CHAPTER THREE

ASSESSING RHETORICAL DYNAMICS

CHAPTER THREE

ASSESSING RHETORICAL DYNAMICS

The previous chapter introduced you to the multiple dynamics of tutorial sessions, presenting a means by which tutors can quickly greet their students, build rapport, define roles, assess tasks, and set an agenda for the tutorial. This third chapter focuses more exclusively and precisely on the variables that together comprise both the text and the context that occasions a given piece of writing. In chapter two, we introduced the rhetorical situation briefly by addressing the student's understanding of the task. In doing so, we aimed primarily to introduce prospective tutors to a means of getting started with tutoring—both in the general sense, of beginning one's career as a tutor of writing, and in the more specific sense of what to do when undertaking any given tutorial session.

Now that you have developed a strong sense of how to initiate sessions that foster purposeful dialogue and collaboration, in this chapter and those that follow, we turn to the specifics of the sessions themselves. Subsequent chapters will demonstrate strategies for helping writers develop arguments and attend to matters of style and correctness. But prerequisite to helping a writer generate ideas, articulate a thesis, or improve sentence stylistics is an important matter: *assessing the rhetorical dynamics* of the writer's task. Experienced tutors will develop an ability to do so implicitly and intuitively. New tutors, meanwhile, will benefit from some careful consideration of the variables that comprise any rhetorical situation—and, with time and practice, learn to employ this analysis productively in any of their tutorial sessions.

THE RHETORICAL SITUATION

Our focus turns now from the interpersonal dynamics of the session addressed in chapter two towards *the rhetorical situation* itself. In doing so, we note that writing is astonishingly rich in variety and possibility—so rich, in fact, that the variables that comprise a given rhetorical situation themselves present a near-infinite array of possibilities. While that richness of possibility might well be part of what attracts us to the joint venture of tutoring writing, it also presents a source of potential difficulty. If the writing tutor makes an incorrect assumption about any of the variables at play in his writer's situation, the outcome will almost certainly be an inefficient session, with considerable energy invested in the wrong direction: towards adopting an inappropriate role, perhaps, or invoking an inappropriate audience. Or, worse, the writer could leave with a work-in-progress aimed in the wrong direction and later dutifully undertake the tutor's advice—only to learn later, and at some cost, that the tutor had misunderstood the rhetorical situation.

This chapter, then, offers a *heuristic* for examining and understanding rhetorical situations. A means of understanding and solving a problem, heuristics are important to composition studies, where they are commonly employed for generating ideas, assessing arguments, and revising and editing. Also employed commonly in mathematics, philosophy, and psychology, heuristics offer systematic ways of addressing complex problems. In essence, our approach to chapter two was heuristic in nature, providing a systematic means of beginning the first few minutes of a tutorial session; this chapter also functions heuristically, offering a systematic approach to assessing rhetorical dynamics. With this heuristic in mind, a tutor can efficiently and effectively understand the writer's task—and, it follows, assist a writer from there through the process of addressing it.

WRITING AS HUMAN COMMUNICATION

To understand any given writing task, we must first understand that writing is not merely a simple artifact or a technology. It *is*, of course, both, an object and a tool, but our focus here is less on the material and technological aspects of writing than on its communicative nature. All writing is, whatever its technology or materiality, an *act of human communication*. And as such, it is governed by a set of principles common to any such interaction. To illustrate, we observe that every interaction featuring writing involves—at its most basic level—a *writer* employing a *form* to convey a *message about a subject* to his *readers*. There are other dynamics at play as well, ones which we address shortly: the communication, of course, takes place over a period of time as the writer composes; it is occasioned by a certain moment when the writing seems appropriate or necessary; and it may be subject to certain conditions or rules for publication or evaluation. But setting aside briefly these more contextual dynamics of the rhetorical situation, the basic elements present in any writing task are **writer**, the **reader**, the **subject matter**, and the **form or format**. Consideration of these provides writing tutors with what can be an efficient heuristic for decoding/understanding rhetorical situations.

The Writer. To state that every writing task requires a writer may seem blissfully obvious, but we think it worth our attention to focus on both the writers with whom tutors work and the roles they adopt as they write. Even if every writer you work with in the years to come is, say, a college student, you'll observe a wide range of talents, abilities, dispositions, and origins among them. (This variety is not necessarily to bemoan but potentially something to embrace.) If you are too a college student, you are in one sense a peer to the students you tutor, but in another, and very real, sense, your roles are *not* the same: you've arrived at your position by virtue of some *aptitude*, whereas your student has arrived by a perceived *need*. Secondly, you can not assume, necessarily, that your students are all (or even should be) equally capable of certain kinds of intellectual thought. You cannot necessarily expect, for instance, that every student with whom you work is capable of the same kind of analysis, interpretation, or evaluation as the next: some students may struggle to interpret texts, critique positions, or arrive at syntheses, and well-designed curricula should pose increasingly complex problems of their students. At higher levels of instruction, you might see a greater focus on increasingly more sophisticated theories, texts, and taxonomies.

It is difficult today to generalize much about "the writer," so we will refrain from doing so. There is a good deal of reportage characterizing today's college generation as that of the "millennial" student. So goes the description, today's college students have greater technological proficiency than previous generations; possess access to greater amounts of information, yet fewer opportunities for in-depth study; experience community and intimacy as members of a group, rather than paired off in couples; experience increasingly high levels of stress and anxiety; work part-time and earn credits at more than one institution; profess high ambitions and unrealistic expectations about achieving them; and resist or defy traditionally-defined boundaries of public and private life (Newton, 2000). All of these characteristics are grounded in reality, and it helps, certainly, to understand that each generation indeed possesses its own defining experiences and values.

Yet at the same time, it is dangerous to assume too much about a student you'll meet. In our experience, we have observed an incredibly wide variety of writers in both our classrooms and our writing center—and tutoring writing is, after all, more about responding to the needs of the individual than it is about managing those of the group. Generational difference theories notwithstanding, writing tutors can expect to work with writers who may be more or less "traditional" (in terms of age, social class, life situation), native, experienced, fluent, and/or willing.

- **Traditional or nontraditional.** If a traditional college student is college age (18-22), enrolled full-time, nonmarried, without dependents, and not working outside campus, the nontraditional student might be an older or returning student enrolled part-time, might be married (or divorced), might have children, and may well be working part- or even full-time. It may be his or her first venture into the college classroom in years, or, perhaps, ever. Your institution may aim to serve one population more than the other, but you can expect to work with both traditional and nontraditional students. Since not every student will have equal access to, or experience with, all of the various technologies and resources used for writing and research, it can be helpful to try to gain a sense of your student's experience and situation as your tutorial begins.

- **First- or second- (or third- or fourth-) language.** While most college writers are native-born speakers of English, the number of students whose first language is not English increases yearly, as a result both of an increasing international presence in the academy and a burgeoning bilingualism nationwide. As we have noted in chapter one, the challenges a second-language (or L2) writer faces are many as she adapts her rhetoric and usage to the conventions of the foreign language that is English (and perhaps especially the academic variants thereof). In the chapters that follow on argumentation and grammar, we bring these challenges into closer focus. For now, please note the "Tips for Working with ESL Writers."

- **Novice or experienced.** Even today's traditional *in loco parentis* students, straight from high school and into the first year of college, can demonstrate widely varying levels of experience in writing. You'll meet some who are already experienced, with dozens of successful papers and projects completed in the course of their studies, and some who are even more accomplished, having published or presented their work or even having won awards. Such experience and accomplishment are usually—though not always—virtues. Others are simply more novice: in some high schools, the writing curricula is lax enough that students have written rarely, if ever, and sometimes not at all in situations requiring research or documentation. We will note that all of us are novices in given endeavors at some point in our lives, though, and that many a new task requires even the experienced to become novice once again.

- **"Fully abled" or learning disabled.** While most writers, regardless of their ability level, are not affected by disability, some students have a learning disability that impacts the process or the product of their writing. A learning disability is not a disorder that a student outgrows; rather, it is a permanent disorder that affects how students with normal or above- average intelligence process information—whether that be incoming information, outgoing information, and/or categorization of information in memory, all of which are vital to success in writing.

Sometimes, such disabilities can linger undiagnosed for years, with performance problems mistakenly attributed to attitudinal or cognitive causes. Fortunately, in many circumstances learning disabilities are diagnosed early enough in a student's career that accommodations can be made. Many students overcome these disabilities well, and some employ alternative print formats, taped lectures, peer note-takers, alternative plans to complete assignments, time extensions for assignments and exams, and/or consultations regarding study skills and strategies. A writing tutor—in providing an evaluation-free setting focusing intently on the developing work-in-progress with careful explanations and helpful examples—can be a great service to the writer whose efforts are impacted by disability.

If you work in an institutional setting, there is likely an office providing services for all students with disabilities, including those with learning disabilities. In fact, federal law requires that educational institutions must make reasonable accommodations for students with physical and learning disabilities, and tutoring services may be an important element of those accommodations. So we recommend strongly doing a bit of research to learn what kinds of services are available or whether in your position you can or should make referrals to such services. If you will be expected to work with learning-disabled writers with any frequency, your local experts can serve as a rich source of support for your work. If you suspect that a writer you are working with exhibits symptoms of a learning disability—such as inordinate struggles with time management, correct spelling, deciphering instructions, recalling sequences, or legible handwriting—you may want to inquire whether the student has been diagnosed or whether she might be. But in any case, it is worth remembering that principled tutoring practices apply well to all types of writers, not just the "fully abled."

- **Basic, blocked, reticent, apprehensive—or fluent**. Scholarship in composition and rhetoric in the 1970s and '80s focused particular attention on some of the kinds of problems and attitudes unsuccessful writers faced. Though often used with some reluctance, the descriptor *basic writer* has been most commonly employed to describe those students who do not or can not (for any of a number of reasons) compose conventional academic discourse (Kasden, 1980). With some greater specificity, other research has focused more on writers who are blocked, reticent, or apprehensive, and the considerable emphasis on the writing process in scholarship and pedagogy has provided a wealth of means of assisting writers who struggle to generate and articulate ideas. (In chapter four, we present a catalog of generative heuristics that can be especially helpful for such writers.)

Resistant—or willing. The term *resistance* is relatively new to composition studies, referring to a general opposition to authority. For the writing tutorial, opposition might be made manifest in resistance to the classroom instructor; to the subject matter or text; or even to the tutor. Resistance can be well- or ill-founded, and it can mask itself in one guise while originating from another. A writing tutor might work with a writer who expresses resistance to her teacher's authority or methodology. Or one who is resistant to classroom texts or reading assignments. Or, ironically enough, to the tutor's suggestions. Although in our experience the vast majority of students coming to seek tutorial help express a grateful willingness to the tutor, some situations might require a disarming tutorial approach.

Working with ESL Writers

Begin by building rapport, engaging dialogue, and assessing the task and text.

It may be tempting to assume that your job will be to correct errors, and the sooner you get started the better. But treat your student *as a student*, not just as a second-language learner with a text to fix. Everything we've suggested about session dynamics and dialogue, about assessing rhetorical dynamics, applies here as well. Make an effort to learn what you can about the writer and the task, and make an effort to build rapport and engage dialogue as you begin.

Recognize cultural differences.

A subfield of linguistics, contrastive rhetoric, explores the ways in which certain rhetorical patterns are typically preferred in certain cultures. For instance, American predilections for directness in business communication, an argumentative thesis in essay writing, and fastidiousness in source citation—all of these are cultural preferences, and by no means universal. Tutors can help articulate the preferred, valued patterns in their host country, simply by saying "In American academic English, it's more typical to ...." And they need to be aware that values toward authority, citation, and gender may differ considerably across cultures.

Provide context, practice, and feedback.

Typically, second-language writers find skill/drill work (that is, worksheet-style sentence problems removed from purpose and context) easy, but *writing* much more difficult. After all, these students are doing higher-order work in a second (or third or fifth!) language. Simply engaging your student in dialogue about the task and the text is helpful, and as an experienced writer in your native country, you can be a valuable source of information for a student whose native language is not English. In any case, "more basics" is rarely what a second-language writer needs most; instead, more practice, more writing, more feedback, more dialogue is what tutors can provide.

Read for the message.

As you begin your sessions, strive first to understand the student's message and approach to the task, and do not let yourself be too distracted by the fact that the paper's syntax, diction, or style may be something other than that to which you're accustomed. While many ESL writers have been studying English in classrooms for years, the range of skills you encounter can be wide. Sometimes, if a second-language writer has yet to master fully some aspect of writing in English, a simple pattern of error—article use, pronoun case or gender, for instance—could result in innumerable surface errors. Even then, make sure you read for the message first.

Address error through example.

A tutor's first priorities should always be to understand the rhetorical context, the writer's purpose and message, the gist and the direction of the paper. When errors are addressed, though, trying to "clean up" second-language writing sentence-by-sentence can result in confused, disorganized tutoring, where you might be forced to address a variety of different rules in a single sentence or two. Instead, as we advocate in chapter seven, diagnose, isolate, and discuss just one or two patterns of error you see most prevalent in the text. Limit your discussion to just a few patterns of error, then provide clear explanations and examples. Drawing attention to patterns of error will help students isolate and address problems more systematically.

Acknowledge the idioms and idiosyncrasies of the English language.

As we note in a later chapter, the English language is remarkably idiomatic—and idiosyncratic. Who among us can explain with confidence whether and why to use "the" in front of Mississippi River, Lake Erie, Fox News Network, or Ohio State University? In your tutorials, try to distinguish *rules* from *idioms*. With a rule, note the pattern of error by isolating examples, demonstrating corrections, and asking the student to demonstrate understanding. But with an idiomatic expression, the best approach is to just be a "tour guide": tell your student "this is how we say it," and don't worry as much about the principle that governs the usage.

Accept that second-language learning—and tutoring—is often slow going.

Quite simply, second-language learning is slower, and frequently more arduous, than first-language learning. After all, most native speakers of English would probably prefer reading Allende, Dostoyevsky, and Maupassant in translation, and writing about them in English, to doing so in Spanish, Russian, or French. But no one would want simply to have errors corrected without explanation or work rewritten without permission or discussion. So: acknowledge up front that the entire process may take more time, and do not "short-circuit" a second-language tutorial by simply correcting errors or fixing sentences.

Since a student writer might be more or less traditional, more or less fluent in English, more or less experienced, or more or less willing to participate in the enterprise, you can see why we are hesitant to generalize too quickly about "the writer." A more helpful approach, we think, is to take the initial minutes of the tutorial to learn what you can about the writer and the task he is undertaking. Note how in the following dialogue our tutor, Mel, invites her student, Sourdi, to contribute some helpful information about her circumstance and experience.

Mel: Hi, Sourdi, nice to meet you. Am I pronouncing your name correctly? It's new to me. I'm Mel, by the way.

Sourdi: Yes, Sourdi is right. It's Cambodian. Is Mel short for Melanie? Or Melissa?

Mel: No, you're right, it's Melanie. But no one calls me that. I don't think I've met anyone from Cambodia. Did you grow up there?

Sourdi: Yes, my hometown is called Ta Khmau.

Mel: You studied English in school?

Sourdi: Oh, yes, since I was young. I went to an International English School for a year before coming here.

Mel: Okay. Is your paper for a class here?

Sourdi: Yes. I am taking the freshman seminar.

Mel: Okay, well, welcome to college! That can be a real transition. How is it going so far? Have you gotten off to a good start?

Sourdi: The class, you mean? It's fine, but this paper is really hard. Here, I have a copy of the assignment. [*hands assignment to Mel*] I'm really hoping you can help me out a bit because right now I'm not sure how to get going.

Mel: [*reads assignment*] Okay, this sounds straightforward — "using field researched observations and interviews, investigate and describe a campus or community place that is new to you" — have you chosen a place to write about?

Sourdi: I was planning to write on the campus Counseling Center. Here, I have some research.

Mel: Let's take a look.

Not every student will be as forthcoming as Sourdi is here, but her volunteering information is hardly an exception to the typical tutorial dialogue. With only a few innocuous inquiries, Mel is able to learn that Sourdi is a non-native speaker of English, a first-year international student, and, apparently, struggling with either apprehension or writer's block; at the same time, she also seems optimistic about her class and willing to work on the assignment. Note that although Mel's goal is, of course, to discern what she can about the assignment and

Sourdi's response to it, she does not begin there. Instead, she exchanges pleasantries, inquires about Sourdi's background, and asks about her work in general beforehand. Note that Mel assumes from Sourdi's name that she is a second-language writer, and this assumption turns out to be correct But Mel does not proceed from there to assuming that Sourdi's experience will be limited or her writing flawed; instead, she continues to build rapport, engage dialogue, and invite Sourdi to provide information that will help them both understand the task. From here, Mel might need next to help Sourdi assess the dynamics of the rhetorical situation, and Mel will need to be alert to any misunderstandings about the assignment that might arise from Sourdi's transition to college—and to America. If and when Mel reviews Sourdi's work-in-progress, she will need to focus first on broader rhetorical concerns and only later on correctness. But as an exchange like this might occur in only a minute or two of real time, Mel has a basic understanding of Sourdi's situation as they begin their session.

Roles Writers Adopt. Every student with whom you work is, without exception, a unique individual with a unique set of experiences, values, and abilities. But it follows too that every rhetorical situation requires its own *role* of the writer. A writer might, in one context, offer the wisdom of years of experience; in another, explore a subject area in which he is completely novice; and in a third, report dispassionately on an observed phenomenon. (In fact, in college, a student might be expected to perform each of these roles in a single day!) In our experience, we've observed writers working in situations where they were expected to play each of the following roles.

- **The Sage: Writer as Expert.** By their very nature, students are immersed in the discourse of expertise: a majority of the textbooks they read and lectures they hear offer the wisdom of expertise. Written by experts for an audience of novices, their psychology texts offer introductory overviews of knowledge in the field; prepared and delivered by professors, their lectures dispense authoritative perspectives on the subject matters of their disciplines.

The very fact that students are immersed in this discourse can lead them to the assumption that its rhetorical stance is one they ought adopt. In some cases, of course, they are expected to do just that: to develop an expertise on a subject they are studying and to profess their knowledge of that subject in their writing. An explication of a sonnet, a historical narrative, a business plan—all of these tasks demand that writers develop and profess their expertise. These kinds of tasks can, we note, bring with them their own set of problems (*what to say to the Donne scholar who literally wrote the book?*) as students assume rhetorical positions that are fraught with difficulty. As David Barholomae (1985) observes:

> Every time a student sits down to write for us, he has to invent the university for the occasion—invent the university, that is, or a branch of it, like history or anthropology or economics or English. The student has to learn to speak our language, to speak as we do, to try on the peculiar ways of knowing, selecting, evaluating, reporting, concluding, and arguing that define the discourse of our community. Or perhaps I should say the *various* discourses of our community, since it is in the nature of a liberal arts education that a student, after the first year or two, must learn to try on a variety of voices and interpretive schemes—to write, for example, as a literary critic one day and as an experimental psychologist the next; to work within fields where the rules governing the presentation of examples or the development of an argument are both distinct and, even to the professional, mysterious. (p. 134)

Also, we note, such roles can be especially uncomfortable for second-language writers, as in some cultures authority is to be neither inappropriately assumed nor quickly challenged.

- **The Seeker: Writer as Inquirer.** In other rhetorical situations, students can adopt a different role, one in which they are not necessarily expected to profess a confident expertise about their subjects—or to profess their own expertise to the expert—but instead to present their developing line of inquiry as they approach, and begin to understand, their subjects. In such situations, writers do not assume the rhetorical stance of expert but that of a seeker, one in search of knowledge. Here, for instance, is Jonathan Kozol (1988), from *Rachel and Her Children:*

The Martinique Hotel, at Sixth Avenue and Thirty-second Street, is one of the largest hotels for homeless people in New York City. When I visited it, in December of 1985, nearly four hundred homeless families, including some twelve hundred children, were lodged in the hotel, by arrangement with the city's Human Resources Administration. One woman—I will call her Laura, but her name, certain other names, and certain details have been changed—is so fragile that I find it hard to start a conversation when we are introduced, a few nights later. Before I begin, she asks if I will read her a letter from the hospital. The oldest of her four children, a seven-year-old boy named Matthew, has been sick for several weeks. He was tested for lead poisoning in November, and the letter she hands me, from Roosevelt Hospital, says that the child has a dangerous lead level. She is told to bring him back for treatment. She received the letter some weeks ago. It has been buried in a pile of other documents that she cannot read. (p. 102)

Students tend to be less immersed in this particular kind of discourse, and as a result, less likely to recognize it as a rhetorical stance that might, in some circumstances—such as in our student Sourdi's field-research assignment described in the dialogue above—be appropriate for their own writing.

▪ **The Observer: Writer as Impartial Recorder.** This is a rhetorical stance commonly found in the traditional sciences, where a writer might record observations in a logbook or report on an experiment. The ability to compose intelligible discourse from such a perspective is one infrequently practiced—and not easily developed. In such situations, writers need to take care to remove themselves from their prose and to avoid unnecessarily evaluative or subjective descriptions in their analysis.

▪ **The Advocate: Writer as Promoter or Activist.** Certainly, the role of writer as promoter or activist will not be foreign to the students you tutor. With television talking heads incessantly advocating for one side or the other and bloggers advocating for or against any of the day's hot-button topics, anyone immersed in today's media will be familiar with the rhetorical stance advocates adopt. In academic situations, rhetorical situations requiring such a stance may be more nuanced: based on the evidence provided in a textbook, case study, or research project, a writer might advocate for a political position, economic theory, or course of action. Generally speaking, in academic situations calling for such a stance, a writer is frequently expected to offer clear claims, carefully-examined evidence, and consideration of counterarguments or alternatives in offering her own position. (These nuances of argument are discussed in greater detail in chapter five.)

A writer who adopts the role of promoter or activist will not necessarily present herself as an absolute expert in her subject matter, but she will nonetheless need to build credibility and project authority—and the most effective means of doing so will be with the careful mounting of an intelligible case built on strong evidence. A writer may, we note, adopt a position somewhere along a continuum between a cautious endorsement and an unshakable belief in her own position, but the former is more common to academic prose, even if the latter might be more familiar—and more tempting—to most of the students you tutor. Some second-language writers, on the other hand, may find Americans' predilection for straightforwardness inelegant, or even crass, and may hesitate to adopt such a stance even when appropriate.

- **The Participant: Writer as Narrator.** Although students might not be too familiar with the rhetorical stance where the writer is more a participant than an expert, there are more than a few situations in which their role is to describe and narrate an experience of their own. Expressivist and autobiographical writing assignments, to be certain, do so, when they require students to narrate and reflect on events from their past. (Just as you might see a James Baldwin, Mary Karr, or Amy Sedaris recall their childhoods.) These kinds of assignments still frequent the first-year curriculum, but might be seen more rarely outside of it, having been relegated to something of a niche of creative writing.

Of increasing frequency, though, are those tasks which ask their writers to familiarize themselves with a new experience—an intellectual endeavor like a lecture series, perhaps, or a physical or social activity. Sometimes, such assignments are located in a first-year experience curriculum aimed at introducing the student to the campus community; sometimes you will see them in health, teacher, or business education programs as a means of learning about a certain approach or paradigm.

As you meet your writer and begin to assess the role(s) expected of her in her writing, you should recognize the following.

- Writers may be more or less "traditional," native-language, able, fluent, experienced, or willing.

- Writers are always called upon to adopt and perform a role in their writing.

- Writers may be more or less familiar or comfortable with the role they are expected to adopt.

- Writers can misunderstand or misinterpret the role they are to adopt.

- The writer's preferred role may not always be evident from her text or understanding of the task.

- A writer may be resistant to the very notion of adapting her persona to adopt a given role as a writer.

- The tutor's task is to assess the role—as efficiently and accurately as possible—and assist the writer in adapting to it.

The Reader. Savvy readers will note from the above discussion of the writer's roles that each is dependent upon other variables in the rhetorical situation: there is no writer's role, so to speak, without a subject, form, or audience that helps determine it. The reader of a piece of discourse is similarly "dependent" upon those other variables: the subject, the form, and to no lesser extent, the writer.

From classical rhetoric to contemporary theories of composition, the notion of audience has always been something of a vexing topic. In the *Rhetoric*, Aristotle proposed that the character of an audience might be measured by analysis of its salient characteristics (wealth, power, age), and that a speaker might then employ those strategies best aimed at a particular audience. For much of the last four decades, composition theorists have increasingly focused their attention on both the kinds of audience analysis Aristotle presented and on the ways that writers understand and conceptualize their readers.

Perhaps the most commonly acknowledged understanding of audience comes from Lisa Ede and Andrea Lunsford (1984), who noted an important distinction between "audience addressed" and "audience invoked." The former of these follows rather directly from Aristotle to emphasize the need for a concrete reality of the audience's situation and assumes that such knowledge of its characteristics (including those Aristotle mentioned but also, more broadly, attitude, belief, disposition) is essential to successful persuasive discourse. This conceptualization of *audience addressed* has been much discussed: some (e.g. Elbow, 1987; Armstrong, 1986) have posited the audience as an inhibiting force, others (e.g. Long, 1980; Berkenkotter, 1981) as a more generative one.

Whether seen as essentially inhibitive or productive, though, this understanding of audience addressed is but one means of understanding the audience for a piece of writing. A second is what Ede and Lunsford called *audience invoked*, and it follows the work of Walter Ong. For Ong (1975), the term *audience* does not so much represent the concrete reality of his readers' positions as it does the process of his constructing, "in his imagination, vaguely or clearly, an audience cast in some sort of role" (p. 12). And it is the successful writer who can best "fictionalize" an audience that he has learned about—not so much from the present writing situation but from ones addressed earlier, and from reading others' successful fictionalizations of the same.

This understanding of audience as simultaneously addressed and invoked has been incredibly useful to composition instructors, as from it students have been encouraged "to see themselves as social beings in a social situation" (Park, 1986, p. 488). If one of the means by which a writer moves from novice to experienced is learning to conceptualize his prose more for his readers and less for himself, then coming to understand that he can move his readers in certain directions through his prose can be a considerable step in a positive direction. And as students are encouraged to understand their audience as one means of understanding rhetorical situations, so too do we encourage tutors to foster this understanding of audience as one that is both directly addressed and rhetorically invoked.

Whether or not the student is writing for a professor has a considerable impact on how she will address and invoke an audience. In non-academic situations—when one writes, for example, a proposal for the workplace, a letter to the editor, or a grant proposal—the audiences may be multiple or possess conflicting values, but the writer's approach to them is uncomplicated by the lurking presence of the professor-as-evaluator.

When writing in an academic situation, the writer's audience may be more or less defined. The student may be told, for instance, to address a community of peers, a high school senior, the readership of a specific publication, or a particular individual. And his writing may (or may not) succeed in part based on his ability to *invoke* that specified audience persuasively. Yet at the same time, both tutor and student know well that he is writing, really, *for* the course professor who will evaluate his work. The student must not only invoke the described audience but keep in mind his more immediate one—and navigate any substantial differences between the two. And that artificiality of the situation can create difficulties not just for novice writers but for experienced ones as well.

Many academic situations, on the other hand, specify no such audience to be invoked. Rather, they leave the writer to his own devices to imagine an appropriate audience and interpret the appropriate role to play. While many writers can do so, of course, successfully, that very lack of clarity will cause some writers to mistake, say, their subject for the audience. We remember a little too fondly the writer whose formal academic literature review on premarital sex frequency among college students concluded with the admonition that "you should always wear a condom." He had, simply, lapsed into the mistake of thinking that the population *about which* he was writing was the same as the one *to whom* he was writing.

But such misunderstandings are, in part, the *raison d'être* of the writing tutor. As Harris (1995) notes, "misunderstanding the assignment happens with such astonishing regularity that we ought more properly to view it properly as part of the educational process" (p. 149). With their proximity to the writer's process and work-in-progress, writing tutors are in a unique position to be able to help writers move towards better, more complete understandings of their tasks. A clear understanding of both the particulars of the audience your writer will *address* and the ways he can appropriately *invoke* that audience will help you help your writer navigate those situations well.

The Subject. A third element of any communicative interaction is a subject matter: writers not only compose for readers, they aim to communicate a particular message about their subjects as they do so. When, for instance, a writing tutor asks the writer to clarify the thesis, the focus, or the interpretation of a piece of writing, she is asking for a clearer iteration of the message.

The subject can prove vexing for academic writing. As we note above in the discussion of audience, many academic writing assignments require that the writer assume a role of expert: the writer adopts this role in the fashion of the apprentice, constructing authority for herself by skillfully presenting details and evidence that demonstrate a level of expertise. Yet her reader, ironically, may be far more expert than she in the subject matter: her professor has almost certainly developed an expertise in the area he is teaching, and in some cases may literally have authored the book on the subject. Consider this exchange from Margaret Edson's Pulitzer-Prize winning stage play *Wit*, between her protagonist, Vivian Bearing, in this scenario the student, and E. M. Ashford, her professor. Here, poor Vivian is faced with the task of writing about a John Donne sonnet for a reader who is far more expert in the topic than she:

> Ashford: Please sit down. Your essay on Holy Sonnet Six, Miss Bearing, is a melodrama, with a veneer of scholarship unworthy of you—to say nothing of Donne. Do it again.
>
> Vivian: I, ah …
>
> Ashford: You must begin with a text, Miss Bearing, not with a feeling.
>
> > *Death be not proud, though some have called thee*
> > *Mighty and dreadfull, for thou art not soe.*

You have entirely missed the point of the poem, because, I must tell you, you have used an edition of the text that is inauthentically punctuated. In the Gardner edition —

Vivian: That edition was checked out of the library —

Ashford: Miss Bearing!

Vivian: Sorry.

Ashford: You take this too lightly, Miss Bearing. This is Metaphysical Poetry, not the Modern Novel. The standards of scholarship and critical reading which one would apply to any other text are simply insufficient. The effort must be total for the results to be meaningful. Do you think the punctuation of the last line of this sonnet is merely an insignificant detail?

The sonnet begins with a valiant struggle with death, calling on all the forces of intellect and drama to vanquish the enemy. But it is ultimately about overcoming the seemingly insuperable barriers separating life, death, and eternal life.

To write an interpretation of "Death Be Not Proud" for a reader who knows vastly more about the Holy Sonnets than the writer is—as Vivian Bearing begins to realize in the exchange above—no easy task. The writing tutor, on the other hand, will almost never be as expert in the writer's subject as the writer herself. In a given shift, a tutor might work with students who are writing not only about Donne's Holy Sonnets, but also the turbulent economics of postwar Hollywood, the polyandrous mating rituals of the Spotted Sandpiper, the local politics of a community development initiative, and Lacan's theory of *le stade du miroir*. While in each case the professor typically knows the subject matter well, a tutor may be at best only middlingly familiar with its existence—and in some cases, completely unaware of it at all. Can a tutor assist a writer when he knows, literally, nothing of the writer's subject?

In a word, yes. (We will address the corollary question—can a tutor assist a writer when the tutor knows the subject well?—shortly.) Most of the tutors we know express some anxiety about tutoring when they lack knowledge of (or even familiarity with!) the writer's subject. We advise them that, when this is the case, first to relax. Students can't reasonably expect a writing tutor to know everything, after all. The tutor's expertise is developed in the craft of writing, not Lacanian theory or avian reproduction. Secondly, we advise tutors faced with an unfamiliar or daunting subject matter to use their own lack of knowledge itself as a heuristic: that is to say, to systematically invite discussion of the subject matter through a patterned line of questioning.

- **Introductory questions**: What are you writing about? What class is that for? How or why did you decide on your topic? Did you discuss that in class? Are you doing research on it? Are you applying a theory or method?

- **Summary questions**: How do you define, describe, or explain it? What's the main point or theme? What are its major components, events, or elements? Are there important scholars, theories, or contexts to consider?

- **Interpretive / evaluative questions:** Do you agree with the position or reasoning? How useful, verifiable, or accurate is this information? What are the counterarguments or alternatives? Why are they less valid or acceptable?

- **Applicative questions:** Are there relevant theories, perspectives, or frameworks that apply to the subject? How does the subject appear or change when viewed from another perspective?

This line of questioning as a means of inviting dialogue about the subject matter serves a number of purposes. First, it can help establish rapport: with a demonstrably sincere inquiry about the writer's subject, you can indicate that you are motivated to learn about the writer's task and topic. Second, it can help the writer articulate and clarify her thinking on the subject, thus serving a generative purpose for her writing. Third, it can teach you—and in a reasonably short time span—the essentials of the topic so that your tutorial can proceed in the direction you both determine. And last, it can help focus the session on the matter at hand by drawing immediate and concentrated attention to the writer's subject.

Note how in the following dialogue the tutor, Kai, uses a mix of types of questions to promote his student Joe's development of an interpretive thesis on the book *Gang of One: Memoirs of a Red Guard* for his Asian history course. This exchange takes place a few minutes into the tutorial, after Kai and Joe are settled into the routine of paperwork, greetings, and task assessment.

Kai:	So what is the book you're writing about?
Joe:	It's called *Gang of One*, and it's by this author named Fan Shen. I guess a lot of classes are reading it this year. The author's going to be on campus next month, so that's cool.
Kai:	Okay, I've heard of that.
Joe:	Have you read it?
Kai:	No, but I think I'd like to. What's your assignment?
Joe:	We have to discuss the author's perspective on political systems.
Kai:	So what's the book about?
Joe:	Well, it starts with the author growing up in China. He was 12 when the Cultural Revolution started, and he was a Red Guard when he was just a kid, though he didn't really know what he was doing.
Kai:	So it's a memoir?
Joe:	Yeah, that's the right word — it's all true, all first-person, but written kind of like a novel, you know, with characters and theme and everything.
Kai:	So what's the main conflict, then?
Joe:	Well, the author, he isn't too sure he should be participating in the Revolution. It's like he's caught up in it but doesn't fully believe in it. And then in one situation after another he has to use his wits to get out of things.
Kai:	Like what?
Joe:	Well, for one, to get out of manual labor, and in another, to get a better assignment, and later, to get an education.
Kai:	So how does he use his wits?
Joe:	That's kind of the funny thing: sometimes he gives his superiors what they want just by going on and on with stories that honor the Party. He tells them what they want to hear, but he does so in a way that after a while, they don't want to hear it any more, and they basically give him what he wants to get rid of him.
Kai:	Funny.
Joe:	It is, yeah.
Kai:	So do you think there's a point to it?
Joe:	Well, we discussed it in class. I said that I thought it was his way of rebelling against the Revolution because he didn't fully agree with its philosophies. Or its methods, for that matter.
Kai:	Oh, good. So is that the direction you think you might take in your paper?
Joe:	Could. How's it sound to you?
Kai:	Should work. Here's what I hear you saying so far: that the author uses his wits to rebel against the Party because he doesn't subscribe to either its philosophies or its methods. Is that close?
Joe:	Well, yeah. "Subscribe"?
Kai:	You need to use your own words, but I was thinking he didn't agree with them—make sense?
Joe:	Yeah, okay.

Kai:	So let's try to flesh this out a bit. Okay, what's the author's name again? [*starts building a table*]
Joe:	Fan Shen.
Kai:	Okay, Fan Shen ... what does he disagree with?
Joe:	Well, we said the Party's philosophies and methods.
Kai:	[*writes down "philosophies" and "methods"*] Let's try to get more specific. What are some of the philosophies he disagrees with?
Joe:	Well, he doesn't really completely believe that the Red Guards' actions were any better than the counter-revolutionaries they were trying to keep down ...
Kai:	[*makes notes in table*] Okay. What does he do in response?

From here, Kai would be likely to continue the line of questioning, asking of Joe (1) what other political philosophies or methods Fan Shen questioned; (2) what kinds of actions he took in response to each of them; and (3) how Joe interprets or evaluates those actions. From those responses, Kai and Joe can fill in the rest of the table and, from there, prompt Joe towards an analytical thesis articulating political perspectives in the book *Gang of One*.

In these kinds of exchanges, take special care to sequence and articulate your inquiries thoughtfully, as our tutor Kai does well. It will help to make certain that your student can introduce and summarize the subject well before moving towards more higher-level analysis and application. These conversations can proceed more slowly, if necessary, than does our scenario above. There's no need to rush through an exhaustive taxonomy of rote interrogation, and there's no need to subject your "witness" to an excruciating cross-examination. Instead, we suggest, ask what follows naturally from your writer's responses so that you can learn more about this new subject, and listen carefully to the responses your questions elicit.

While all of these benefits can follow from a few minutes of dialogic exchange on the subject matter, we should note that, on infrequent occasion, a student may balk at the questions. He may bristle, perhaps, that you haven't read the same book as he, or doubt your intellect if you're not up on your Lacan. These cases, though you may on occasion encounter them, are rare, and a demonstrably sincere effort to learn more about the subject of your student's writing is almost always enough to persuade him that you are working in his best interests.

We promised to address the corollary to our earlier question: can a tutor assist a writer if he knows the subject well? The answer is, of course, yes, though we raise the question to address a specific concern. It would seem, on the surface, that such knowledge can only help—if, for instance, you studied Lacan in your psychology minor and had applied his insights to literary works in a number of instances. Yet we caution tutors against the temptation of using that knowledge to short-circuit the dialogue we advocate. We've already noted the benefits of the extended dialogue about the subject, and we hate to see those lost just because, well, you're up on your Lacan. Secondly, your own application of *le stade du miroir* to Hamlet's melancholic self-loathing—however successful it might have been—means little to the tutorial session at hand. Your student is striving to develop his own thesis, his own understanding of the material, and *your* knowledge of *his* subject matter here matters, frankly, hardly at all. You might acknowledge your interest and experience with the subject—but that really is as much time as you can afford in a session to devote to *your* thinking on it. The focus of the tutorial needs to be, as it always must, on the *writer's* developing thought and writing processes. In a session like Kai and Joe's above, even if Kai has himself read and written about *Gang of One,* his own interpretations, no matter how thoughtfully-developed, need to take a backseat in the tutorial to Joe's more emergent thinking.

Form and Format. From Donne's Holy Sonnets to avian mating rituals and Lacanian theory, the contemporary academy is something of a marketplace of ideas, with specialists in each discipline having developed deep knowledge of each field and thousands of apprentices building their own. If there is any site that bears more regular witness than the writing center to the rich array of topics discussed in the contemporary academy, we are unaware of its existence. We noted above how a writing tutor must be well prepared to assist any writer on virtually any topic; so too must a tutor be aware of, and able to assist with, the variety of forms and formats student writers employ.

There is, we note first, something of an implicit standard for conventional thesis-driven essays, the type one sees commonly assigned in first-year composition. Ranging from some three to five pages, driven by a central and unifying thesis, supported with evidence from authoritative and documented sources, aimed at an indeterminate audience, these essays are a staple of the academy (you can recognize them even by their double-spacing, pagination, titles, structure, and yes, that staple in the upper left-hand corner). And every writing tutor, we note, works with many a student on essays just like these: within a minute or two, you will need to know all you need to about the details of the form.

But at the same time, a writing tutor cannot always assume that these are the parameters within which any given student is working. A writing center typically promises to assist all writers, from all disciplines, at all levels. And each discipline will have not only some common (or sometimes contested) rhetorical patterns and maneuvers, but also some frequently employed genres and specific formats for documentation.

The array of expectations can sometimes prove bewildering, and not only to the student, but even to the tutor. Each of the following genres commonly exhibits features different from the others and may be assigned in the study of one discipline or another:

- Essays
- Examinations
- Editorials
- Reviews
- Letters
- Memoranda
- Résumés
- Proposals

- Manuals or directions
- Laboratory reports
- Journal entries
- Abstracts or summaries
- Research papers
- Case studies
- Bibliographies
- Profiles

And each of these may feature subgenres as well—the broad category of "essays," for instance, might range from autobiographical narrative to historiography to literary explication to scientific explanation, just as a "letter" could complain to the editor, seek resolution to a conflict, or request admission to a school or program. And all of these subgenres feature rhetorical strategies that differ from one to the next. Just consider how a single feature thereof—for instance, the location, articulation, and support of a central idea or thesis statement—might manifest itself very differently from one subgenre to the next.

We acknowledge that this diversity may seem daunting, but we also note that it will seem even more so to your students than it might to you. Your own experience working in some of these diverse genres can prove invaluable, as can a resource like a good handbook of grammar and usage. Many of today's handbooks feature separate sections on the conventions of lab reports and other genres of writing, and these can be used as a helpful aid in your tutoring. Last, we note, part of the experience of developing as a writer and a learner is, simply, developing expertise and experience working and writing within a diversity of genres and subgenres, and this is a fact you can help communicate to your students. Learning to write with confidence and success is in no small part a matter of gaining opportunities to write on different subjects, to different audiences, and in different genres.

There is one last consideration with regard to format we wish to raise. The conventions for documenting sources are not at all standard across disciplines, and this fact is one students often learn more by trial and error than by design. First-year writing curricula typically do require, and teach students the basics of, acknowledgement and documentation of sources. Yet, we find, too few students understand that each discipline has developed its own conventions and expectations, and that the details of documentation learned in first-year composition may not suffice well for upper-division work in the social or natural sciences. These are the documentation systems in most widespread use in today's academy:

- **MLA (Modern Language Association).** Typically employed in the humanities, the author-page MLA documentation system includes parenthetical citations and a separate list of works cited. Conventions in these fields—literature, religion, art, philosophy, music, film—tend to be less commonly agreed upon than in others, but in some fields, especially literary studies, students are expected to adhere strictly to published rules and conventions. See the *MLA Handbook for Writers of Research Papers*, 6th ed.

- **APA (American Psychological Association).** Used in the social science fields, the author-date APA documentation system also uses parenthetical citation—though in a format different from that of MLA—and includes a separate list of references. "APA Style" may be used to mean only this system of documentation, or it may mean every detail of formatting, pagination, division, and manuscript preparation. Some fields, especially behavioral and health sciences such as psychology and nursing, use APA format exclusively and strictly. In other fields, students may be allowed to use either APA or MLA documentation. *The Publication Manual of the American Psychological Association*, 5th ed., provides details, as does a newer pocket guide, *Concise Rules of APA Style*.

- **CSE (Council of Science Editors; formerly, CBE, for Council of Biology Editors).** The details of documenting scientific information can vary from publication to publication. Research in the sciences generally involves describing a problem, setting up an experiment, and interpreting results in the context of other scientific knowledge. Library resources are used to review existing knowledge and/or present information specific to an experiment. Some scientists use an author-date system of documentation like APA; others use the number system presented by the CSE, where each source cited in the paper is given a number in the text, and a separate list of references provides full publication information for each numbered source. The full details of CSE style are presented in *Scientific Style and Format: The CSE Manual for Authors, Editors, and Publishers*, 7th ed.

- **Chicago Manual of Style (aka Turabian).** Once the primary documentation system for all of the humanities, the "Chicago Style" is now more exclusively used by historians. This documentation style employs either footnotes or endnotes (typically at the instructor's discretion) and a separate, usually abbreviated, bibliography. *The Chicago Manual of Style*, 15th ed., provides details not only of the note-and-bibliography system but of all aspects of usage and manuscript preparation. A popular handbook based upon the Chicago style is Kate Turabian's *A Manual for Writers of Term Papers, Theses, and Dissertations*, 7th ed. Like the *Chicago Manual of Style* on which it is based, Turabian offers those in the natural and social sciences the option of using an author-date system with notes and parenthetical references, albeit slightly simplified for student use.

The style manuals that describe every nuance of manuscript preparation can be daunting for the novice. We do not recommend, as a matter of course, turning directly to the 680-page *CSE Manual* or the 1000-page *Chicago Manual* for basic directions and instructions for documenting simple sources. Rather, an up-to-date handbook of usage and documentation will provide an organized overview of each of the above systems with enough advice and examples to sustain the vast majority of your inquiries. Sometimes your student's questions regarding documentation format will be quite precise. For instance, you might be asked how to format Work Cited entries for published interviews in MLA format, or how to structure parenthetical citations framing quotations in APA format. In other cases, however, your student might be unsure which format to use—or why—or even that multiple formats exist. Here our tutor, Tucker, working with Maya, a first-year student enrolled in a general-education theatre arts course, provides some basic direction for citing sources:

Tucker: So, it looks like you've done some research for your paper. Are those all your sources?

Maya: Yeah, he said we needed to use three sources for our paper on the Guthrie's production of *Gatsby*.

Tucker: You saw the play?

Maya: We all did. It was actually very good.

Tucker: I heard that. I've never seen a play of *Gatsby*. I can't quite imagine it. So what's your angle on the paper?

Maya: I'm comparing it to two previous productions of the play, one from the 80s and one from the 70s.

Tucker: How'd you learn about those?

Maya: Well, the playbill mentioned them, and I didn't know anything about them, and I asked the prof, and he seemed kinda surprised to hear it, so I thought I'd just go with it. I found three different reviews of both in the newspaper archives, and then this other article about "performance adaptation" of *Gatsby* in general. It kind of talks about the challenges of putting it on stage or in movie or radio form.

Tucker: Nice.

Maya: So the prof is always saying that a performance has to find a way to communicate something to its audience, so I think I can make that part of my thesis.

Tucker: Sounds good. How can I help?

Maya: I don't know how to footnote the sources. Can you help?

Tucker: Footnote?

Maya: Well, yeah, footnote. I have to footnote, don't I? And the others?

Tucker: You do have to cite your sources, yeah. You'll be quoting parts of those reviews?

Maya: Mmm-hmmh. Look. [*shows him her draft*]

Tucker: Good, okay. I can show you a couple ways to introduce those quotations a little better, I think. And yes, you do have to cite your sources, but you don't have to use footnotes. Did your professor tell you you needed a certain format?

Maya: I don't think so...

Tucker: This is for a theatre class, right?

Maya: Yes ...

Tucker: Did you get a handout for the assignment?

Maya: Yeah, but it didn't say anything about that.

Tucker: Really? Hmm. [*looks it over*] How about your course syllabus?

Maya: I don't think so ... [*she shuffles to look for it*] Okay, it says here, three performance analyses, 1000 words each, MLA format, dates TBA ... Is that it?

Tucker: Yes, that's what we need to know. MLA is one way to format sources. Theatre usually uses it, so I was going to be surprised to see if he didn't mention it. I thought maybe it got taken for granted. Anyway, it's pretty easy. You need to give just short parenthetical citations ...

Maya: [*interrupts*] What?

Tucker: Sorry — just a page number, usually, in parentheses, when you quote a source. Or if you're quoting a line from the play, the act, scene, and line number. Let's look at your draft ... [*shows her an example*] Here — when you quote this review, you'll need to cite it, but it's pretty easy to do ... [*pulls a handbook from the self*]

Okay, here's the section on MLA documentation. See, it shows how to use these parenthetical citations in the text. All you need afterwards is the page number in parentheses afterwards. Now look at this quotation, what would you need here?

Maya: Same thing? Just the page number?

Tucker: If the author's name is in the sentence, yes. If not, add that to the citation. Like if you didn't have the name [*points to reviewer's name*] here in the sentence.

Maya: Is that all? Don't I need footnotes and a bibliography, too?

Tucker: MLA has what it calls a list of "Works Cited" instead of a bibliography, but it's the same concept. I can show you how to do the entries. And no, no footnotes. The handbook shows how.

Maya: Is that all I need?

Tucker: Well, maybe. A handbook like this has the basics in it, and it's pretty to use. I'm an English major, so I have a copy of the *MLA Handbook*, 'cause that's what we use. It's more comprehensive, but it doesn't show how to do the other formats.

Maya: Other formats?

Tucker: Sorry, yes, there's others. Like APA for nursing. Or Chicago for history. What's your major?

Maya: I'm not sure, but I was thinking maybe psychology as a possibility. Is there a book I should get for that?

Tucker: Psychology uses APA format, too, but until you're certain, just a general handbook like this might be enough, as long as it has both APA and MLA formats in it.

Maya: Okay. Does theatre always use MLA?

Tucker: As far as I know, yes.

Maya: Well, I guess that makes that a little easier. We were going to look at the bibliography or whatever, too, right?

Tucker: Yep. There's a specific format to use for reviews, if I remember. And a different one for a regular periodical article. Let's take a look. [*reaches for the handbook*] Okay, here's where to look for advice on putting together the Works Cited list in MLA format. It shows how to do the entries for all different types of sources, like books, interviews, articles, reviews. Which should we do first?

In this tutorial, Tucker does not simply assume that the student should know which system to use—or the details of how it works. Rather, with patient questions and explanations, he helps her discover which system to use for her theatre courses. (It would be easy enough to overlook, as Maya has, the syllabus requirement that papers use MLA format.) And he then helps guide her through the basics of the format. His student does not expect him to be a walking style manual, and instead the tutorial features, as sessions focusing on documentation conventions often will, writer and tutor consulting a handbook side-by-side.

THE RHETORICAL CONTEXT

If every writing situation features common elements of writer and reader, subject and form, so too does every situation occur in a specific context. As you work with your students to determine the dynamics of each of the rhetorical situations they face, certainly you should use the first minutes of your sessions to assess the variables we've discussed: your student writer, the intended audience, the subject matter of her writing, and the dictates of form and format. With practice and experience, you will find yourself able to assess these dynamics quickly, confidently, and accurately, helping to ensure that all that follows in your session will be based on an informed, reliable assessment of the situation.

Yet these four variables do not by themselves account adequately for all that affects or determines the ultimate shape of a piece of writing. Tutors and writers alike must also account for the *context* that warrants the writing.

***Kairos:* occasion and purpose.** One important consideration comes from classical rhetoric: *kairos*. A classical term with roots in both tapestry and archery, *kairos* can be defined as "the appropriateness of the discourse to the particular circumstances of the time, place, speaker, and audience involved" (Kinneavy, 1986, p. 213). In a sense, then, for the writer *kairos* functions both as the opportune occasion for rhetoric and the way a given context both calls for and constrains one's rhetoric. Most academic assignments, curiously, pay little heed to the notion of *kairos*: they are simply assigned to be completed by a certain date. But in the public sphere, *kairos* is crucial to the writer: he must determine what might be said, how he might say it appropriately, and select the right place and time to deliver his message.

For the writing tutor, understanding *kairos* can be very helpful in assessing the dynamics of the rhetorical situation. You might ask, either directly or indirectly of your writer, why she has chosen this particular subject, this particular thesis, this particular message, to deliver in this particular way to this particular audience. While some students in some situations are, simply, going through the motions of fulfilling a requirement, the answers in many other situations will be surprisingly enlightening, both for you and for your student. As students move upward and outward throughout their curriculum, they gain more and more opportunities to write in situations that affect and determine the quality of their lives—and others.

Process, sequence, and schedule. A second element of the rhetorical context is more procedural, involving the stages and sequences of the writer's work. Oftentimes, assignment handouts or class syllabi will give indications of a preferred sequence of stages for the writer's work. If you don't see dates assigned for the completion of bibliographies, drafts, reviews, or submissions, you will want to inquire of your student how much work has been completed, what stage of the writing process she is (roughly) immersed in, and what her (and her professor's) expectations or plans are.

As you'll find that writers will seek assistance at virtually any stage of the writing process, you can never assume that writers are "on time" with their schedules. Some, certainly, will postpone drafting until the last possible second, while others might begin the process literally months before anything is due; some will be oblivious to published deadlines, and others will seem to have structured the entirety of their lives around impending deadlines. We caution tutors to pay attention to their writers' timelines, to help them understand their professors' deadlines and requirements, and to foster realistic expectations for completing their assignments. Managing time effectively can be especially difficult for the first-year student, and only with an accurate understanding of the writer's time and schedule constraints can you help your writer move successfully from the early stages of the process to the final submission.

Assessment and evaluation. A last consideration in assessing the rhetorical context is the assessment and evaluation of the student's writing. Doing so is made reasonably simple when an assignment handout lists specific criteria for evaluation. For instance, the following grading criteria from a marketing research report assignment can serve the tutor and student both as a kind of a checklist for review as the work reaches its latter stages.

- *20 points: Quality of narrative.* Is the chronology of the case made clear? Is it factually accurate? Is the research thorough? Are facts documented accurately?

- *30 points: Quality of causal analysis.* Are causes stated clearly? Is support plausible and convincing? Do the facts support the analysis?

- *20 points: Readability.* Are claims foregrounded? Do headings guide the reader? Are sentences clear and efficient?

- *20 points: Visuals and design.* Are charts, graphics, tables, and/or other visuals presented simply and correctly? Is each purposeful? Is the report designed, formatted, and delivered in a way that promotes readability and professionalism?

- *10 points: Grammar and correctness.* Is the language of the report grammatically correct, with no errors, oversights, or gaffes?

As Harris (1995) points out, tutors often serve very useful roles in helping students interpret the language of evaluation. In the following dialogue Tania, the tutor, guides her student, Alex, through a brief analysis of the assessment criteria for the marketing research report:

Tania: So this is the assignment sheet?

Alex: [poring over his own paper] Mmm-hmmh.

Tania: I see your professor has kind of a grading checklist here.

Alex: She does?

Tania: This section called "evaluation criteria." Did you look at it?

Alex: Not really. Should I?

Tania: Well, it's worth looking at. Sounds like she really emphasizes clarity and presentation.

Alex: She talked about that in class.

Tania: Not just in the prose, either.

Alex: Huh?

Tania: Well, she says she wants to see clear and efficient sentences, and there's a separate section on correctness, but she also emphasizes the design of the report and visuals, too.

Alex: Yeah, that sounds right. I have a couple of tables I want to put in, and a photograph. So I'd like to look at that — and the headings.

Tania: Good. But I wonder if the others should come first?

Alex: You mean like the sentences.

Tania: That, yeah, but also just making sure that the material is strong, the citations are correct, and maybe before that that the analysis is as good as it can be. The way she's set these up, it's almost like a checklist for submission.

Alex: Okay, what's first?

You'll note that what Tania aims to do in this conversation is to draw Alex's attention to the existence of the grading criteria she's observed. Both tutor and writer are correct to note that the correctness and presentation are later-stage concerns, addressed better after more careful analysis of the case itself and whatever causes the writer proposes. But even in situations where you and your student lack such concrete information about grading criteria, a discussion of evaluation might well be warranted. Such conversations often can focus your writer's attention and help the two of you negotiate a purposeful agenda for your session.

SUMMARY

As a means of human communication, every writing task features a writer using a certain form to communicate a message about a subject to a reader. This simple interplay of variables—*writer, reader, subject, form*—serves as a powerful heuristic for assessing rhetorical situations. The process of thinking through these variables might be conducted within minutes of beginning a tutorial session. In some circumstances, the analysis can further help identify and provide a clear agenda for a given session: a tutor might need to address the needs or the role of the writer, help him invoke or address an audience, think critically about the subject matter, or attend to the demands of the genre or documentation format. Other considerations in rhetorical analysis can include the *kairos*, or timing and occasion of the writing; the sequence or schedule of the writer's process; and the means by which the writing will be evaluated or assessed.

In short, tutors should always strive to learn all that they can about the dynamics of the rhetorical situation and context as they undertake their sessions. (The "Heuristic for Assessing Rhetorical Dynamics" provides a concise overview of those variables.) Unfounded assumptions or unexamined perceptions about the task can result in the tutor doing more harm than good; conversely, a careful assessment of the rhetorical dynamics can place both tutor and writer on solid ground for the work that follows.

SUGGESTIONS FOR FURTHER READING

Bartholomae, David. (1985). Inventing the university. In Mike Rose (Ed.), *When a writer can't write* (pp. 134-165). New York: Guilford.

Ede, Lisa, and Andrea Lunsford. (1984). Audience addressed/audience invoked: The role of audience in composition theory and pedagogy. *College Composition and Communication 35*, 155-71.

Harris, Muriel, and Tony Silva. (1993). Tutoring ESL students: Issues and options. *College Composition and Communication 44*, 525-37.

Kasden, Lawrence N. (1980). An introduction to basic writing. In Lawrence N. Kasden and Daniel R. Hoeber (Eds.), *Basic writing: Essays for teachers, researchers, administrators* (pp. 1-9). Urbana, IL: NCTE.

Kinneavy, James E. (1986). *Kairos:* a neglected concept in classical rhetoric. In Jean Dietz Moss (Ed.), *Rhetoric and praxis: The contribution of classical rhetoric to practical reasoning.* (pp. 79-105). Washington, DC: Catholic University of America Press.

Kinneavy, James E. (1969). The basic aims of discourse. *College Composition and Communication 20*(4), 297-304.

Leki, Ilona. (1992). *Understanding ESL writers: A guide for teachers.* Portsmouth, NH: Boynton/Cook.

Ong, Walter J., S. J. (1975). The writer's audience is always a fiction. *PMLA 90*(1), 9-21.

Park, Douglas B. (1982). The meanings of "audience." *College Composition and Communication 44*, 247-257.

Reiff, Mary Jo. (1996). Rereading "invoked" and "addressed" readers through a social lens: Towards a recognition of multiple audiences. *JAC Journal of Composition Theory 16*, 407-424.

CASE 3.1: MEETING YOUR WRITER

Earlier in this chapter you were introduced to an exchange between a tutor, Mel, and a student, Sourdi, which illustrated the need for the tutor to explore the writer's background, experience, and comfort level with the assigned task. You will recall that the assignment sheet read that students were to "use field researched observations and interviews to investigate and describe a campus or community place," and that Sourdi had elected to write about the campus counseling center. Although Sourdi appears to express some ambivalence or apprehension about the task, to this point the session appears on track. But how might the session with Sourdi progress if, say, Mel had learned something different from what was volunteered in the original dialogue? Or, if immediately following, Sourdi's understanding of the rhetorical dynamics appears confused or incomplete. Using what you have learned about these variables in chapter three, consider how the dialogue might progress, and what the tutor might do to promote a thorough understanding of the rhetorical situation, if Sourdi volunteered any or all of the following:

- *I haven't been to the counseling center for research, but I have time. My paper is due at the end of the day.*

- *My new roommate is getting some help in the Counseling Center, so I might write about her experience.*

- *I'm going to the counseling center later today. I will ask the students what kind of problems they faced.*

- *I have research from the library on the difficulties that college students face, so I have what I need to write my paper. Do I use APA format? I need to use that for my major.*

- *We had a book called* Rachel and Her Children *that's supposed to be like what we write for our paper, but it took me too long to read. I don't understand how to do this.*

- *In American writing you always have a thesis sentence, right?*

- *Can you look over the grammar? I need good marks on this essay.*

CASE STUDY 3.2: BACK TO SCHOOL

A student in the same class as Sourdi (Case Study 3.1) is your next appointment. Frank, a nontraditional student who appears to be in his thirties, seems less than forthcoming with his responses to your questions and less than enthused about his work on the same assignment. Again, the assignment sheet read that students were to "use field researched observations and interviews to investigate and describe a campus or community place," and according to it, students are supposed to model their approach on Jonathan Kozol's writer-as-seeker-of-knowledge approach in *Rachel and Her Children.*

Using what you have learned in this chapter, consider how you might promote a thorough understanding of the rhetorical dynamics of Frank's task, were he to volunteer any or all of the following:

- *Here's the assignment. Someone please tell me why we have to do this.*

- *I haven't written anything for ten years, so I don't know how I'm supposed to start now.*

- *I checked out the Career Services office for a topic, but all they did was give me a bunch of handouts.*

- *The professor assigned a book for us to read, but I didn't get too far. It didn't have anything to do with what we're writing, anyway.*

- *I read one kid's paper and he sounded like a pro. No matter how hard I try to write all I come up with is crap.*

- *I tried to get started on this. So I sat in the library for two hours last night, and this is what I've got.*

> Career Services is the place to help JSU students prepare for a successful future. The staff can help you explore careers and choose one that is best for you. If you are like me you will want to pick a major that will guarantee a good future, so go to Career Services to pick a major, build leadership skills, and find a real job. Career Services has this new thing called FutureLinks that could of helped you get a job. In this system, you will be able to search for jobs, learn about events, and get alerts for job postings. Career services is one place every student needs to go to.

CASE 3.3: ASSESSING RHETORICAL DYNAMICS

Based on the "Heuristic for Assessing Rhetorical Dynamics," your task here is to create a scenario where a writer comes to you for assistance with the assignment below. Describe the writer, the reader, the subject matter, and the form in terms of the variables presented in this chapter, and then examine how you would assist the writer in the opening minutes of a tutorial session. Your student is enrolled in an introductory Physics course and has been assigned the following, due one week from today.

> According to The Insultingly Stupid Movie Physics website, "movies and physics have a lot in common: neither are completely realistic, both are simulations of reality."
>
> Your assignment is to examine the presentation/understanding/importance of physics in one of the following films: *October Sky; Apollo 13; I.Q.; The Abyss; The Right Stuff; Saving Private Ryan; Unforgiven; The Fugitive; The Net; The Usual Suspects;* or *Blade Runner.*
>
> Write a five-page essay that (1) discusses how a specific scene (or scenes) from the film depicts physical science, including helpful descriptions, illustrations, and/or diagrams, and (2) evaluates the presentation of that science according to the principles we have discussed in class, including references to physical laws, course texts, and appropriate equations.
>
> It is important to your success in this paper that you present a clear introduction to the film and the concepts you will examine; that you describe the scene(s) in strong and accurate detail; and that you demonstrate a clear understanding of the relevant physical science.
>
> When referring to course texts, use parenthetical citations in the following format: (Casek, 1996). You do not need to document scenes from the films, and a bibliography is not required unless you use outside research (which is not recommended).
>
> All papers must be double-spaced in 12-point fonts with one-inch margins. No cover page is necessary. Put your name and the assignment at the top of the first page. Number your pages. Proper writing (grammar, organization, style) counts.
>
> Written assignments for this class may not be submitted by e-mail or in any other electronic form. Papers are due in class **Wednesday, March 1**, and late papers will be penalized one-half letter grade per class day.
>
> Beginning the following week, we will discuss the papers in class. I will show selected scenes from some of the films and require students to comment on those they've written on, so please be familiar with and prepared to discuss the contents of your paper.

CASE 3.4 WRITING IN THE DISCIPLINES

The first few weeks of tutoring have been reasonably predictable, with most students seeking help with the panoply of standard first-year composition assignments, but that predictability changes with the arrival of Vera, a fast-talking bundle of energy enrolled in the nursing program. Breathlessly, Vera plunks down, in order, her laptop, a file packet labeled "case study," a set of photocopied research articles, one *very* large hardcover nursing textbook, and what appears to be an assignment sheet. "Hi," she says, "I am *so* glad you can help me with this." She aims the last piece of paper (the assignment sheet reproduced below) at you. "Here's my assignment, and here's where I am so far," she says, before launching nearly immediately into the introduction transcribed below. Based on what you have learned about assessing rhetorical dynamics, determine how you could help her assess the rhetorical situation and focus your session productively. Where would you start, and how would you progress through your session?

What Vera says as you get started: *Okay, my patient is a twelve-year-old boy with respiratory distress due to pneumonia. After two visits to the clinic, he had severely decreased oxygen levels, and his chest x-ray revealed pneumonia. He was admitted to the hospital to maintain his oxygen levels and to begin intravenous antibiotic therapy. Now, my sources basically say that the important considerations for his care include maintaining oxygen levels in the 90s, being alert to signs of increasing respiratory distress, ensuring that intravenous solutions remain patent (open) and uninfiltrated, and I know our professor has emphasized the need for careful monitoring of vital signs and observation of any distress or discomfort. Another source I found emphasized the need to make parents part of the decision-making process and to help them feel comfortable in the hospital setting. So I think I have what I need, at least according to my assignment sheet. What I need to know is how to put this together ...*

DR. D'ANGELO'S ASSIGNMENT: As a new staff nurse at St. Elegius, an acute-care facility, you have recently been assigned care of a patient named _____. Information about your individual patient will be provided separately in a case file. Consult the data provided regarding your patient's admitting information, history and physical data, progress notes, nursing notes, and social services report. Carefully consider all data relevant to the patient's care.

YOUR TASK: After reading, studying, and analyzing the facts regarding your patient's history, prepare your care plan. The basic outline of a care plan is to provide the following, in order: Overview; Data; Diagnosis; Goals; Interventions; and Assessment. Additionally, you must use a title page; write in third-person scientific style; and cite sources in APA format. See Pinka 897-902 for examples.

CHAPTER FOUR

GENERATING AND DEVELOPING IDEAS

CHAPTER FOUR

GENERATING AND DEVELOPING IDEAS

In her national bestseller *Bird By Bird*, a guidebook for aspiring creative writers, author Anne Lamott (1994) portrays the process of generating and developing ideas with refreshing candor: "Very few writers really know what they are doing until they've done it. Nor do they go about their business feeling dewy and thrilled. They do not type a few stiff warm-up sentences and then find themselves bounding along like huskies across the snow" (p. 22). Rather, speaking for herself and the published writers she knows, she reports that "We all often feel like we are pulling teeth, even those writers whose prose ends up being the most natural and fluid. The right words and sentences just do not come pouring out like ticker tape" (1994, p. 22). Lamott (1994) goes on to say that even accomplished writers reach points where they "come to a screeching halt, and all of a sudden [they] realize [they're] Wile E. Coyote and [they've] run off a cliff and are a second away from having to look down" (p. 177).

In these colorful passages Lamott evokes a central truth about writing: at times, all writers struggle to know both what to write and how to write it. In chapter one of this book we surmised that as someone who aspires to tutor writing, you are likely to have experienced success as a writer in the past. Perhaps when reading your work, your professors and peers have found your prose lucid, your attention to detail admirable, and—germane to the present chapter—your ideas interesting and worthwhile. In making this assumption about our readers, we do not mean to suggest that you believe writing well is a simple or easy undertaking. Quite to the contrary, one of the reasons most good writers are good at writing is that they appreciate just how difficult it is to write well. And they often use this appreciation to explore strategies for more effectively navigating the rhetorical dynamics that virtually all writing tasks present. Chief among the abilities of most good writers is that in addition to having firm command over the grammar and structure of writing, they also are usually able to generate and develop workable, original, and appropriate ideas in their writing, regardless of whether writing tasks call for narration, description, argumentation, analysis, research, or a combination of these or other modes of writing. Put more simply, when they sit down to write, good writers are often able to find and sustain something worth saying.

As a writing tutor, you will frequently be in positions where the student with whom you are working is struggling mightily to discover what it is that she wants or needs to write. Sometimes faced with assignments they cannot figure out how to undertake, students work with tutors to try to discover and evaluate ideas for their writing projects. Other times students enter tutorials with nascent or incomplete ideas, and in their work with tutors they try to extend them so that the writing more fully meets the rhetorical demands of their project. It's also not uncommon for students well underway with their work to run into difficulty when they lose sight of where they need to go and what they need to do. As a writing tutor, you can count on encountering these scenarios as well as any number of variations on them on a regular basis.

Chapter four provides prospective tutors with a clear understanding of their role with regard to idea generation and development in student writing. To this end, the chapter opens with a description of the relationship between composing and processes of invention before offering a number of generative heuristics that tutors can use to help students productively develop and enrich their ideas.

INVENTION AND THE COMPOSING PROCESS

> *In Xanadu did Kubla Khan*
> *A stately pleasure-dome decree:*
> *Where Alph, the sacred river, ran*
> *Though caverns measureless to man*
>   *Down to a sunless sea.*

With these famous lines, Samuel Taylor Coleridge opens his fifty-four line poem "Kubla Khan: A Vision in a Dream," a work whose considerable literary reputation in part rests on its reported method of composition. As Coleridge tells it, the poem is but a transcribed "fragment" from a longer work he claimed to have "composed" entirely in his mind while asleep in his chair during the summer of 1797 at a lonely farmhouse outside of London (p. 729). Coleridge's account of how he wrote "Kubla Khan" is a dramatic example of the romantic notion of the solitary genius for whom composing involves, as William Wordsworth would memorably put it in his 1802 preface to the Lyrical Ballads, "the spontaneous overflow of powerful feelings . . . recollected in tranquility" (p. 611). Interestingly, this version of composition—that of the lone author finding ideas by looking deep within—is one that retains remarkable traction in the minds of many writers more than two hundred years later.

In our conversations with students (and some colleagues) over the years we have met no small number of writers who hold firmly the idea that writers discover what it is they want to write by looking inward, fixing their gaze upon their topic, and then waiting for the rush of material that will spring forth as inspiration strikes. While there are times when looking inward can yield desirable results, more often, and especially for beginning or developing writers, this practice by itself seldom approaches the sort of "spontaneous overflow" Wordsworth describes. And yet, having said that, we would be remiss if we failed to note here that many good writers certainly do spend time turning their ideas over in their head, testing, stretching, and revising them until they feel they will adequately meet an audience's needs. Mike Rose (1985) has described this process as the "necessary mulling and rehearsing periods in our composing processes" (p. 227). (Curiously, quite a number of the writers we know do this while cleaning the house.)

Composition scholar Karen Burke LeFevre (1987) has noted holdovers from the Romantic notion of the genius writing in isolation. Characterizing views of invention in contemporary composition theory, LeFevre notes that "rhetorical invention is commonly viewed as the private act of an individual writer for the particular event of producing a text," a perspective she criticizes because it "sketches an incomplete picture of what happens when writers invent" (p. 1). For LeFevre, invention "occurs through the socially learned process of an internal dialogue with an imagined other" (p. 2), leading her to contend that "the invention process is enabled by an internal social construct of audience, which supplies premises and structures of beliefs that guide the writer" (p. 2). In other words, writers generate and develop ideas by making determinations about their intended audience's rhetorical needs and preferences and shaping their discourse to fit accordingly. In this way, LeFevre's (1987) work is predicated on her recognition that writers "often invent by involving other people" (p. 34), perhaps in face-to-face interactions and most certainly through the exchange of ideas that comes about through reading other writers' work.

As a writer, part of your success likely hinges on how effectively your internal dialogue helps you to generate and develop ideas that meet your audience's rhetorical needs and expectations. Perhaps, as LeFevre writes, you build your ideas by consulting with others— maybe the authors as presented in the texts you read, perhaps your professors or peers, maybe someone so removed from the writing context that he or she can offer a completely fresh perspective. From a more procedural standpoint, to facilitate your invention process you might turn to lists, outlines, thought webs, freewriting or some other graphic or verbal recording of thought. Regardless of which of these or other invention strategies you employ, the salient point is that part of most successful writers' skill set is a reasonably stable procedure for creating and following through on ideas that meet the rhetorical demands of a given audience.

For many beginning and developing writers, however, the process of generating and developing ideas is shrouded in mystery. Linda Flower and John R. Hayes, two scholars whose research is foundational to much of what we know about the writing process, have articulated a thoughtful and elaborate model describing how writers find ideas for their work. Specifically, Flower and Hayes (1980) argue that less experienced writers frequently run into trouble generating and developing ideas because they are inexperienced in "the act of finding or defining the problem to be 'solved'" (p. 22). Put another way, unseasoned writers receive writing assignments and are unable to frame them rhetorically, and, as a result, they struggle to know what their audience expects of them, a shortcoming that effects their ability to make informed decisions about what to write let alone how to write it.

Flower and Hayes (1980) have further observed that writers "only solve the problem they give themselves to solve," (p. 22), a tenet that is at the heart of many of the student papers that professors characterize as rhetorically immature, insufficient, or misdirected. When faced with assignments whose intricacies they are struggling to understand rhetorically, students understandably simplify or redirect the project into something they can comprehend and complete, in the process producing text that, rhetorically speaking, does not meet expectations. While on the one hand simplifications and redirections are wrapped up in inaccurate task representations, they are also intricately enmeshed in the writer's troubles with generating ideas that will fulfill the assignment.

As a writing tutor, you will see rhetorical simplification or redirection in student writing with regularity. For example, a student facing an assignment asking her to analyze the narrative structure of William Faulkner's *As I Lay Dying* may struggle to figure out how to undertake such a complicated analysis and instead produce a paper that simply summarizes the novel. A student in a philosophy seminar assigned to compare rationalism with empiricism might feel uncertain how to approach such a subject and end up with a text that argues why rationalism is superior to empiricism. A geography student overwhelmed by an assignment that requires him to produce a flood hazard reduction plan for coastal North Carolina may end up writing a paper that only explains why flooding can be a problem at certain times of the year in that region. What all of these scenarios and others like them have in common is this: the writers face tasks that leave them unsure how to go about generating and developing ideas and, as a result, they represent the task as something they feel they can handle. But in doing so, these writers produce writing that does not meet the demands of their audience.

For many students, a number of affective factors can further complicate the difficulties of generating workable ideas. Robert Boice (1985) has written about the ways that a writer's fear—of failing, of appearing stupid or naive, of simply not knowing what to do—can stymie the development of ideas. John A. Daly (1985) and also Cynthia L. Selfe (1985) have both showed how student apprehension about writing frequently hamstrings their creative ability. Mike Rose (1984) has described the ways that "writer's block" emerges as a significant problem for writers, resulting in texts that, if they do get moving, are little more than associational streams of ideas. What these studies collectively suggest is that on top of the challenges associated with accurately responding to an audience's rhetorical expectations, a number of affective factors can subvert even well-meaning and hard-working students' efforts to write well.

Addressing ways that instructors can assist writers experiencing difficulty with topic generation and development, Flower and Hayes (1980) maintain that "If we teach students to explore and define their own problems, even within the constraints of an assignment, we can help them to create inspiration instead of wait for it" (p.32). Predicated on the tutor's and writer's collective understanding of rhetorical situation (chapter three), the generative heuristics in this chapter are meant to serve as a productive means for tutors to assist in students' invention processes.

INTRODUCING HEURISTICS

James Berlin (1988) has pointed out that heuristics are only as good or bad as the person using them. Put another way, heuristics are generally only helpful if the user of the heuristic understands and invests in its utility. Thus, before employing generative heuristics to help students find and develop ideas, tutors need to check for the student's understanding of and receptiveness to trying the heuristic that the tutor is recommending. Also, tutors must keep in mind that the finding and developing of ideas is something over which the student must retain control. At no point should a tutor feed ideas to students, even in those instances when the tutor can clearly see a workable direction for the project under consideration. While offering your own ideas might occasionally feel like the right thing to do, to do so would be to usurp the student's ownership of the writing project, in the process denying the student an opportunity to develop her own strategies for finding and extending writing ideas.

Tutors also need to recognize that it is not their job to be the final arbiter of the quality and potential of the ideas students generate. After all, as we observed in chapter three, very often students are working on topics about which their tutors know very little. (A particularly memorable example that comes to mind is a time when one of our tutors worked with a student who was trying to generate ideas for a paper in her art history class on the aesthetic vision of Hans Holbein, a German Renaissance artist of the 16th century.) As with all other aspects of tutoring, the tutor's role with regard to student invention is to ask questions and reflect statements—usually within the context of a generative heuristic—in the process creating space for students to more productively and fully examine and extend their thinking.

Brainstorming

Many of the students with whom you work will have had some experience with brainstorming. An invention heuristic focused more on generation than on development, in brainstorming the goal is for the writer to think associatively, listing as many ideas as pop into his head with the understanding that after a period of time he will sort back through those ideas in search of ones that might have potential. Sometimes employed to locate a starting focus for a paper, other times utilized to subordinate ideas to an already established focus, brainstorming can be of considerable use to writers who are in search of more or better ideas for their writing.

Although in general most students you tutor will know what brainstorming is—and many will have done it in the past—they may be uncertain about exactly how to go about sifting through and weighing the merits of the various ideas they write down. In the following dialogue, our tutor, Darnell, suggests brainstorming in his work with Seth, a student who is having trouble with an assignment that asks him to take a side on a controversial issue for his freshman composition class. Seth has been lamenting his inability come up with a topic.

Darnell: You know, listening to you talk, it sounds to me like it might be helpful for us to just take some time to try to generate some possibilities for your paper.

Seth: Yeah. I just don't know how to do that. All the ideas I come up with seem lousy.

Darnell: Have you ever tried brainstorming?

Seth: Yeah, but in the past nothing has really come of it. I make lists but still don't feel like my ideas are any better.

Darnell: I understand. It can sometimes be tough to know where to go with the ideas you write down. Would you be willing to take another shot at it anyway?

Seth: Sure, why not.

Darnell: Good. Okay, at the top of a blank piece of paper, write the word "controversies." I'm going to give you some time to write down everything that comes into your mind—words or phrases—associated with that word. You might be tempted to evaluate the ideas before writing them down, but I want you to resist doing that. Just get thoughts down. We'll go back through them later to see which ones have potential.

Seth: Okay, I'll do my best.

Darnell: While you're working, I'm just going to give you some time on your own. I'll be back in a bit.

[*ten minutes later*]

Darnell: [*Returning to the table*] Okay, let's see what you came up with.

Seth: Well, I don't know if any of these are good. I don't see how I could get three to five pages out of any of them.

Darnell: Let's just take a look at what you've got. We'll work more on whatever looks good. To get started, why don't you read through your list and put a mark next to the ones that you think are interesting or might have potential.

Seth: Okay.

Controversies		
*Abortion	Politics	Legalization of drugs
*Teen pregnancy	No real alternatives	Marijuana
Promoting abstinence	Belief in democracy	Safer than alcohol
*Capital punishment	*Leaving Iraq	Traffic
Texas	*Patriotism	Legal in other parts of
Dead Man Walking	Hand guns	the world
Mercy killing	Kids with guns	Parental responsibility
*War in Iraq	Bowling for Columbine	*Weapons of mass
President Bush	Gun control	destruction
Role of media	Trigger locks	*Right to disagree
Liberal media?	Parental responsibility	

Darnell: Okay, I see you've marked a number of different things on your list. Why did you mark the ones you did?

Seth: Well, I marked "Abortion" and "Teen pregnancy" and also "Capital punishment" because they seem like they'd be easy. I mean, they're clear controversies, ones everyone knows about. But, I don't know. I don't want to write about something that everyone else will do. I just thought they'd be easy.

Darnell: Okay, so if you're not that invested in them, let's see what else you marked.

Seth: Well, as I read the list now, there are some that seem related, the ones that are connected to "Patriotism" and the war in Iraq. I also marked "Dissent" because this seems connected.

Darnell: How so?

Seth: Well, ever since September 11th, it seems like it's hard to disagree with the government because then you'll be accused of being unpatriotic.

Darnell: So, how is that a controversy?

Seth: It's a controversy because one of the things we're supposed to have as Americans is the right to say what we want, to question our government. But right now, with the war in Iraq, a lot of people say that you can't question our government because it hurts the war effort. I don't agree with that. I think you can disagree with the government but also be supportive of the troops. Do you think this might be something I could argue for in a paper?

Darnell: Maybe. Is there something about it you don't like?

Seth: Well, it's not a "normal" controversial topic like the other ones on my list: abortion, gun control, legalizing drugs, death penalty.

Darnell: That's true. What you're talking about is different than those others, but I think that that may be a good thing. You won't be doing something that's already been overdone.

Seth: So, I could write about this?

Darnell: It depends. What would you call this controversy?

Seth: I don't know. Maybe something about the whether or not it's all right to disagree with the government during a time of war.

Darnell: That's good. Earlier you mentioned you were concerned about your topic being long enough to satisfy the length requirement. So let's see if this has potential. Let's get out another sheet of paper and make a new list. At the top of this one, write "difficulty disagreeing with the war." And then I'll give you some time to generate a list of ideas like you did the first time, only now all of them related to that idea.

Seth: That sounds good. I can do that.

As with any generative heuristic, Darnell makes sure that Seth understands how brainstorming is supposed to work and also that he is willing to give it a try. After Seth spends time listing ideas that fit a broad category ("controversies"), Darnell invites Seth to talk through his thinking, in the process helping him come to the realization that he may have a set of ideas that revolve around a usable focus for his paper. Note too that Darnell ends the above dialogue by inviting Seth into a second round of brainstorming, only this time with a narrower starting point. Presumably, Seth will come away from this work with a larger set of ideas that fit within a focus that he finds interesting and worthwhile. It is also worth noticing that Darnell's contributions—supportive questions and some restatement of ideas—have not usurped Seth's control of his topic development. As a result, Seth enters the next phase of the tutorial with ownership of where his current line of thought might take him.

It bears mentioning here that some students will struggle more than Seth does in the above scenario, requiring the tutor to ask additional and more specific questions about the student's brainstorming to try to help the student open up some workable conceptual space.

Freewriting

Freewriting is an invention technique predicated on the idea that when writers write they give themselves opportunities to discover, extend, and combine ideas that previously were inaccessible. The basic idea behind freewriting is that the writer spends ten to fifteen minutes writing nonstop and without regard to spelling, grammar, organization, or style.

The object is for the writer to write as quickly as she can, recording ideas as they emerge. Many writers find that when freewriting they reach places where they are not sure what else to write; to keep moving, writers can write "I don't know what else to write" or "Relax and breathe" over and over until more ideas come. Freewriting often resembles stream of consciousness, with ideas that may have relevance interspersed with stray thoughts whose only purpose was to keep the writer writing. To get students started on a freewrite, tutors can help the writer to generate a starting question or idea and then leave the student to respond to that idea. After an agreed upon amount of time, the tutor can return to help the student sift back through the freewrite in search of promising ideas. The following dialogue picks up with the tutor, Sondra, returning after the student, Diane, has been freewriting for ten minutes. The assignment Diane is working on is an analysis of Yann Martel's *Life of Pi* for her philosophy of religion class. She's struggling to determine what to write about.

Diane's Freewriting

What is going on in Martel's *Life of Pi*?

Okay, Life of Pi. Let's see. Well, the things that strike me as important in the book all have to do with religion. Because Pi is a Christian, a Hindu, and a Buddhist, as he tells us early on. Plus in the preface or whatever it's called the author writes that this is a story that's supposed to make us believe in God. I don't know if it does that or not. But, maybe that's the point. I mean, we've got a main character who says he follows three of the major world religions but at the end of the day, none of them are what save him or really even offer him all that much comfort. I mean, once he's lost at sea with a tiger on his lifeboat, religion doesn't really help him at all. The only thing that saves him is his own ingenuity. The author, Martel, gives us some places where Pi thinks religious thoughts, but religion for Pi seems to just be a diversion, almost like a drug, from the true terror of his situation. In actuality, the book is as much about the horrors of humanity— especially if we interpret the novel as being about humans in the lifeboat instead of animals—rather than being about how religion could save Pi. It's interesting though, because the book is full of all this religious imagery. It's like window-dressing. Religion is fine theoretically, but it won't help you get through an ordeal like Pi faces. Hmmm. So, what's that mean? I don't know. This line of thought might not be any good. What's the analytical angle here? Maybe it's just that the book tries to show us how religion is only something humans turn to as a way to try to impose meaning on a world where the only thing that's real is suffering and uncertainty? So, Pi's following all three religions isn't what gets him through his ordeal. What gets him through is his ability to understand humanity, to manipulate others, to use his wits. It's almost like his own ingenuity becomes his religion, the thing he follows with almost religious zeal. Hmmm. I wonder if that's the angle. The book seems to be about religion until you look more closely, at which point you see it's really about how the only thing we can depend on is ourselves. That feels bleak, but it's what I see going on in the novel.

Sondra: It's been ten minutes now. How'd it go?

Diane: Well, it's hard to say. I don't if I know what I'll focus on yet, but I have a feeling that this helped me at least clarify what I think.

Sondra: That's good. To try to see if there's anything that will work in here, do you think you could go back through the freewrite and underline any sentences or ideas that feel like they might get at what you want to say in your analysis?

Diane: I can do that. [*Diane underlines several sections*]

Sondra: Why did you underline those things?

Diane: When I was working on a topic before, I kept trying to come up with something about what the book said about religion. I was trying to force myself to see the book as supportive of religion. But, when I started writing just now, the thoughts that kept coming out felt like they were about how the book shows how religion failed Pi. I mean, he was lost at sea and religion just wasn't practical. So, the thing he followed in its place was his own ingenuity. There's so much of the second half of the novel focused on Pi's almost ritual-like behaviors. And, like a religion, these rituals are what give Pi's life meaning and hope.

Sondra: So, if you were put it in a sentence or two, what would you say your idea is for this analysis? Perhaps beginning with: "An analysis of Yann Martel's *Life of Pi* reveals..."

Diane: An analysis of Yann Martel's *Life of Pi* reveals that the book seems to be about how religion gives Pi's life meaning, but once you look more carefully you see that the "religion" Pi follows has nothing to do with religions in the usual sense. It has to do with Pi's belief in his own ingenuity.

Sondra: That sounds interesting. Why don't you write that idea down, and we'll keep going from there to try to tease out some more pieces.

Diane: That sounds like a good plan.

Note that once the freewrite has concluded Sondra is careful to let Diane do the work here. Diane, not her tutor, is the one who is explaining and amplifying her thoughts, talking through what seems to be at the crux of her thinking about the novel. Sondra's role is to clarify, prompt, encourage—and listen. To help Diane develop her idea further, Sondra might invite her to freewrite again, this time with a prompt that focuses specifically on the idea Diane has generated. Another way to continue is to ask the student to respond to a sentence or idea in the initial freewrite that appears to have the most potential or interest behind it.

When some students try freewriting they produce texts that are much more incoherent than Diane's. In such cases, the tutor can help the student unpack the freewrite by seeking clarifications and explanations of the ideas that have been written down. Very often the process of talking through the freewriting gives the student an additional chance to sift through and weigh the ideas that he has generated.

Idea Mapping

Another technique for building and exploring ideas, idea mapping offers students a more visual representation of their thinking. To make an idea map, in the center of a page the writer writes a central idea or question that they intend to develop or explore. Like spokes off of a wheel, related or subordinate ideas come out of the starting thought. Often times these satellite ideas warrant additional spokes, some of which might themselves yield ideas. The goal of this strategy is to produce a graphic representation of how ideas are related to one another, often in a hierarchical manner.

In inviting students to try idea mapping, tutors should advise the student to pursue each line of thought until no new ideas arise. Somewhat related to the listing activity that characterizes brainstorming, idea mapping produces many more ideas than freewriting, though they tend to be less fully articulated and developed. Students can sometimes use an idea map as a heuristic for discovering how various ideas are related to one another. On the next page is a sample idea map for Diane's *Life of Pi* paper.

As the tutor, Sondra might probe some of the features of the map, asking Diane to explain what she means and also to articulate more precisely how some of her ideas are connected to one another. The following dialogue shows how a tutor might carry out this line of questioning.

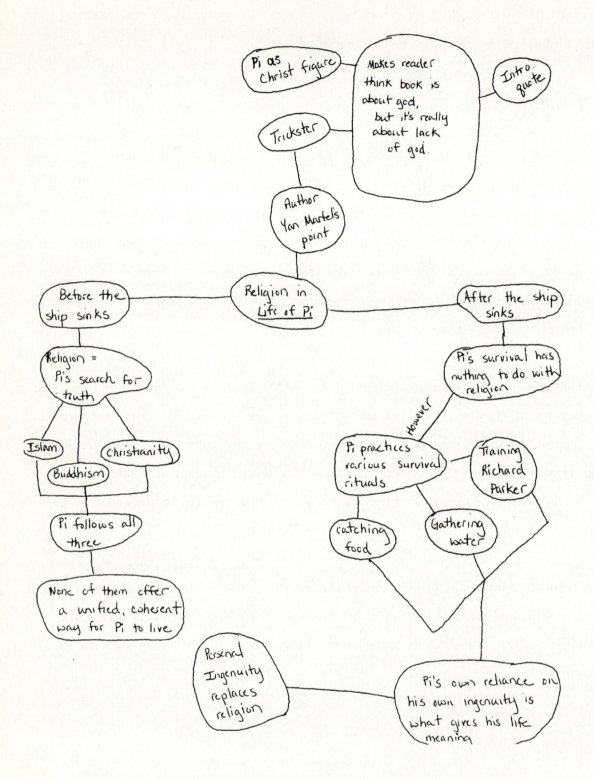

Sondra: [*returning after Diane has completed the map*] So, how'd it go?

Diane: I think it went all right. Does it make sense?

Sondra: It depends on how well you understand it. I see you've got three main ideas coming out of the center. Can you see a way that they're related to each other?

Diane: Yeah, I think so. There's the first part of the novel when Pi was practicing all these religions. And then, there's the second part after the boat sinks and Pi is lost at sea.

Sondra: What's the relationship between those two?

Diane: Before the boat goes down, Pi is safe and comfortable, so it's like he has the luxury of pursuing religion. But, after the boat goes down, all the religions he has supposedly been following have to be forgotten because they won't help him survive.

Sondra: Okay, so you've got a structural break in the novel, before and after the boat goes down. What about that third idea, the one about the author?

Diane: Well, I think that's the really important part. Because Martel sets the reader up to think the novel is about religion but in actuality, it's about how religion isn't all that practical.

Sondra: How does that figure into the paper?

Diane: I want to show how Martel makes it look like he's giving the reader a clear and easy religious allegory, but when we look at it more carefully we see that it's about the inadequacy of religion.

Sondra: So, what's this about Pi as Christ figure?

Diane: I think that could just be an example of Martel trying to get the reader to fall into an interpretation that is too simple. It's like he wants to stir the waters with all these religious ideas, but in the end he wants to say how religion doesn't get Pi anywhere.

Sondra: This is all sounding very interesting. I think it sounds like you might be ready to start writing.

Diane: Yeah, I think I am. Can I come back after I've got a draft done?

Sondra: Sure. I'll look forward to reading your work.

Sometimes idea maps can be quite specific, linking quotes from or precise observations about texts the student has read to the larger ideas to which they connect. Other times, idea maps can remain on the surface and still be productive, as when the student is merely trying to gain an overall sense of how their ideas are related to one another.

HDWDWW

An acronym for **How Does Who Do What and Why?**, HDWDWW (Berthoff, 1978) helps students consider their topic thoroughly and from a variety of potentially productive angles. The basic idea behind HDWDWW is for the student to create ideas by identifying an agent (who?), an action (does), an object (what?), a manner (how?) and also a purpose (why?). At first glance this heuristic may appear unwieldy: it's true that HDWDWW isn't exactly a smooth or pronounceable acronym. But in our experience tutors can put HDWDWW to good use when working with students who need to think more expansively and carefully about their topic. Additionally, as you will see in chapters five and six, variations on the strategy can be used to help articulate claims and clarify meaning. In a tutorial focused on generating ideas, tutors can use HDWDWW in one of two basic ways: either by helping students to fill in a chart answering the HDWDWW questions to their fullest extent, or simply by prompting students in dialogue to respond to the questions verbally.

The following example shows how Seth, the student in one of our previous scenarios, might answer the HDWDWW questions to develop his ideas about a paper exploring the difficulties of disagreeing with the government during a time of war.

How Does	Who	Do What	Why?
1. By writing letters 2. By voting and encouraging others to vote 3. With an understanding of how complicated things are	Citizens against the war	1. Voice opposition to policies 2. Support troops even though they criticize the war	1. To try to end the conflict 2. To separate the war from the soldiers who have to fight it
1. By writing letters 2. By voting and encouraging others to vote 3. By questioning dissenters' patriotism	Citizens who support the war	1. Criticize those who disagree 2. Support President Bush and Dick Cheney	1. Because they believe that if don't support the war you are hurting the troops 2. To show patriotism
1. In debates with each other 2. By using the media to gain support for their ideas	Politicians	1. support the war 2. call for an end to the war	1. To get re-elected 2. To deflect blame 3. To try to do some good
1. By following orders 2. By using their combat skills	Soldiers	Fight the war	1. though they have no choice 2. because they believe they are doing the right thing 3. because they are honorable men and women

Seth could continue to build the chart further, listing additional, more precisely differentiated agents and providing fuller details in each of the cells. As the tutor working with Seth, Darnell would want to ask questions to elicit clearer, fuller explanations regarding some elements, in the process drawing out additional ideas. For instance, one line of questioning might be to try to get Seth to explain how loyalty to political party (as implied by the "with their votes" item) might also influence opinions about the war, in the process revealing a potential source for the controversy about which he is writing. Another possibility is that Darnell would ask Seth what he means about politicians' use of the media and its relation to the topic. Darnell would also do well to question Seth's assumption that only citizens who are against the war understand the situation's complications.

Once Darnell's questions have pushed Seth to examine his work in more fine detail, Darnell would want to take Seth through some further analysis. Notice how each row in the table yields the seeds of a grammatically complete (if not necessarily syntactically elegant) sentence: *By questioning dissenters' patriotism, citizens who support the war support President Bush to show [their own] patriotism.* Darnell might prompt Seth to examine each of these potential claims for their clarity and potential, looking to find examples that might support claims that could appear in a subsequent draft. In doing so, Seth will be well on his way to writing a paper that presents a controversial issue with an appropriate level of complexity.

One of the advantages, then, of HDWDWW is that its highly structured nature can help keep writers from getting lost in or discouraged by the intricacies of the relationships among the material they generate. It can also be used for fairly straightforward comparisons, and its strength is that in a short amount of time, it can reveal surprising insights. In the dialogue that follows, the tutor, Bree, assists her student, Aaron, with his paper on James Joyce's famous short story, "The Dead." Aaron's choice for a topic is the similarities between Joyce himself and his protagonist in the story, Gabriel Conroy.

Aaron: We read a story called "The Dead" and I was thinking that the author based the main character, Gabriel, off of himself. I know there are a lot of similarities between them and I'd like to expand on that more.

Bree: Okay. Have you done any research, or do you need to?

Aaron: I just have what we heard in class so far, but based on it, there seem like some similarities, and no one mentioned them.

Bree: So that should make for a good topic.

Aaron: There's a lot of ways that the two are similar, but I'm having a hard time sorting it out.

Bree: Okay. If you want, we can try something called HDWDWW, which stands for "how does who do what and why." It sorts out your ideas a bit.

Aaron: Never heard of that before... but sure, I'll try it.

Bree: Let's start with the easy part: "who". So who is involved in the topic you want to write about? Write their names here.

Aaron: [writes "*Gabriel Conroy and James Joyce*"]

Bree: Okay, next is "does what", as in what do they do?

Aaron: Well a big idea in this book is the idea of "nationalists" and "West Britons". Both the character and the author are "West Britons", which basically means their sympathies lie towards Great Britain and they aren't supportive of Ireland's independent culture. [writes "*they both are not nationalists*"]

Bree: Okay, that's a good start. Next, "how," we want to know how they are West Britons and do not support nationalism.

Aaron: Well they both write for papers that are definitely not supportive of nationalism. They are both kind of detached from the country. I know Joyce did a lot of traveling and liked to spend time outside of the country. Gabriel did as well. Gabriel seems very detached from the party guests. There really is no conversation between them except for with one character, but it gives me the impression that he is different from the rest of the group with them being nationalists. [*writes "detached from country" for both*]. Also that they write for newspapers that do not support the nationalist movement.

Bree: Good, write that down, too. Okay, what else do you want to add? You already have that they "write for newspapers that don't support nationalism". Anything else that they do?

Aaron: Well I know Gabriel argues with Miss Ivors about it. [*writes "argues about nationalism/West Briton views"*].

Bree: Who's she?

Aaron: A character at the party. A foil, basically—she irritates him by pointing out how stuffy and old-school his thinking is, and it gets under his skin.

Bree: If she's important, you might want to add a line for her, but for now, just put down her name, and we can come back to her later. Let's go on. Now we want to focus on the effect of their beliefs. What effect do their actions produce?

Aaron: Again, Miss Ivors arguing with him. More specifically though, people expressing their contempt towards "West Britons". [*writes "nationalists are anti-West Britons"*]. Their differing views also produce detachment from the country [*writes "produces detachment"*].

Bree: The last question is "why." Why do they do what they do?

Aaron: Well I know Joyce had exiled himself, possibly because of the slum life in Dublin. Everything had changed since his childhood, and he no longer recognized the Ireland that he grew up in. [*writes "a changed Ireland"*].

Bree: How about the main character? Why does he do what he does?

Aaron: Well, I'm not sure, but I think it's different for him. He seems like he's trying to hold on to the past in some ways.

Bree: Sounds like you might need to think that one through a bit more.

Aaron: Now I think I want to focus on the nationalist/West Briton conflict. I think it's especially interesting how they are so detached from their own country. I would like to look up more about the driving force behind it.

Bree: Sounds like a plan. We do have some time left, is there anything else you want to discuss or go over before our time is up?

Here, Bree's role is to motivate Aaron to deepen his inquiry. She begins with simple reconstructive question: *who* will the paper discuss? But it is Aaron who is generating and developing the ideas that link James Joyce, the author, to Gabriel Conroy, his fictional creation. Using HDWDWW more as a general guide than a strict protocol, Bree prompts Aaron towards a fuller understanding of each of their actions and purposes. When suggesting this strategy to students, tutors would do well to remember that the more numerous and detailed the answers to HDWDWW are, the more likely that the ideas will be usable to the student. Though HDWDWW will not apply to all writing assignments, the heuristic can be useful for students who are struggling to see and articulate a more complete set of ideas on their topic.

SUMMARY

Helping student writers generate and develop ideas can be a regular part of a tutor's work. When employing generative heuristics with students, tutors need to remember that, as with other aspects of tutoring, they must allow students to bear the responsibility for rhetorical invention, even in those instances when they can offer quality ideas for the student's writing. With practice, students can gain confidence and flexibility in their invention work, particularly when they receive the sort of structured mentoring that a writing tutor can provide. Each of the heuristics we present—brainstorming, freewriting, idea mapping, and HDWDWW—serves its own unique purpose in the writing process and can be purposeful at different moments. At the same time, however, no tutor can rightfully expect that every such generative heuristic will work for every student or for every rhetorical situation. A more realistic approach is to view these heuristics as useful starting points for tutors to begin conversations with students about their writing topics and their ideas for developing them. Since a considerable responsibility of the writing tutor is to be ready and able to work with students at any stage of the process, knowing a set of heuristics well—and being able to promote their writers' thoughtful invention work through collaborative dialogue—is essential to the process of becoming an effective and confident tutor.

SUGGESTIONS FOR FURTHER READING

Berlin, James. (1988). Rhetoric and ideology in the writing class. *College English, 50*(5), 477-494.

Berthoff, Ann E. (1978). *Forming thinking writing: The composing imagination.* Portsomouth, NH: Heinemann.

Boice, Robert. (1985). Psychotherapies for writing blocks. In Mike Rose (Ed.), *When a writer can't write: Studies in writer's black and other composing-process problems* (pp. 182-218). New York: Guilford.

Daly, John A. (1985). Writing apprehension. In Mike Rose (Ed.), *When a writer can't write: Studies in writer's black and other composing-process problems* (pp. 43-82). New York: Guilford.

Flower, Linda, and John R. Hayes. (1980). The cognition of discovery: Defining a rhetorical problem. *College Composition and Communication, 31*(1), 21-32.

Lamott, Anne. (1994). *Bird by bird: Some instructions on writing and life.* New York: Anchor.

LeFevre, Karen Burke. (1987). *Invention as a social act.* Carbondale, IL: Southern Illinois University Press.

Rose, Mike. (1984). *Writer's block: The cognitive dimension.* Carbondale, IL: Southern Illinois University Press.

Rose, Mike. (1985). Complexity, rigor, evolving method, and the puzzle of writer's block: Thoughts on composing-process research. In Mike Rose (Ed.), *When a writer can't write: Studies in writer's black and other composing-process problems* (pp. 227-260). New York: Guilford.

Selfe, Cynthia. (1985). An apprehensive writer composes. In Mike Rose (Ed.), *When a writer can't write: Studies in writer's black and other composing-process problems* (pp. 83-95). New York: Guilford.

Spack, Ruth. (1984). Invention strategies and the ESL college composition student. *TESOL Quarterly, 18*(4), 649-670.

CASE STUDY 4.1: IN SEARCH OF A VIABLE IDEA

You are working in the writing center when your 4:00 appointment arrives. The student, Joanna, is struggling to come up with an idea for a paper in her freshman writing class. Here's are the instructions from her professor:

> In an essay of 1000 words, argue for or against the validity of a common maxim or saying. To do this, the first thing you will need to do is select a maxim with which you have a reasonable level of familiarity and comfort. As for the maxim/saying you choose, it can be classic (e.g., Beauty is only skin deep) or something more contemporary (e.g., No guts, no glory). Your essay should demonstrate the supposed wisdom or logic behind the maxim and evaluate its truthfulness or relevance.

While Joanna appears to have a solid understanding of the assignment, when it comes to developing ideas for approaching it, she is unsure how to proceed. She's brought in the list of maxims below but doesn't know quite what do next. Based on what you have read about invention processes in chapter four, determine a course of action for helping Joanna evaluate and develop ideas for getting started on her paper.

Easier said than done.
Curiosity killed the cat.
Discretion is the better part of valor.
Don't wash dirty linen in public.
Fools rush in where angels fear to tread.
Every dog has his day.
It never rains, but it pours.
Waste not, want not.
One good turn deserves another.
Necessity is the mother of invention.
Too many cooks spoil the broth.
There's no honor among thieves.

Familiarity breeds contempt.
He who hesitates is lost.
Let sleeping dogs lie.
Every picture tells a story.
Good fences make good neighbors.
Ignorance is bliss.
No news is good news.
You can't take it with you.
Penny wise, pound foolish.
The proof of the pudding is in the eating.
Virtue is its own reward.
There's more than one way to skin a cat.

CASE STUDY 4.2: EMPLOYING GENERATIVE HEURISTICS

Earlier in this chapter you read a dialogue between Darnell (the tutor) and Seth (a student). Recall that Seth's assignment was rather broad: he had to articulate a position on the controversial issue of his choice. This case study revisits their interaction. However, in the options below, we have altered the course of the dialogue. Based on what you have read about invention strategies (and also calling back on your knowledge of session dynamics and assessing the rhetorical situation), how should Darnell respond to Seth in the following scenarios?

OPTION A

Darnell: You know, listening to you talk, it sounds to me like it might be helpful for us to just take some time to try to generate some possibilities for your paper.

Seth: Yeah. I just don't know how to do that. All the ideas I come up with seem lousy.

Darnell: Have you ever tried brainstorming?

Seth: Of course, but in the past nothing has really come of it. I make lists but still don't feel like my ideas are any better.

Darnell: I understand. It can sometimes be tough to know where to go with the ideas your write down. Would you be willing to take another shot at it anyway?

Seth: You know, I'm really not that interested in doing anything like that. I just want you to tell me what a good topic would be. I really don't care what it is, I just need something that you think will work okay.

OPTION B

Darnell: At the top of a blank piece of paper, write the word "controversies." I'm going to give you some time to write down everything that comes into your mind—words or phrases—associated with that word. You might be tempted to evaluate the ideas before writing them down, but I want you to resist doing that. Just get thoughts down. We'll go back through them later to see which ones have potential.

Seth: Okay, I'll do my best.

Darnell: While you're working, I'm just going to give you some time on your own. I'll be back in a bit.

[ten minutes later]

Darnell: [Returning to the table] Okay, let's see what you came up with.

Seth: Well, I only wrote down five things: abortion, hand gun control, euthanasia, capital punishment, and cloning. That's all I've got, and they're all lame and overdone. I just can't get anything going.

OPTION C

Darnell: [*Returning to the table*] Okay, let's see what you came up with.

Seth: Well, I don't know if any of these are good. I don't see how I could get three to five pages out of any of them.

Darnell: Let's just take a look at what you've got. We'll work more on whatever looks good. To get started, why don't you read through your list and put a mark next to the ones that you think are interesting or might have potential.

Seth: Well, as I look as this list, the only one I see that looks like it could work is *Traffic*. Have you seen that movie? It's got all sorts of controversies in it. So does *Dead Man Walking*, the other movie I wrote down. I think I could write a really good paper explaining what the controversies are in either one of those movies.

CASE STUDY 4.3: UTILIZING HDWDWW TO DEVELOP IDEAS

During your shift in the writing center a student comes in asking for help with a comparison/contrast paper he is trying to get started on. The student, a freshman named Andrew enrolled in a 100-level general education course, reports that he has some potential topics but can't come up with anything he feels will work.

Andrew's assignment:

> This assignment asks you to compare one of the major figures we have studied in class with one of his or her (or their) contemporaries (or influences, predecessors, or followers) in an essay of 1000 words. For your analysis, choose something that allows you to present a fair amount of complexity and depth (rather than something overly simplistic). Your comparison must be motivated by a purpose for the comparison, with a carefully selected and intellectually genuine connection between the two figures prompting your analysis. Research outside the course text may include library or internet sources, but they must be incorporated sparingly and acknowledged carefully in a recognized documentation format such as MLA, APA, or Chicago.

How would you guide Andrew through a careful comparison of two figures using HDWDWW to try to help him develop an elaborated analysis that might serve as the basis for a successful essay? Based on your own interests and knowledge base, select a pair of figures for analysis that one might encounter in a first-year general education elective: you might select two literary authors, two musicians or composers, two philosophers, two scientists or other intellectuals, two politicians, two historical figures (e.g. reformers or inventors), or two film directors or actors. Compose a dialogue that demonstrates how you would help him to understand and use HDWDWW. To do this, as part of the scenario you will want to prompt Andrew to complete the chart so that you can also help him analyze the results of his invention work.

CASE STUDY 4.4: BUILDING ON A FIRST DRAFT

Crina, an ESL student from Romania, shows up for her 11:00 appointment having already started on a paper for her ESL writing course. As you are sitting down, she informs you that she has written very few papers in English, and never one that is as long as her current assignment needs to be. She also lets you know that it has taken her several painful hours to produce her current draft. After reading her work, select one (or more) of the invention heuristics described in this chapter and construct a dialogue demonstrating how you would help Crina develop her ideas.

Crina's assignment:

> Prompt: Many students choose to attend schools or universities outside their home countries. Why do some students study abroad? Use specific reasons, details, and examples to support and develop your answer. Length: 2-3 pages.

Crina's draft:

> As learners, students long for knowing more about the world we all live in. That's the reason why there are more and more students choose to study abroad far from their home countries.
>
> Take me for example. I am also one of those students who desire greatly to learn more. As a English major, I learned a lot about American culture from history, literature, poetry, etc. However, the things I learned from textbooks did not make me content. So I started to search for other sources, such as movies, music, drama, news, TV shows, etc. Nevertheless, it seems not to be enough to me after all. I finally realized that is it impossible to "learn" another culture completely. The only way to know the culture well is to "be" a part of it!
>
> It is the idea that brought me here to America, and I am glad to be one of the parts in the culture, although I am not quite used to it. But I am still happy to be here and to experience more in this brand new world.

CHAPTER FIVE

DEVELOPING ARGUMENTS

CHAPTER FIVE

DEVELOPING ARGUMENTS

"Argument" is something of a loaded word. In popular parlance, it implies a battle, a skirmish between combatants, each equipped with opposing sides. One will win, the other lose. Such an argument is considered "won" when one arguer demonstrates the superiority of his argument to the opposition's. To do so he might point out the inaccuracy of evidence, cast doubt on a premise, or find a fallacy in the conclusions reached. In part, such views of argument—that it is to be *fought* and *won*—are perpetuated by political debate and reinforced by the quasi-intellectual "debate" of television news shows featuring a guest from "each side" of an issue trying desperately, in three minutes of airtime, to talk down the other.

As argument is more typically taught in the modern academy, however, it focuses less on fighting and winning than on constructing a reasonable position. In this chapter we present a brief overview of the most prominent approaches to argument, so as to familiarize tutors with the language that might be familiar to students. Following this overview, the chapter provides a set of strategies for helping writers attend thoughtfully to many of the most common concerns of developing arguments: developing a thesis, articulating claims, evaluating evidence, and acknowledging sources. Equipped with these heuristic strategies in mind, a tutor can lend a critical eye—and a thoughtful mind—to most student writers' attempts to argue with success.

APPROACHES TO ARGUMENT

The view of argument we observe above originates at least in part from classical rhetoric and its essentially agonistic nature. Yet this win-lose view of argument is one that most of today's writing teachers and composition scholars have come to reject. While argument of course retains strong roots in classical rhetoric, most teachers today rely at least as much on the works of psychologist Carl Rogers and philosopher Stephen Toulmin. The more *dialogic* approach to argument that is taught today typically seeks more to invite dialogue rather than to end it; to convey understanding rather than to dismiss an opposing position; and to seek and find means of identification with the audience and opposition. And as a writing tutor, deeply engaged in dialogue with others' arguments, you will likely have many opportunities to help writers develop, extend, and refine their positions.

As conceived today, argument is central to the college writer: from explications of literary works and narratives of historical events to evaluations of business plans and proposals for community initiatives, most writing tasks can be seen as arguments in which the writer puts forth a proposition of some sort, offers evidence in support, considers alternatives and counterarguments, and rests the case based on argument provided.

The Aristotelian Approach to Argument

Given that our contemporary understanding of an Aristotelian approach to argument is likely to be based on partial readings of a variety of his treatises, it is probably not possible for us to provide a single source (as there is no sole source outlining his theory of argument) or a simple definition of Aristotelian argument. There is a great deal of Aristotelian thinking that still informs the teaching of writing today. In particular, Aristotle's appeals of ethos, logos, and pathos still provide powerful means of rhetorical analysis and invention for many writers. And, we note, the broad conception of the argument as vital to democratic decision-making thrives in the modern university. Yet at the same time, we observe, the Aristotelian approach has waned in part because of its combative nature: if Aristotle felt that rhetoric was employed by speakers "to defend themselves and attack," then teachers of writing have felt the apparent need to distance themselves from such an agonistic—and antagonistic—understanding of argument.

The logic of the syllogism, a restrictive kind of argument in which a conclusion inevitably follows from two premises, can also be traced to Aristotle. You may have encountered this example of the syllogism:

- *All men are mortal.*
- *Socrates is a man.*
- *Therefore, Socrates is mortal.*

Its premises (*All men are mortal, Socrates is a man*) and its conclusion (*Socrates is mortal*) are ones with which we feel compelled to agree. Such is the inescapable logic of the syllogism. Yet who in their right mind, we wonder, would feel particularly compelled to argue that Socrates was, indeed, a mortal? As any introductory primer on logic will demonstrate, the examples with which syllogistic argument are taught infrequently resemble genuine discourse. And furthermore, the conclusion to the syllogism ultimately proves only another unquestioned assertion. For these reasons, strictly syllogistic logic is a second Aristotelian approach to argument from which most writing teachers have distanced themselves.

When the logic of the syllogism is faulty—if, say, a premise can be disproved or a conclusion reached in error—the reasoning is said to be fallacious. Lists of these fallacies, accompanied by examples of their faulty reasoning, can be found in more than a few writing textbooks and curricula. Yet the use of "logical fallacies" to name flaws in arguments is also of questionable value to the writer. The study of such fallacies, especially as it applies to writing, would seem to imply that arguments absent such fallacies are by definition successful, while any argument featuring any of them can be deemed invalid. As Fulkerson (1995) notes, the approach is essentially negative: it aims only to label flaws. The approach does not help writers who typically need to generate, not simply dismiss, ideas. For these reasons, such syllogistic logic has generally proved unappealing to teachers of writing, even if other elements of Aristotelian rhetoric remain powerful and vital.

The Rogerian Approach to Argument

Rogerian argument was introduced to the teaching of writing in the 1970s by Richard Young, Alton Becker, and Kenneth Pike (1970) in a textbook entitled *Rhetoric: Discovery and Change*. Proposed as an alternative to the agonistic nature of traditional argument, the Rogerian approach focused instead on methods of psychotherapeutic discourse made famous by Carl Rogers (1961). For Young, Becker, and Pike (1970), rather than aiming to discredit the opposition by invalidating opposing viewpoints, a person employing Rogerian argument would seek instead ...

1. to convey to the reader that he is understood,

2. to delineate the area within which he believes the reader's position to be valid, and

3. to induce him to believe that he and the writer share similar moral qualities (honesty, integrity, and good will) and aspirations (the desire to discover a mutually acceptable situation). (p. 275)

Following Young, Becker, and Pike's important work, Rogerian argument made considerable inroads into the teaching of composition towards the end of the 20th century, in part because it offered a viable and pedagogically flexible alternative to traditional models. Also, with the benefit of hindsight, we can recognize today a certain kind of Cold War logic in the 1970s ascendancy of Rogerian discourse. As Douglas Brent (1991) has noted, an approach to argument based more on negotiation and identification with your enemies than on obliteration and annihilation of them could hardly have helped but resonate with some audiences. Rogerian argument never has fully supplanted Aristotelian in the academy, and in the 1980s and 90s, feminists among others critiqued its self-effacing nature as problematically submissive. Yet aspects of it remain frequently taught today, most of them focusing more on its generative power—its exhortation to try to perceive the subject as others might—than on its analytical framework.

The Toulmin Model Of Argument

An even more widely-adopted model is based on the work of the British philosopher Stephen Toulmin, who in *The Uses of Argument* (1958) offered a complex method of understanding and strengthening arguments. Based more on the genuine (if codified) discourse of legal arguments than on the abstractions of syllogisms, Toulmin's model rejects absolutism and objectivism and thus questions the Aristotelian structure of the syllogism. Given that Aristotelian syllogizing seemed too divorced from actual arguments in real rhetorical situations, the fact that Toulmin's model was based on legal arguments proved especially appealing to teachers of composition. Today, many composition programs and textbooks devote themselves nearly exclusively to the study of argument, and for them, Toulmin's model—or, in some cases, a simplification thereof—provides a teachable framework.

Toulmin's model consists of the following key terms, the most important of which are the claims and the data. In contrast to Aristotle, who began with premises and then syllogizing about the conclusions that must necessarily follow, Toulmin's model begins with what he called the claim. The **claim,** for Toulmin, is the main point a writer hopes to assert, and it is central to his model. The **evidence** (what Toulmin called the data; we prefer *evidence* here) offers support for the claim. Evidence may take the form of examples, statistics, testimony, and/or analogy; evidence may be offered in different forms, quantities, or combinations, depending upon the rhetorical situation.

A third element of Toulmin's model is what he called the **warrant;** a warrant is what the reader must believe in order to agree that the data supports the claim. Warrants may be stated explicitly, but more often than not they are implicit. (A careful study of an argument's warrant may offer a close understanding of a writer's unstated premises.)

The claim, the data (or evidence), and the warrant are central to Toulmin's model, and an understanding of their function will probably suffice for almost every tutorial situation. Toulmin's model also includes what he called the **backing** (the evidence offered to support the warrant) and notes the uses of **qualifiers** (for instance, exceptions which limit the strength of the claim or the data) and **rebuttals**. These three last elements of Toulmin's scheme help us to understand the nuances of an argument more so than its structure.

To demonstrate Toulmin's model in action, here is an example of a short passage from Tim Flannery (2005), *The Weather Makers: How Man is Changing the Climate and What It Means for Life on Earth*:

> It's inevitable that human changes to the environment will obstruct migration. A striking example of this is provided by Edith's checkerspot butterfly (*Euphydryas editha*). A distinctive subspecies inhabits northern Mexico and southern California, and increased temperatures in spring have caused the plant that its caterpillars feed on—a type of snapdragon—to wilt early, starving the larvae so they cannot pupate. Suitable habitat once abounded to the north, and the population might have migrated if the sprawl of San Diego didn't stand in its path. With only 20 percent of its original range now able to support it, without human help the southern subspecies of Edith's checkerspot will not see out the century. Most of the world's more fertile regions are now occupied by human-modified environments, so many, many more as yet undocumented instances of species and populations facing extinction may already be occurring. (pp. 88-89)

At a glance, the primary elements of Toulmin's scheme should be evident in Flannery's argument. The evidence provided supports the claim articulated in the paragraph's first sentence.

claim:	Human changes to the environment will obstruct migration.
primary evidence:	(The southern subspecies of) Edith's checkerspot butterfly cannot pupate.
secondary evidence:	Many, many more as yet undocumented instances of species and populations facing extinction may already be occurring.

One virtue of the Toulmin approach is that it lets us discern an overarching structure to the argument: identifying the claim and the evidence offered in support of the claim provides us with a shorthand "gloss" of the argument's structure. Even armed with only this deep an analysis, we can from here consider the value of the claim and the appropriateness of the evidence. And in a tutorial setting, a writer can work to make his own claims stronger and the evidence more compelling using the strategies we outline below. In many tutorials, the simple analysis of claims and evidence, their sequence and interrelationships, their articulation and presentation, will prove formative for the writers you work with. Yet Toulmin's model allows for an even deeper analysis when one considers the interplay of its warrants, backing, and qualifiers. Below follows a more complete dissection of its components:

claim:	Human changes to the environment will obstruct migration.
primary evidence:	(The southern subspecies of) Edith's checkerspot butterfly cannot pupate.
explicit warrant:	Without human help the southern subspecies of Edith's checkerspot will not see out the century.
backing:	Increased temperatures in spring have caused the plant that the *Euphydryas editha* caterpillars feed on—a type of snapdragon—to wilt early, starving the larvae.
secondary evidence:	Many, many more as yet undocumented instances of species and populations facing extinction may already be occurring.
implicit warrants:	These instances exist even if undocumented. These extinctions may be occurring already.
qualifier:	Suitable habitat once abounded to the north, and the population might have migrated if the sprawl of San Diego didn't stand in its path.

As you can observe from the analysis above, discerning the warrants, backing, and qualifiers in an argument allows us to understand not only its structure but its nuance. In the Flannery example, our analysis helps us to understand that the claim rests on a single primary example which is well warranted and backed—a means by which Flannery demonstrates his own authority—but presented also as a representative example when others are unnamed and undocumented.

It is important to note that in Toulmin's model, the presence of all six components of an argument does not necessarily signify a successful argument; nor does the absence of one or more components suggest an unsuccessful argument. But Toulmin's model helps us to understand how the various components of the argument work together. When critiquing the argument above, we might take note of the effectiveness of the data (one example, albeit a persuasive one), its relationship to the claim, and the validity of the premises on which the argument is based. For instance, do you find the example compelling?—or sufficient? Do you need more evidence in order to accept the claim? Do you accept the warrants, especially the implicit ones, on which the argument is based? Do you accept the ambiguous and inexact nature of the secondary evidence provided, which implies that Edith's checkerspot is just one of many eventual, if undocumented, potential extinctions?

The benefit for writers using Toulmin's model—even if their analysis and discussion is limited to the primary elements of claim, evidence, and warrant—is that it requires them, in their own writing, to articulate a clear claim; to provide sufficient evidence to support the claim; and to consider the tacit assumptions that allow the evidence to support the claim. As we illustrate strategies for helping writers develop thesis statements, write clear claims, and evaluate and present their evidence, we rely to no small degree on Toulmin's model, especially its primary elements.

HELPING WRITERS DEVELOP A THESIS

A considerable number of tutorial sessions focus on the writer's development and articulation of a thesis. While some sessions focus on understanding the rhetorical situation, some on generating ideas, and still others on lower-order concerns such as sentence stylistics, appropriate usage, and mechanical correctness, writing tutors must always be ready to assist their writers as they process their thinking and move from inchoate to working to more fully articulated thesis statements. The dialogic nature of tutorial sessions can be especially helpful for such work: in a sense, the tutor can examine the writer's work, question her assertions, press her for evidence, and assess her developing thinking. If a writer has, through critical reading, invention, and/or drafting, developed at least a partial draft, a tutor can almost always guide the writer towards a more fully articulated thesis, employing one or more of the strategies we present below.

Glossing

One strategy we have observed nearly all of our tutors adopting with success is **glossing**. In her *Forming Thinking Writing* (1978), Ann Berthoff presents this method of labeling and grouping ideas: a gloss can be a single word, a phrase, or—potentially—a complete sentence, typically a predicated claim that offers an arguable statement about the topic. Tutors can help writers gloss their own drafts, in essence mining them for the essence of their ideas in an attempt to articulate claims that are—as we advocate above—clear, concise, and conspicuous. And once a draft has been fully glossed, tutors can help their writers work those new or revised claims into the structure of their papers, both as signal sentences that lead (or perhaps conclude) paragraphs and as the scaffolding for a potential thesis.

In a tutorial session, glossing typically consists of the tutor asking the writer one or more of a set of questions about each paragraph of the draft. (Glossing can be conducted every bit as purposefully from invention notes or outlines as well, but we will illustrate the process with the example of a writer who has completed an initial draft.) For each paragraph or division, the tutor can ask the writer the following questions:

- What is the point of this paragraph? *(names the topic)*
- What does the content of the paragraph suggest about that subject? *(predicates the claim)*
- What's the primary function of this paragraph? *(clarifies the purpose)*
- How does this paragraph relate to what precedes and follows? *(examines the order)*

We should note that while a tutor would almost never ask exactly these four questions, as worded above, of each paragraph of any writer's draft, the process implied here can be invaluable, especially for the writer who has worked through some of the material for a paper but who struggles to make good sense of it.

In the following scenario, our tutor, Seb, is working with a writer, Cara, who is struggling with an explication of an Emily Dickinson poem, "Because I could not stop for Death—." Here is Cara's draft, and as you will observe, her introductory paragraph is little more than a placeholder for what follows, and she has not yet composed a conclusion:

Emily Dickinson's poem "Because I could not stop for Death—" employs the formal elements of imagery, symbolism, figures of speech, and diction to convey its theme. These formal elements help lend meaning to Dickinson's poem.

Imagery debuts in the poem's first stanza as Death is introduced. Death is personified as a civil and leisurely carriage driver. He is shown to be kind and personal toward the speaker. The image of Death as a thoughtful person (after all he did stop to pick her up) provides rich imagery in contradicting the more common view of death as an enemy. Meaning is established through the personification of Death early on in the poem. The tone is also set for the poem: it will be a slow and pleasant journey rather than a brutal and grotesque view of death and exile into the afterlife.

One reason Dickinson may have chosen to portray Death in a positive manner stems from her upbringing. She was raised in an orthodox Christian family whose beliefs stated that death and the afterlife are a pleasant addition to life on earth. As she spent most of her later years alone she must have had plenty of time to speculate about death and the afterlife.

The poem's literary, or contextual, symbolism gives the images meaning. The school and children at recess in the poem are symbolic of the beginning of life. The speaker is looking at the children, while also reflecting on her time growing up. Grain fields are often associated with life and prosperity, which, in this context, are representative of the speaker's middle-age years. In turn, the end of life is represented by the setting sun. Because they lend meaning to the poem that goes beyond their meaning in other situations and works, these symbols are contextual rather than conventional.

In the final two verses of her poem, Dickinson's figures of speech provide the reader with clear and unexpected visualizations of eternity: "We paused before a House that seemed / A swelling of the Ground— / The Roof was scarcely visible— / The Cornice— in the Ground— "(lines 17-20). Here Dickinson uses metonymy to represent the speaker's grave. Speaking metonymically rather than bluntly stating that the poem's speaker is viewing her own tombstone helps soften the fact that she is dead. The speaker sees her gravesite but she speaks of it somberly as a house furthering the theme that Death is a friend rather than a foe. In the final verse the speaker says, "Since then—'tis Centuries—and yet / Feels shorter than the Day" (21, 22). Death has treated her well, the time has passed so quickly that she has hardly noticed her stay in the afterlife. The reader too is convinced of the speaker's contentment in Death through the poet's choice of words.

In the dialogue that follows, Seb has already begun the session with the kinds of rapport-building and task-assessing dialogue we advocate in chapters two and three. He has learned that Cara's paper is written for an introduction to poetry course, that her explication is to focus on at least four of the formal elements of poetry the class has studied to date, and that the paper, due in a week, is to be no longer than 1,000 words. Seb's goal is to guide Cara through a careful glossing of each of the essay's paragraphs, all with the aim of helping her develop clearer claims and a stronger thesis.

Seb: Well, let's take a look at what you have so far. How is it going?

Cara: Okay, I guess. I mean, I think I understand the poem—honestly, it's pretty straightforward. I think I have some good material and I'm doing what I'm supposed to. The problem is more that it just seems really dry and factual so far.

Seb: Short introduction, no conclusion?

Cara: That's about it. I just wrote the intro to get going.

Seb: Okay, let's get started. Let me slide you a sheet of paper to work with. I think what we'll do is take a look at each paragraph you have, see what it says and does, and from there we might be able to come up with a stronger intro and thesis.

Cara: You mean my thesis won't do?

Seb: Well, if you wrote the intro just to get started, as you say, my guess is it's worth working on more. Okay, let's start with the first paragraph of the body. [points to paragraph 2] What's the main idea or topic here?

Cara: I put the imagery first.

Seb: Okay, imagery. Write that down. And what does the paragraph say about the imagery?

Cara: That it debuts in the first stanza?

Seb: Okay, so it does. Write that down next to it. We'll follow this pattern a bit. [looks at the paragraph quizzically] Though when I look at the paragraph …

Cara: I should say more than that?

Seb: Well, to say that it appears in the first stanza is pretty cut-and-dried.

Cara: True enough.

Seb: What gets accomplished through that first presentation of imagery?

Cara: I said here that it helps personify Death as civil, even courteous.

Seb: I think that's better—it's more about the function than the fact. Though I think it would help if you provided some evidence to support that claim. Otherwise, I suppose, your readers would doubt your interpretation.

Cara: Okay, yeah, I didn't do that at all there, did I?

Seb: That's all right, we'll address that a bit later, if that's okay—just make a note that you want to provide evidence there. Let's keep going for now. How about this paragraph? [points to paragraph 3] What's the topic here?

Cara: Dickinson's upbringing. Our instructor said that biographical information can be helpful as long as our case doesn't depend on it.

Seb: All right. Again, write that down. And what does your evidence suggest about Dickinson's upbringing?

Cara: That it might help us understand her personification?

Seb: Okay. [*gestures to Cara to write this down, too*] And why does this paragraph follow the previous?

Cara: Shouldn't it?

Seb: I'm not necessarily saying that. Just asking for the rationale.

Cara: Well, I guess I'm providing further support for the other paragraph about imagery and personification.

Seb: Interesting. What's the connection?

Cara: It's just speculation, since she was so private. But I thought it might show how she would maybe have had the time and the upbringing to think this way. Is that too much of a stretch? Or is it in the wrong place?

Seb: Those are the right questions to ask of it, but let's come back to that. How about paragraph four—what's the topic there?

Cara: Symbolism.

Seb: And the point about the symbolism?

Cara: That it's literary rather than conventional.

Seb: Is that an important distinction?

Cara: Well, we talked about it in class. But it may not be the most important thing to say.

Seb: What do the symbols accomplish?

Cara: They suggest a process of growth or aging—they go from youth to maturity and prosperity to old age.

Seb: Good. Let's try to work this out in a sentence. If the subject is "the poem's symbols," what do those symbols accomplish or illustrate?

Cara: Something like "the poem's symbols illustrate the natural processes of aging from childhood to maturity and old age."

Seb: You know, I think that's strong, you should write it down. Don't forget to cite the poem itself as you discuss these. You make the point here that the symbols are literary rather than conventional, which I think is worth doing, but now your claim is more interpretive, and I think that'll help you with the thesis. You might rework it a bit later, but let's go on.

As their session continues, Seb leads Cara through the process of glossing the next paragraph as well, and in the process, Cara concludes that this paragraph can be divided into two subclaims, one presenting Dickinson's use of metonymy (which she's named) and hyperbole (which she hasn't). The two of them conclude that her broader generalization introducing the two subclaims—that "Dickinson's figures of speech provide the reader with clear and unexpected visualizations of eternity"—is appropriately interpretive and not merely factual. From here, let's fast-forward ahead to a later stage in the session, as Cara and Seb examine her notes from the glossing:

¶	topic	Claim	evidence
1	poem	poem employs the formal elements of imagery, symbolism, figures of speech, and diction to convey its theme	n/a
2	imagery	personifies Death as civil, even courteous	need to quote!
3	Christian upbringing	helps us understand personification of Death	orthodox Christian family, beliefs about afterlife, solitary adulthood (time to speculate). Need to cite!
4	symbols	illustrate the natural processes of aging from childhood to maturity and old age	schoolyard, children playing, grain fields, setting sun. Need to quote!
5	figures of speech	provide the reader with clear and unexpected visualizations of eternity	metonymy, hyperbole
5a	metonymy	helps soften the fact that she is dead	cornice in the ground
5b	hyperbole	emphasizes the speaker's contentment	centuries feel shorter than the day

Seb: So, let's look at what you came up with. Want to go through it?

Cara: Well, I reworked some of the claims a bit. Like we said, I wanted to make sure they were all interpretive. That one about imagery was terrible! I can't believe I wrote that. And in a couple of the paragraphs, I just made a note that I need to provide more evidence in support. Right?

Seb: Yep. Now, with the claims, to you, does the order seem appropriate?

Cara: Mostly. In general, I'm following the order that these topics show up in the poem. But I wonder about the part about her upbringing.

Seb: I agree that it almost seems to interrupt the discussion of the poem itself. But it seems like it's helpful. Where does it come from?

Cara: This is my textbook for the course. Oh — of course I need to cite that, don't I?

Seb: Yep. Know how?

Cara: Yeah, MLA is a piece of cake.

Seb: Good. Now let's look at the claims. Just read them to me in sequence.

Cara: [reads] Imagery personifies Death as civil, even courteous. Dickinson's Christian upbringing helps us understand personification of Death. Her symbols illustrate the natural processes of aging from childhood to maturity and old age. Her figures of speech provide the reader with clear and unexpected visualizations of eternity, as metonymy helps soften the fact that she is dead and hyperbole emphasizes her speaker's contentment.

Seb: Now compare that to the thesis you had stated in your intro.

Cara: Wow. Much better. But I can't just use these for my intro.

Seb: Not in so many words, no. But if you can rework the language slightly, and still keep the same keywords—imagery, symbols, figures—in the same order, it should guide the readers through the order of your paper and make your case for your interpretation.

For what it's worth, though, it always takes me a few tries to get that language right. Let me ask you this: what's the most surprising or illuminating aspect of your reading?

Cara: That the speaker is so accepting and positive about Death?

Seb: Good—that provides something unexpected. Could that help you in the beginning?

Cara: Okay, I see. Maybe I could use the biographical information to begin the paper, then lead from there into that thesis?

Seb: That's certainly a possibility. I think then her background wouldn't seem like an interruption, and it would still do what you want: suggest how plausible your interpretation is. What else should your introduction do?

Cara: Our professor said that we had to introduce the poem by naming its speaker, setting, and situation—he's big on that. But I think I can work that in with the biographical information and the thesis.

Seb: Good. What else do you plan to do, based on what we've looked at?

Cara: I guess I need to rework the claims like we talked about. In a couple of paragraphs I still need to quote the poem. And I guess I might end up with two paragraphs on the figures of speech.

Seb: That's a really solid plan. We're out of time, but if you want, you could work here on some of that and I can look at it.

Cara: Thanks! I have another 20 minutes before class—maybe I can make some progress.

Before we look at the revisions that Cara prepares, let's reflect on Seb's use of glossing during the session. We first note that depending upon a number of factors, a session using glossing may go slowly, as this one does, or quickly. The process is deliberate here, in part because at most steps in the process Cara learns that she can improve her claim, provide more evidence, or re-consider the sequence of her material. Seb's continual prompting of her to move her claims from the merely factual to the more interpretive reinforces her original desire to make her paper "less cut-and-dried." The benefits of glossing should be clear: it draws attention to individual sections, identifies those in need of stronger claims (or evidence), and provides the opportunity to question the purpose of each section. Here is Cara's revised introduction:

> The poet Emily Dickinson was raised in an orthodox Christian family whose beliefs stated that death and the afterlife are a pleasant addition to life on earth. As she spent most of her later years alone, she must have had plenty of time to speculate about death and the afterlife (Meyer 138). This speculation is the subject of her poem "Because I could not stop for Death—." In it, Dickinson's speaker recalls, from beyond the grave, both Death's calling for her and her journey with him into eternity. But rather than depict the experience as terrifying, Dickinson uses imagery, symbolism, metonymy, and hyperbole to personify Death as civil and courteous servant whose "carriage ride" will offer a slow and pleasant journey across time and into the afterlife.

Certainly, Cara's introduction, though it may still be revised further, has made considerable leaps forward from the prior version: it now offers a clearer, more challenging, and certainly more interpretive thesis. Furthermore, her thesis is now more specific to the Dickinson poem itself. Contrast the new version with the old, which said merely that the poem "employs the formal elements of imagery, symbolism, figures of speech, and diction to convey its theme." (What poetry of Dickinson's—or of anyone's, for that matter—would not similarly employ formal elements to convey thematic meaning?) Cara's revised thesis will guide the reader more adroitly through her explication, and her explication will rest on a scaffolding of significantly stronger claims and a more consistent, persuasive presentation of textual evidence in support.

It's worth mentioning as well that glossing can be used in almost any kind of session with any kind of writer on any kind of topic. A writer need not be working on a traditional argument (of which Cara's explication assignment is just one subgenre) to benefit: glossing can be every bit as helpful in a session where the genre is more narrative or expository. Since glossing can reveal inconsistencies or idiosyncrasies in the order or choice of material, it can be employed in any session attending to structure or development, as long as the writer has a thorough plan or a near-completed draft in place. Glossing helps writers to see more clearly what they have written and more precisely what they need to do, whether that is a matter of shifting emphases, deleting ideas, adding new material, or re-ordering paragraphs.

Depending upon the dynamics of the session, a tutor using the glossing strategy might or might not choose to name and discuss the strategy itself. One possibility would be for the tutor to re-examine the strategy as the end of the session draws near, illustrating it so that the writer could use it herself as a heuristic for revision. Doing so might help the student understand—and apply—its basic premises: that revision is largely a matter of clarifying, sharpening, and supporting the paper's claims and thesis.

HELPING WRITERS ARTICULATE CLAIMS

In Toulmin's scheme, the claim is, as we state and illustrate above, the proposition that is being argued. Tutors can typically offer considerable assistance with a writer's claims, especially at the introductory and intermediate levels of composition. In a great deal of academic discourse, the sentences that function as claims constitute the structure of the paper. As such, writers will want their claims to be articulate and memorable: they should be *conspicuous, arguable, clear,* and *concise.* Working with writers, tutors can use strategies like glossing, as Seb does above, to isolate and examine individual claims, and from there to subject them to careful revision. Writing effective claims, we note, is as much a matter of diligent revision as it is of careful planning.

As you work with writers and examine the claims they make, you can urge them to …

1. *Aim for "conspicuousness."* We don't advocate a slavish obeisance to the old elementary-school saw that every paragraph must begin with a topic sentence. In fact, research on professional writing demonstrates that such paragraphs are more the exception than the rule (Irmscher, 1979). But we will advocate for writing that is transparent in its argument because its claims are conspicuous: that is to say, they are prominently located—usually near the beginning or endings of paragraphs or other section breaks—and they are immediately recognizable as claims, in part because they offer brief, emphatic, and syntactically straightforward propositions. There are always instances when a writer will choose to leave a claim implicit rather than explicit, or occluded rather than conspicuous. But for the most part, when claims are absent from, buried deep within, or indiscernible amongst the text, the writer's case is lost.

2. *Aim for "arguability."* In Toulmin's scheme, an essential quality of the claim is that it is arguable rather than factual. If you remember Cara's concern about her explication of Dickinson's poem being "really dry and factual," that entirely

accurate observation may be based on statements like "imagery debuts in the first stanza." We note that especially for novice writers, the willingness to take an intellectual stand is one that does not come easily. Many writers hide behind oblique or obvious statements like those we've seen in first year-themes: "another amazing statistic is quite shocking," wrote one student, apparently unwilling to articulate just what that particular statistic implies. Yet in a tutorial, such statements may serve a generative purpose, and it is often not too difficult to prompt such writers towards more arguable claims that make more genuine propositions.

3. *Aim for clarity and brevity.* Another benefit of Toulmin's model is that it highlights the claim and makes it the center of the model, the origin from which the others follow. As such, the claim ought be distinguishable from the evidence not only by its conspicuousness but also by its clarity and brevity. You can urge writers to use precise language; to omit overly long qualifiers and exceptions; and to use clear subject-verb patterns like "competitive sports pose psychological dangers for children" or, in the case of our student Cara's explication of Dickinson, "hyperbole emphasizes the speaker's contentment."

4. *Aim for appropriate qualification and exception.* Although we've given them lesser attention here, Toulmin's qualifiers and exceptions are crucial to his model. If syllogistic logic is too based on absolute conditions to serve the purposes of actual discourse well, Toulmin's model features an ability to qualify claims and acknowledge exceptions that proves invaluable to writers. Sometimes, a claim will need no exception—such as in the case of Cara's claim that "hyperbole emphasizes the speaker's contentment." Hers here is an interpretive claim based appropriately on a single instance of figurative language. Other claims, though, such as "competitive sports pose psychological dangers for children," though concise, may need qualification: Do all such sports pose dangers? Must they? Are distinctions to be made between team and individual sports? Is the age,

competition level, or country of origin relevant? Once she has established the appropriate subject-verb-object structure of her claim, our writer in this instance might need to qualify her claim to increase her chances of supporting it effectively with the evidence that is to follow.

HDWDWW (How Does Who Do What and Why?)

You will remember that in chapter four, we present the HDWDWW (How Does Who Do What and Why?) strategy as a generative heuristic for invention, and in Case Study 4.3, you've practiced lending its methodology to a topic for comparison and contrast. The same strategy, though, can be every bit as powerful a heuristic for articulating clear claims as it is for generating ideas, in part because it calls upon the writer to name a specific subject, locate that subject as the subject of a claim sentence, and predicate that subject beginning with an active verb.

To demonstrate, let's imagine that you are working with a writer in a first-year seminar course and that she and the other students in the class have been asked to write papers explaining positions based on data from the recent annual report of the National Study of Student Engagement. Her notes from the NSSE include the following, listed as the first three bulleted points, which she intends to combine with her own anecdotal information gleaned from her roommate and her campus's assessment office.

- *By their own admission, three of ten first-year students do just enough academic work to get by.*

- *Less than one-fifth of first-year students spend more than 25 hours per week studying, which approximates the amount of time faculty say is needed to do well in college.*

- *40 percent of first-year students spend fewer than ten hours per week studying.* (NSSE, 2005, p. 12)

- *My roommate estimates she will need to spend ...*
    - *about 25 hours per week in class and at required activities*
    - *about 12 hours per week in athletics*
    - *about 25 hours per week working*

- o *at most 10-12 hours per week studying.*
- *Our Campus Assessment Coordinator says our first-year students underestimate the amount of recommended study time by half, and that retention here is 65% from first to second year.*

Based on her data, how might you encourage her to use HDWDWW to articulate a claim based on her findings? Even a few minutes' worth of experimentation with the strategy ought to demonstrate how it can be used to help writers articulate claims that exhibit the characteristics we list above. Aside from its use as a more generative heuristic, the HDWDWW strategy can be especially helpful in assisting writers who are struggling to articulate claims, and used in tandem with Berthoff's glossing technique, it can offer a consistently productive means of clarifying the structure and content of an argument.

HELPING WRITERS EVALUATE EVIDENCE

As writers develop arguments, they ought to be constantly in the process of examining and re-examining the interrelationships of their claims and the evidence they provide in support. The types and quantity of evidence used will, of course, depend upon a number of variables, including the expectations of the discipline, the length of the piece of writing, and the quality of research or invention work. No matter the specifics of the situation, though, a tutor can almost always assist a writer in evaluating and presenting the evidence that supports her claims.

STAR (Sufficient, Typical, Accurate, Relevant)

An especially elegant and flexible method for evaluating the evidence in an argument is offered in rhetorician Richard Fulkerson's *Teaching the Argument in Writing*. There, Fulkerson presents what he calls the **STAR** criteria for evaluating evidence in an argument. **STAR** serves as an acronym for the criteria themselves: to support a claim, a writer should offer a Sufficient number of Typical, Accurate, and Relevant examples. Fulkerson suggests asking of any claim if the evidence provided is ...

- *Sufficient?* Is there enough evidence to support the claim? Does the claim require more evidence than is provided?

- *Typical?* Is the evidence typical, or rather atypical—e.g., hyperbolic, idiosyncratic, unlikely, or extreme?

- *Accurate?* Is the evidence provided factual, verifiable, and trustworthy? Is there reason to believe it may have been distorted or taken out of context?

- *Relevant?* Is the evidence directly supportive of the claim, or does its relevance depend upon various unstated assumptions? Can the relevance or assumptions be made more explicit?

To demonstrate how Fulkerson's STAR criteria might be used in a tutorial, let's first apply it to a piece of professional writing, in this case an excerpt from Edward Jay Epstein (2005), *The Big Picture: The New Logic of Money and Power in Hollywood*. Here, in a chapter examining the social order and logic of Hollywood, Epstein examines the ways that various players in the film industry—agents, actors, directors, producers—occupy varying but well-established positions in the social strata of power there. In this paragraph, Epstein claims that writers saw themselves as victims of the studio's uncontrollable capitalism. As you read, apply the STAR criteria. Is Epstein's supporting evidence sufficient? typical? accurate? reliable?

> Whatever their original motivation, writers eventually came to see themselves as poorly-treated pawns in a money-driven system. Their writing about Hollywood—such as Budd Schulberg's *What Makes Sammy Run?*, F. Scott Fitzgerald's *The Last Tycoon*, Nathanael West's *The Day of the Locust*, and William Faulkner's "Golden Land"—often expressed contempt, if not outright loathing, for the values of the studios. A principal theme of such works is that financial calculation was systematically destroying the artistic integrity of movies. The same contempt, it should be noted, has also pervaded movies about Hollywood over the years; in *The Big Knife, The Bad and the Beautiful, Barton Fink, The Player*, and *State and Main*, the studio is constantly portrayed as run by philistines maximizing their earnings on the back of the writer's integrity. In Jean-Luc Godard's *Contempt* (1965), insult is further heaped on injury: the heroine, Camille (Brigitte Bardot), holds her screenwriter husband in such contempt for writing a movie for a Hollywood producer that she can no longer bear to be in his company. (pp. 259-260)

Of course, as a professional writer who makes his living by researching and analyzing information, and one who has the benefits of a professional publishing house and editorial staff, Epstein ought to be held to a reasonably high standard of rhetorical aptitude. Does his evidence here meet the STAR criteria? He has elected to list a number of works, both written and filmed, that support his claim about the beleaguered scriptwriter. He might have presented instead a longer analysis of one of these works to make his case, but he certainly seems to meet the criteria for *sufficiency*, with no fewer than ten examples to make his case.

Epstein's evidence can be said to be *typical* as well; after all, it's not as if these works mentioned are at all atypical, or that there are dozens of others treating the studio system instead as a paragon of artistic integrity. The criterion of *accuracy* is more complex: we might quibble that Bardot's character in Godard's film has motives for her contempt that are not as transparent as Epstein proposes. But to say so is to quibble: for the most part, Epstein's representation of these works is entirely accurate. Just as he suggests, these works indeed portray the studio system as corrupt and the writers employed there as little more than disempowered, disrespected pawns.

The last criterion proves the most interesting here: is Epstein's evidence *relevant*? Well, its relevance depends upon an unstated assumption—a warrant, in Toulmin's scheme—that fictional works are appropriately illustrative of the reality Epstein proposes. Do these fictional representations support that claim? We might be satisfied that they do, or we might ask for other kinds of evidence. Epstein might have, for instance, referred to nonfiction narratives like John Gregory Dunne's *Monster* and *The Studio*; John Irving's *My Movie Business*; Brian Michael Bendis's graphic (nonfiction) novel *Fortune and Glory: A True Hollywood Comic Story*; or the anthropologist Hortense Powdermaker's early ethnography of Hollywood culture, *The Dream Factory*. Any of these would have further substantiated his claim.

But would any of these, or any more than Epstein has already provided, have been necessary? Is Epstein's claim best built on fictional narratives? The evidence's ability to satisfy the criterion of *relevance* is debatable. And in part, a conclusion, if one can be reached, must necessarily be based on an understanding of the rhetorical task and context. If Epstein's book were focused more specifically on an analysis of the writer's place in Hollywood or an explication of the role of the writer in its fictional treatments, his list of examples would seem disappointingly abrupt. Yet his book is neither: it is an examination of the power roles and economic logic of the current system, of which the role of the writer is but a minor part. His point is not to illustrate fictional depictions of the writer in Hollywood but to use examples that will persuade his readers of the value of his claim, and he must believe that these fictional examples will do so better than their lesser-known non-fiction counterparts.

We expect that the writers you tutor won't typically offer up such elegantly composed and skillfully argued paragraphs as Epstein's—a fact that will make the applicability of the STAR criteria all the more valuable to you as a tutor. When you are working with a writer on the strength of her evidence, though, we recommend that you consider the degree to which she seems willing to examine it closely. Our tutors often present the heuristic, mentioning that STAR can be a good way to examine the evidence provided in an argument, asking the writer's cooperation, and from there determining the degree to which the evidence supports the claim.

With novice and recalcitrant writers, employing the STAR criteria will often reveal that they haven't provided sufficient evidence, or that the evidence provided is atypical, inaccurate, or irrelevant. When this occurs, it's important to remind your writer that no argument is "airtight," that fulfilling the criteria doesn't "prove" the claim, and that finding a weakness doesn't mean that the claim is disproved. Rather, when you and your writer find that evidence in a given section is less than sufficient, this finding should motivate the next question: what other evidence might be provided in support? Similarly, if the two of you find the evidence lacking in its accuracy, or relevance, the writer might be prompted to turn back towards invention work or conduct further research to cull stronger evidence—or, in many cases, to revisit the claim.

HELPING WRITERS USE SOURCES

The excerpt above from Epstein's *The Big Picture* is representative of the kind of expository prose that illustrates its claims primarily with examples. In other circumstances, the writers with whom you work will rely not only on examples to support their claims, but on evidence culled from library and field research. When writers are making their cases with statistics, authoritative opinions, researched studies, expert testimony, or other published data, the presentation of evidence raises a double concern: how to present the information so that its authority is clear, and how to acknowledge the source of the information appropriately. As we've observed, many writers, especially at the introductory levels, are satisfied enough to have simply found the information and are not particularly concerned about its presentation. Therefore, another promising avenue of exploration for your sessions is addressing their use of source material.

Some sources are designed merely to present contextual or factual information, so writers need not "engage in conversation" with every source they use. But to write argumentatively, they must be able to use sources as a means of deepening their analysis of the subject. When working with writers who are using material from published sources, you can encourage them to try to *respond* to their sources, rather than merely to *present* them. You can encourage your writers to try to explore the implications of what's been said; to apply the idea to another instance or scenario; to take issue with a part of what the source material says; and/or to provide evidence that complicates the analysis in some way. Any of these strategies might be used in circumstances where your writers simply present cited material in support of a claim without actually engaging that material in any real intellectual way.

It can help to encourage your writers to quote, paraphrase, or summarize sources only in order to analyze them, to think of sources not so much as self-evident "proof" supporting claims but as invitations to further conversation, as raising questions the writer hopes to address. And when presenting those sources, you can encourage writers to use attribution both in-text (to identify the authority and perspective) and in citation (to fulfill the expectations for documentation).

Consider the case of a writer, Fiona, who in a paper for a child and family studies course has been writing about body shape and self-image among young women. Here is an excerpt from her paper:

> The experts disagree about modern girls' relationship to their bodies. Biology ultimately determines the shape of girls' bodies, and as a result many girls become frustrated and depressed because they never come close to achieving the "ideal body" (Pipher). But even so today's generation believes that the female body is ultimately "perfectable" with the right diet, the right exercise, the right wardrobe, and maybe even the right plastic surgery (Brumberg).

In the dialogue below, our tutor, Jess, has observed how in this passage Fiona is rushing through her source material. Note how she broaches the topic of presenting the researched material and how she prompts Fiona towards a fuller, more authoritative presentation of the content of both books cited.

Jess: [*reading*] ... "they never come close to achieving the 'ideal body.'" Wow. You hear a lot about that these days. What's the source?

Fiona: Pipher. I cited it. See?

Jess: Yes, I do. Is that the name of the author?

Fiona: Yes.

Jess: Is it a book or an article, or what?

Fiona: It's a book. I read it for a class last year. *Reviving Ophelia.*

Jess: Oh, okay. And is the author a nutritionist or ...?

Fiona: I don't know. Does it matter?

Jess: Well, the way the citation is, your readers won't know that it's a book. I mean, I've heard of the book, but I didn't recognize the name right away.

Fiona: It's on my work cited list.

Jess: Yes, I mean here in this paragraph, though. It's an interesting statement and it could be really authoritative, too. Do you have the book? [*Fiona hands her the book.*] Okay, it says that Dr. Mary Pipher is [*reads*] "a clinical psychologist who has treated girls for more than twenty years."

Fiona: So I should put that in?

Jess: Well, would it matter to your readers that she has this expertise? In other words, would adding it make your material more authoritative?

Fiona: How do you mean?

Jess: Because it comes not just from any source, but from an author who's got her PhD in psychology or who's worked with girls.

Fiona: Okay. So what do I write?

Jess: There's really only a couple of basic ways to introduce cited information. One is with the phrase "according to _____," the other with "_____ states that." You can tinker with the verbs a bit for variety's sake, but either works. Then just add what you think you need to about her authority.

Fiona: [writes: According to Dr. Mary Pipher, a clinical psychologist and author of *Reviving Ophelia*, biology ultimately ...] How's this? Do I still need a citation?

Jess: Good, I think. And yes, you do need a citation. Are you supposed to use APA or MLA?

Fiona: APA.

Jess: Then the citation should be a year after the name. I wonder, too: does she give examples that you might cite?

Fiona: Oh, the book is full of them. I wouldn't know which to pick. Would I have to?

Jess: It might help. Or, you could state afterwards if you agree with what she says, or if you find part of it troubling, or if there are examples that disagree with her point.

Fiona: Or what about exceptions to it?

Jess: Good, yeah. You don't need to just put it out there and leave it. Now let's look at the next sentence. Who's Brumberg?

Fiona: Here's her book [*reads title*]: *The Body Project: An Intimate History of American Girls*.

Jess: And what's her authority?

Fiona: It says she's a Professor of History and Gender Studies at Cornell.

Jess: Is that worth adding?

Fiona: I suppose ... right?

Jess: I'd think so, yes. I mean, that way, readers will know it's not just some website or MySpace page. How is what she says different from what Pipher says?

Fiona: I don't follow.

Jess: Well, is she contradicting what Pipher said, or adding to it, or giving an example, or ... ?

Fiona: I guess Pipher says that girls will never achieve an ideal body image, and Brumberg says they're conditioned to try even more so now than ever, in part because of the way we see the body today as ... well ... as "perfectable." So it's kind of a ... I don't know. It doesn't completely disagree, it just complicates it a bit.

Jess: Okay, cool. Now I'm going to suggest that when you revise this section it might be a little longer. Naming each of these persons' authority—like their title, their book, or their expertise—helps you make your case. Also, there's no big rush to go right from one cited sentence to the next. It might help to slow down a bit, present what you have about Pipher, then show what Brumberg says, then show how what she says complicates what Pipher says. Make sense?

Fiona: I think so.

Jess: Cool, because if you can, you can have a really good angle on this. If you can work on it now for a while I can see how it's going, and then we might take a look again at that claim in the first sentence.

The main thrust of Jess's work here is to show Fiona that while her instincts are good in selecting and presenting material from two sources that are directly related to each other (and to a potential claim about body image), she can nonetheless develop greater authority for herself by demonstrating the expertise of the sources she's citing and by engaging in dialogue with them. Like many a novice writer, Fiona has instead simply presented the source material. But with helpful direction from her tutor, Jess, she can now work with that same material to present a fuller, more authoritative, and more nuanced discussion of the changing dynamics of young women's body image.

Tutors can play an important role here as students learn—and struggle—to write with sources. Some novice writers will, like Fiona above, simply present source material without context, introduction, or analysis. Others take an even easier road: simply pretending that the text of a published source is their own. Doing so, though a clear violation of academic integrity, happens all too often, especially in this digital age, and the problem isn't necessarily limited to novice writers. When writers have at their fingertips hundreds, even thousands of texts that might be inserted into a problem spot in a paper, the temptation is apparently too much for some writers to bear. As a writing tutor, your responsibility will often be to show others how to cite source material with accuracy and purpose. And when you perceive a writer to be less than thorough in his citation, you will need to pursue the matter, just as our tutor Jess does above, by indicating with some clarity what needs to happen, and how.

TROUBLESHOOTING ARGUMENT SESSIONS

You may have noted that each of our examples in this chapter proceeds with a deliberate, objective, and matter-of-fact analysis of the writer's work-in-progress. Yet we also observe that working with writers as they develop arguments can present its difficulties. You may work with a writer who holds too emotional or too untenable a position on a subject matter that is itself charged. You may work with writers who, for a variety of potential reasons, may be unfamiliar or unpracticed with the conventions of argument we discuss here—and they are, we note, just that: *conventions*. Your writer may be simply unready for some of the more sophisticated positions that advanced courses or topics require. Your writer may have been given an assignment that is confusing or unworkable. Or your writer might have chosen a topic or argument that is inappropriate or even abhorrent. Thankfully, you're not likely to encounter all of these situations simultaneously, and each can be addressed in tutorials as the situation requires.

When the writer seems unfamiliar or unpracticed with argument conventions: As we noted in chapter three, you may work with a wide range of writers who have a variety of levels of experience and acquaintance with these kinds of argument conventions. For some writers, particularly those who are not native speakers of English, the patterns of American academic argument can be entirely unfamiliar, and even potentially bewildering. Research in contrastive rhetoric has examined the patterns of argument employed in different cultures and noted sources of dissimilarity. Yet at the same time, it is an oversimplification to assume that *all* second-language writers' struggles are due to unfamiliarity with culturally specific rhetorical patterns. While certainly some non-native speaking writers may on occasion exhibit arguments that are more circular or indirect than is acceptable in the American academy, we caution against generalizing about the student or the country of origin. Instead, a better approach is to play "tour guide" when such appears to be the circumstance: as you would for any student, L2 or otherwise, show and explain the conventions of academic discourse that you understand to be most accepted and valued here.

When the writer seems unready for some of the more sophisticated positions that advanced courses or topics require: Speculative research in educational theory suggests that as they mature, writers move through stages of development that allow them to accommodate conflicting points of view (Perry, 1968; Belenky et al., 1986). The approach to argument we advocate here seems to call for a cognitive level of development at least at what Perry called "relativism" and what Belenky et al. termed "procedural knowing." As these theories suggest, college students can expect to find themselves in transition to these stages, where they become more adept at accommodating and even later synthesizing diverse points of view and directly contradictory data. What this means for the tutor is that some students may simply be unready for that transition. In such cases—where your student seems unable to process evidence that contradicts his claims, to address the sufficiency or typicality of examples, or to consider counterarguments—you will need to decide whether you can successfully advocate for his doing so. In some cases, as we've observed, trying to do so will not be worth the effort, and your session time might be better spent simply assisting him with a more basic level of argumentation. If the goal is a better writer, and not just a better piece of writing, you will sometimes need to recognize that the improvement you hope to happen will need to come over time.

When the writer has been given an assignment that is confusing or unworkable. Not every teacher or professor has training in the teaching of writing, and for some, assigning writing is an area where they have little experience and lesser expertise. Faculty development sessions and guidebook training can help, but there are always going to be writing assignments that are simply confusing or unworkable, and if you work in a campus writing or learning center, you are bound to see more than one of these in your career. Even assignments that sound simple on the surface can become irritatingly obtuse when a student plans her response: "compare and contrast Foucault's and Freud's theories of sexuality and repression as explored in the folk tale and film versions of Beauty and the Beast." Even a student who knows her Foucault, Freud, Mme. Le Prince de Beaumont, Cocteau, and Disney well will find no obvious—or even tenable—approach to ordering her argument to suit her professor's request. It may be tempting when working with a student who is faced with such an assignment to want to contact the professor immediately for direction. And in some cases, such discussions can be productive, but they must be couched as seeking information rather than criticizing the assignment. But more often than not, a deliberately-paced working through of a series of potential outlines or plans for the argument will reveal at least one solution that can accommodate the demands of the assignment and at the same time satisfy the rhetorical needs of the writer.

When the writer's topic is inappropriate or even abhorrent. There is no guarantee that writers will select topics that are appropriate to the situation and context, and there is no guarantee that even if their topic selection is workable that their argument itself will be. It helps, as we note in chapter three, to do all that you can to ensure that you and the writer are both proceeding with a full understanding of the rhetorical situation. And it helps, of course, if the writer has worked at careful invention and planning. But in some cases writers will simply choose topics that seem inappropriate to the assignment. If you work with writers whose work-in-progress seems based on a faulty understanding of the task, you do them no favors by pretending otherwise, especially if there exists enough time to undertake a different topic. (Sometimes the best advice, one of our colleagues likes to say, is simple: "Start over." Of course, a sympathetic tutor will explain why, and how, in earnest.)

In other cases, you may find yourself confronted with an argument you find abhorrent. It is no problem to disagree with a writer's claim—as the whole of the chapter should suggest, there are dozens of ways to work with writers on the development of their arguments regardless of whether you agree or disagree with what they say. Yet you may sometimes find a writer's position so abhorrent to your own sensibilities that you find stomaching the discussion difficult. (Even a personal narrative, as our case study 5.3 demonstrates, may present just such a dilemma.) You may have religious beliefs, personal experience, civic responsibilities, or ethical standards that would seem to make it impossible for you to work fairly with a writer who argues in their face. You can sometimes, if this is the case, ask that the writer work with another tutor, though that may not solve the problem (the second tutor might be as similarly predisposed as you). Instead, we urge you to acknowledge that tutor and writer need not agree on a topic in order to work together well. You may benefit from the dialogue that unfolds as much as the writer does, especially if you can use the strategies we discuss here to examine the strength of the argument as it develops.

In some rare cases you may elect, if you think it helpful to the session, to divulge your own interest, and to let your writer know what evidence supports your claims. But we urge extreme caution in such instances. After all, it is often the writer whose stance is abhorrent who is least receptive to alternative explanations or evidence. And it is entirely possible that such a writer will perceive your presentation of alternatives not as a Socratic pedagogical strategy but as a hostile criticism. If she does, she may respond not with a more enlightened, analytical position or an enhanced presentation of evidence but instead with a more firmly entrenched bulwark. In such an instance, you've done neither your writer nor yourself any justice. So when you consider whether you might present the alternative, you need to gauge whether doing so will motivate the writer's better-developed argument and not simply placate your desire to persuade her of the folly of her position.

Though it can be difficult to do so, we've witnessed more than one or two tutors put aside their own perspectives on a topic to work successfully with writers arguing positions counter to those the tutors held: after all, the work of the contemporary argument is not so much to win the skirmish or dismiss the opposition as it is to engage it and offer a reasonable, defensible position. In a more extreme, and thankfully rare, circumstance, you might encounter a paper that is blatantly and unrepentantly racist, misogynist, ethnocentric, or homophobic. In such circumstances, you ought to be prepared to explain why the work is likely to be perceived that way, even as you recognize this is a message your writer is not likely to want to hear. Our advice is to avoid escalating any disagreements that might arise; if you find you cannot respond to the writer's position by using the strategies we present without escalating tensions, the session might not be worth continuing.

When you suspect that the writer has plagiarized all or a part of an assignment. In some sessions, as we indicated above, discussions of source material will be perfectly clear and purposeful. You may note that a writer's citations are incomplete or inaccurate or that his introductions or acknowledgements are insufficient. As our tutor Jess demonstrates in her session with Fiona on her body-image paper, a pattern of questioning focused on the inherent problems with insufficient citation will typically guide the writer to a fuller and more purposeful presentation of the material. In most such cases, calling attention to your own difficulty in reading—*Is that a book? Who's the author? What's her authority?*—will motivate the writer to give more, rather than less.

However, in rare circumstances, you may suspect that a writer has—unlike Fiona—fraudulently pasted in large chunks of others' text, without attribution, apparently as his own. Of course, to encounter such a scenario in a tutorial is unlikely: after all, if a writer hopes to pass off others' work as his own, he can only increase his chances of being found out if he brings it to a writing center or other tutoring service. These are not, typically, the writers who are most likely to seek your help. However, it's not unimaginable that you might encounter such a scenario. There are a few telltale signs, especially if you are reading a student's paper that at some point …

- *Veers off-topic from the proposed topic or thesis;*
- *Presents material with which the writer appears unfamiliar;*
- *Evidences a clear shift in diction, syntax, or tone;*
- *Appears suddenly perfectly copy-edited (when the rest has not been); or*
- *Employs a different font, paragraph, margin, or page style.*

Any of these might be an indication that the writer is lifting material from an outside source. If you suspect that a writer is doing so, you can continue with a line of questioning about source material, and you should do so with the intent of fostering the writer's abilities and awareness. Keep in mind that some writers have little or no experience with academic citation practices, and for some ESL writers, the concept of plagiarism itself is a construct with no equivalent in their home educational culture (Pennycook, 1996). It helps to know what kinds of instruction your student has received. But no writer should be accused of plagiarism without incontrovertible evidence, and even then, such matters are normally better left to your supervisor or the course professor. Our advice is to learn your institution's policies and to ask your supervisor's practices, so that you know in advance how best to respond in the very slight chance that you are presented with work that is fraudulent in nature. (Case Study 5.4 raises this very question for you and your colleagues and supervisor.)

In sum, there are a number of potential areas of difficulty when working with students in the process of argumentation. We feel confident, though, that in most of these instances, the strategies we describe here will help you work comfortably and objectively with writers in these circumstances. Some occasional circumstances can be more extreme, but these are, thankfully, rare, and if you need to take action to end a session prematurely, it can help to know that you've exhausted the other possibilities and that your knowledge of what makes an argument successful is secure.

SUMMARY

What makes a successful argument? We can't say that a successful argument is one with airtight syllogistic logic: after countless iterations of a shopworn syllogism, Socrates has been proved a mortal, but we don't find this much of an argument. Nor is an argument successful simply because it appears to be devoid of logical fallacies. Nor if it evidences each of Rogers's features or Toulmin's elements. Nor even if it satisfies each of the STAR criteria. In short, no application of any individual scheme for analyzing an argument will ever meet every such critierion, of course, and as a result, we draw on both traditional and more contemporary understandings of argument for a synthesis. We conclude this chapter with that synthesis not because we expect that tutors will deliver final summations on whether or not their writers' arguments are indeed successful (or not). Instead, we note, anyone who proposes an argument needs to have a sense of what that argument ought accomplish.

To our thinking, good arguments are ones ...

- *which are carefully developed through an intimate understanding of the rhetorical situation and context;*

- *which present arguable, conspicuous, concise, and appropriately qualified claims;*

- *which present evidence that is varied in type and source according to context, that is well warranted, and that is carefully presented and appropriately documented;.*

- *which present evidence that is not only appropriate to the context but also sufficient in number, providing instances that are reasonably typical, accurate, and relevant;*

- *where evidence that would tend to support a claim different from the writer's is acknowledged and accounted for; and*

- *where the language used is relatively neutral, employed fairly and never pejoratively.*

Tutors can make use of a number of strategies for helping their writers achieve these goals. They can, first and foremost, be aware of the most commonly known schemes for argument (Aristotle, Rogerian, Toulmin) and their respective differences and purposes. They can practice and develop strategies that they can use to help writers articulate thesis statements (like glossing) and clear claims (like HDWDWW). They can use Fulkerson's STAR criteria to guide writers through a careful assessment of the evidence they use to support claims. And they can promote their writers' critical thinking by encouraging them to use their source material thoughtfully and responsively. No less important, they can be aware of the many differences in culture and development that can inhibit successful argumentation—for some writers, advanced levels of argument may simply be too abstruse a concept to manage at any given moment—and they can be attentive to some of the areas of difficulty that can arise when responding to an assignment or questioning a writer's claims. With the ability to assist at any of these stages or levels, though, a writing tutor will be well equipped to move a writer towards a better, fuller, more nuanced, and ultimately more *dialogic* understanding of argument.

SUGGESTIONS FOR FURTHER READING

Belenky, Mary Field, Blythe McVicker Clinchy, Nancy Rule Goldberger, and Jill Mattucki Tarule. (1986). *Women's ways of knowing.* New York: Basic Books.

Berthoff, Ann E. (1978). *Forming thinking writing: The composing imagination.* Portsmouth, NH: Heinemann.

Bouman, Kurt. (2004). Raising questions about plagiarism. In Shanti Bruce and Ben Rafoth (Eds.), *ESL writers: A guide for writing center tutors* (pp. 105-116). Portsmouth, NH: Boynton/Cook.

Brent, Doug. (1991). Young, Becker and Pike's "Rogerian" rhetoric: A twenty-year reassessment. *College English 53,* 452-466.

Clark, Irene. (1999). Writing centers and plagiarism. In Lise Buranen and Alice M. Roy (Eds.), *Perspectives on plagiarism and intellectual property in a postmodern world* (pp. 155-168). Albany, NY: SUNY Press.

Fulkerson, Richard. (1996). *Teaching the argument in writing.* Urbana, IL: NCTE.

Hairston, Maxine. (1976). Carl Rogers' alternative to traditional rhetoric. *College Composition and Communication 27,* 373-377.

Howard, Rebecca Moore. (1995). Plagiarisms, authorships, and the academic death penalty. *College English 57,* 788-805.

Kneupper, Charles W. (1978). Teaching argument: An introduction to the Toulmin model. *College Composition and Communication 29,* 237–241.

Lassner, Phyllis. (1990). Feminist responses to Rogerian argument. *Rhetoric Review 8,* 220-232.

Lunsford, Andrea A. (1979). Aristotelian vs. Rogerian argument: A reassessment. *College Composition and Communication 30,* 146-151.

Pennycook, Alastair. (1996). Borrowing others' words: Text, ownership, memory, and plagiarism. *TESOL Quarterly 30*(2), 201-230.

Perry, William. G. (1970). *Forms of intellectual and ethical development in the college years.* New York: Holt, Rinehart & Winston.

Rogers, Carl R. (1961). *On becoming a person.* Boston: Houghton Mifflin.

Schroeder, Christopher. (1997). Knowledge and power, logic and rhetoric, and other reflections in the Toulmin mirror: A critical consideration of Stephen Toulmin's contributions to composition. *Journal of Advanced Composition 17*, 95–107.

Toulmin, Stephen. (1958). *The uses of argument*. Cambridge: Cambridge University Press.

Young, Richard E., Alton L. Becker, and Kenneth L. Pike. (1970). *Rhetoric: Discovery and change*. New York: Harcourt.

CASE STUDY 5.1: USING GLOSSING TO ARTICULATE A THESIS

Veronica, a sophomore student enrolled in a course called "Intro to Film Art," brings into her tutorial session both a short syllabus description of her assignment and a draft of her paper, which is presented below. Even a cursory glance at her draft should suggest that she has more than a little talent and aptitude for the subject matter. According to the course syllabus, students are to "Analyze a pivotal scene in the week's film, paying attention both to the scene's technical elements and as well to its purpose in the narrative structure." But after describing the assignment and her analysis, Veronica notes the following: "On my last analysis, my professor wrote 'Decent observations but no real thesis.' So I get a C! I never know what my thesis is until I finish writing, so how can I come up with a thesis at the start that sums up all my ideas?"

How could you use the techniques presented in this chapter, especially Berthoff's glossing, to assist Veronica as she struggles to articulate her thesis?

Veronica's Draft:

One of the most memorable and suspenseful murder scenes in film history is *Psycho's* shower scene. *[Help, I'm stuck here, this is where I need to state my thesis better. Here's what I've got: Its technical elements are impressive, and the scene completely changes the direction of the narrative.]*
The scene helps accomplish a number of things. First, the speed of the attack shocks us, punctuating the relief we'd felt with Marion's apparent decision to return and face the consequences of her crime. Second, the result of the attack raises the issue of the attacker's motives: did Mrs. Bates kill Marion for the money—or for the risk to her son's innocence Marion's sexuality posed? And third, Norman's subsequent cleanup gives us reason to admire his cleanliness and thoroughness even as Hitchcock's subjective camera focuses our attention on the money Marion stole.
Cinematically, the harsh high key lighting, rapid montage editing, and extreme close-up camerawork constitute a radical departure from the quiet parlor dialogue of the prior scene. The audience first sees a figure enter the bathroom where an unsuspecting Marion Crane showers in near-silence. Special lighting effects illuminate "Mrs. Bates'" silhouette, creating a central focus on the character. Rapid editing between occasional subjective viewpoints and close-up indirect-subjective shots puts the viewer "in the shower." Brutal knife slashes and close-ups of Marion's mouth, agape with fear, punctuate the scene.
The accompaniment of music heightens—and resolves—the tension. The music is a cacophony of high-pitched strings alerting the audience to danger. Given the cold-blooded murder taking place, the music is abrupt, fast-paced, and high-pitched. The music parallels the fast and violent knife stabs. The silence of the strings after Marion has been murdered results, literally, in a "dead track" interrupted only later by the voice of Norman Bates crying, "Mother...blood!"

The indirect-subjective camera angle changes to a low-angle shot after Marion has been stabbed to death. The camera focuses on Marion's hand. The camera moves to the water and the blood circling around the bathtub drain, symbolizing the finality of her death. There is then the dissolve of the bathtub drain, and a close shot of Marion's eye is brought into focus. A slightly centrifugal fixed-frame movement mimics the water draining from the tub just as Marion's life drains from her eyes. The narrative, it seems, now lacks a clear protagonist. Until, that is, Norman arrives.

During the cleanup scene that follows, Norman becomes our only point of identification. We think him innocent; we root for him to succeed in his grisly task. The use of the moving camera keeps the viewer one step ahead of Norman. As he covers up the murder to "protect his insane mother," we see the newspaper containing the stolen money moments before Norman does. We're conditioned, then, to root for him to remove any incriminating evidence from the crime scene—one of the many ways in which Hitchcock manipulates his audience's sympathies, only to subvert their sympathies in the end.

CASE STUDY 5.2: EXAMINING EVIDENCE

Students in Professor Garson's journalism class are one of those groups that tend to frequent your writing center, in part because the editorial processes of drafting, revising, rereading, and editing prove such a challenge to newcomers there. Jake, a third-year psychology major completing the course as a free elective, has brought in a draft of his final project for the course—an editorial for prospective publication in the campus magazine—with the following concern. "No matter what we say in our editorials, we get shot down," says Jake. Either we have too much evidence, or not enough, or it's not the right kind. Sometimes, I think he enjoys just being able to contradict any point we raise. In any case, maybe you can help me think through what he's going to gripe about when I turn this in."

Jake's draft is presented below. How could you use the methods discussed in this chapter—perhaps most specifically, Fulkerson's STAR criteria for evaluating evidence—to help address Jake's concerns?

Hollywood's Golden Age Long Gone

The magic of Hollywood has long fascinated the American public. From the early silent films to the first talkies, movies resonated with the American audience. In the golden age of Hollywood, from the late 1930s to the end of the 1950s, film art reached its pinnacle. The movies from that period still live as the great accomplishments of the art form. But in contrast, today's movies just don't stack up.

For one thing, look at today's actors. In the golden age, a star's popularity was long and lasting. A leading man like Cary Grant made dozens of successful films. But today's actors are simply pretty faces, cast because they have a certain physique or celebrity spouse. Plum roles go to whoever happens to be dating the celebrity-of-the-month, not to the most talented actors. But when icons like Jimmy Stewart and Grace Kelly starred in a movie, their star power was undeniable. Those stars had an unforgettable quality that you just don't see today.

Moral values have changed for the worse too. In the studio era, nudity was never seen. Married couples had separate beds. The good guy always won (and got the girl!). Prostitutes, thieves, hoodlums, and killers weren't made to be heroes like they are in *Fight Club* or *Chicago*. And we weren't subjected to constant acts of premarital, homosexual, or other illicit kinds of sex onscreen. Even the language used today is worse. In the last installment of the PG-13-rated *X-Men* franchise, for example, practically every one of the heroes used foul language, and the biggest roar of the movie came when one mutant called another "Bitch." Every other movie is a new lesson in vulgarity of one kind or another.

In the golden age, movies were based mostly on quality literary works. Today, it seems like they're based on nothing but comic books, tv shows, video games—and even adventure park rides. Where's the substance? *Casablanca*, *The Maltese Falcon* and *The African Queen* will live forever. But, honestly, how long will people remember *Lara Croft*, *Doom*, or *AVP*, whatever that is supposed to stand for? My bet is not long at all.

Special effects might be new movies' only saving grace. Today, it is possible to transfix a viewer with CGI effects and animatronics. *The Lord of the Rings* and *Harry Potter* films, among others, had excellent special effects. So did the recent *King Kong* remake, even though it didn't surpass the original in any other way. For most of today's movies, however, technical expertise alone can't make up for bad performances, questionable values, and weak subject matter.

There is one answer to the problem. With 500 channels on satellite, growing on-demand options, and DVD prices plummeting, there's no reason to have to settle for mediocrity. Instead, there's a gem like *Rear Window* on Turner Classic Movies or the original *King Kong* re-released on a special edition two-disc set. Don't spend a sour night on tripe like *Snakes on a Plane*—when there's dozens of great classics of Hollywood's Golden Age within arm's reach.

CASE STUDY 5.3: A CHALLENGE TO YOUR BELIEFS

In a 1996 essay, "Teaching and Learning as a Man" (*College English 58*, 137-57), Robert J. Connors discussed a paper submitted by one of his writing students. That student paper—titled "Horsing Around"—has since been one frequently used and discussed in conversations and colloquia for new (and experienced) teachers of writing. As we discussed the prospect of tutoring a writer whose position is one you find abhorrent, we invite you to examine in detail just how you might do so. How would you use the strategies suggested in this chapter to make a session with the writer of "Horsing Around" productive? Present your case in the form of a well-developed and complicated narrative, and show in dialogue how you would respond to the writer's presentation of his experience.

Horsing Around

It was a cold winter day and my two friends, Bill and Jim, decided to skip school with me. I got out of bed and acted as if I were going to school, but instead I went to Bill's house. We sat in his living room drinking alcoholic beverages at 8:00 in the morning, Jim came over at 8:30 to join us.

As we drank beer like fish, we decided we were bored. The three of us had a total of about three dollars, so we could not go anywhere, even out to eat. To help make the time pass, Bill got out his twelve-gauge shotgun and started to clean it. Then a bright idea came to me, so I said, "We have enough guns and ammunition, and we have plenty of wooded area to go shooting in, so let's go!"

We got in Bill's jeep and drove down Party Road to get to the woods. Bill and I both had twelve-gauge shotguns, and Jim had a twenty-two rifle. We were out walking in the woods and Jim saw a crow, black as night, land in a tree. He aimed, shot, and killed the crow. I walked over, picked up the blood-soaked bird, and sat it with its wings spread wide in a small twig tree. I loaded my gun, walked back fifteen to twenty feet, turned, and fired. The bird was blown into about twelve pieces, just like a jigsaw puzzle. The ground was covered with powdery snow, so when the bird was shot a blood spray pattern covered that area.

After this adventure, we walked farther into the woods where we spotted a horse in an open field. Jim dared me to shoot it, but I told him that the horse was too far away to hit. As soon as I said that, though, the huge black and brown horse slowly trotted toward us. Bill was approximately one-hundred feet away from me, and did not know what I was about to attempt. It was a good thing that he did not know, because he is one of those "follow-the-rules" kind of guys. Then Jim said, "Go ahead Adam, I dare you."

Without thinking of the seriousness involved, I raised the gun to my shoulder, took a careful aim, and KABOOM! I nailed him in the left hind quarter and he let out a yelp like a dog getting its tail sliced off. At first I thought I might have killed the animal, but I was too afraid to stick around to find out. All I remember hearing after I shot the gun was the horse yelping and Bill shouting; going into hysterics about what I had done.

At this time we hurried back to the jeep and drove quickly to Bill's house without being caught. Needless to say, Bill doesn't want me to go shooting with him anymore. While in the jeep, Jim was laughing so hard that he wet his jeans. We finished up our unusual and impromptu hunting excursion by cleaning the guns and drinking more beer.

Looking back now, the whole thing seems pretty funny, but I also regret it. I feel bad about hurting the horse and I think the incident probably wouldn't have happened if it hadn't been for the combination of boredom, beer, boyhood.

CASE STUDY 5.4: ENCOUNTERING PLAGIARISM

Stephanie—a first-year student struggling mightily with the transition to college—has been asked to write a paper examining the work of a contemporary artist for her art history class, offered by the chairperson of the department. The assignment specifically stipulates that the students rely on no more than four secondary sources and conduct their own analysis of the artist's work. Having earned a D- on her first paper and been told firmly to "get help" for the next, she appears less than confident as she hands you the following and says: "I really don't care what it says or how it says it. I just need to know if it will be good enough to get a better grade. If I don't do better, I won't be able to stay in school long." As you review Stephanie's draft and source material, it becomes obvious to you that she has neither acknowledged sources fully nor paraphrased appropriately. How would you broach this topic with her? How would you do so had she not attempted to acknowledge her sources at all?

1. Excerpted from Stephanie's draft of her paper:	The original source material from Norden, Linda. "Introduction." *Chihuly Glass.* 1982. <http://www.chihuly.com/essays/introessay.html>.
In her biographical introduction to Chihuly glass, Linda Norden reports that Chihuly's first encounters with glass took place within the context of a weaving assignment for the University of Washington where he was enrolled in an Interior design Program. Asked to incorporate some non-fiber material in a work, Chihuly, with his proclivity for challenge, chose glass because it was the "material most foreign to fiber." Chihuly quickly realized that working with glass meant that it was not at all like fiber: It was very brittle and broke easily. By experimenting and checking around with people who knew more about glass than he did, Chihuly was determined to solve this problem.	As it happened, Chihuly's first encounters with glass took place within the context of a weaving assignment at the University of Washington. Asked to incorporate some non-fiber material in a work, Chihuly, with his proclivity for challenge, chose glass because it was the "material most foreign to fiber." Setting out to control the brittle glass threads, he began testing and improvising, consulting with whatever experts on glass he could scout out. This pattern, of immersing himself in a project and coupling trial-and-error testing with a willingness to seek out and accept the expertise of others, remains as much a Chihuly hallmark as his interest in glass.
2. Excerpted from Stephanie's draft of her paper:	**The original source material from Bernard, Walter Darby. Introduction. *Chihuly: Form from Fire.* Daytona Beach: Portland Press, 1993. 11-12.**
In the introduction to the book *Chihuly: Form from Fire*, Walter Darby Bannard says Chihuly saw some Indian baskets in museum storage room stacked sagging under their own weight, and his imagination associated these effects with glass—by nature not a substance of symmetry but a taffy-like liquid which "prefers" to sag and flow and well and blend. Bannard became very excited when he recognized	In the mid-'70s, Chihuly turned away from large multi-material pieces and began making plain, small cylindrical vessels with drawings formed from threads of hot glass picked up by rolling the semi-molten, red-hot bubble of glass over them. Somewhat later, after recovering from a serious automobile accident, Chihuly saw some Indian baskets in a museum storage room stacked [and] sagging under their own weight,

immediately that Chihuly was taken in by the sight and saw the potential of the sagging baskets for applications to glass, which was an altogether new vision (ii).

and his imagination associated these effects with glass - by nature not a substance of symmetry and applied decoration but a taffy-like liquid which "prefers" to sag and flow and swell and blend. When Chihuly saw these misshapen fiber baskets, he saw the essence of glass.

CHAPTER SIX

SENTENCE STYLE

CHAPTER SIX

SENTENCE STYLE

As we addressed in the previous chapter, many writing tutorials address the nature and structure of argument. Tutors and writers examine evidence, evaluate claims, and assess rhetorical structure and appeals in many such sessions. This kind of work—refining the argument through a dialogic process of reassessing the interplay of claims and evidence— reflects the contemporary emphasis on argument in the contemporary writing curriculum. At an earlier time, that same curriculum was every bit as much focused on *the sentence* as today's is on the *argument*. As Robert Connors (2000) notes, "the sentence itself as an element of composition pedagogy is hardly mentioned today outside of textbooks" (p. 97). But the fact that the sentence is rarely mentioned in classrooms or in scholarship does not necessarily mean that it is absent from the writing tutorial. In fact, many sessions will—and will need to continue to—address sentence style with writers.

There was a time, not too long ago, when the sentence as a unit of composition was at the center of the postsecondary writing curriculum. In fact, from the 1960s to the 1980s, a generation of scholars focused considerable attention on the sentence as a syntactic unit, developing rhetorical grammars and exercises that became the focus of many textbooks and curricula. Among these, perhaps the most prominent were the work of Francis Christensen, known for his "Generative Rhetoric" of the sentence, Edward P. J. Corbett's imitation exercises, and William Strong's pedagogy of sentence combining instruction. Later, rhetoricians like Richard Lanham developed classroom-tested methods of revising prose that also became well integrated into composition courses.

For a time, most noticeably in the 1970s and early 1980s, sentence-based composition pedagogies were more prevalent than any other in college composition classrooms. And when researchers tested and examined their effectiveness, they learned that such pedagogies were indeed demonstrably successful in teaching students to write more mature, sophisticated, and varied prose. The scholarly journals in the field proposed, discussed, examined, and debated these pedagogies as they were laid out in textbooks offering semesters' worth of drill, practice, and experimentation.

However, due to a number of factors, the popularity of sentence-level instruction began to ebb, and then quickly faded, in the 1980s. Connors (2000) details this narrative well in his essay "The Erasure of the Sentence." First, a new generation of Ph.D. scholars in the field critiqued the assumptions on which sentence-level instruction was based. In his *Teaching the Universe of Discourse*, James Moffett (1968) argued that teachers must address the sentence only "within its broader discursive context" (p. 186) and that students can be taught only if "the units of learning are units larger than the hindsight sentence" (p. 205). Moffett's was the first of many such anti-formalist critiques to suggest that any pedagogy based exclusively on form and not attendant to broader patterns of rhetoric and argumentation was suspect. To his thinking, what sentence-level instruction was missing was "meaning and motivation, purpose and point"—just exactly "what are missing from exercises" (p. 205).

As Connors notes, the 1980s also brought prevailing attitudes of anti-behavioralism and anti-empiricism that diminished sentence-level instruction. Pedagogies that aimed to make use of un- or sub-conscious knowledge to foster even something as innocuous as syntactic dexterity (as both Christensen's program and sentence combining did) came to be seen by anti-behavioralists as manipulative and demeaning to students (Connors, 2000, p. 113). To a less demonstrable extent, a growing sentiment of anti-empiricism in composition studies fostered a distrust of pre- and post-test quantification and experimentation (Connors, 2000, p. 116).

This distrust manifested itself eventually in strong critiques of the very research that had demonstrated the successes of sentence-level work. Today, the "erasure of the sentence" is near-complete: only a minority of textbooks address sentence-level concerns and no programs put such instruction at their core (if they address it at all). By the publication of Connors' 2000 article, he was able to liken the sentence to the *Titanic*: struck, and sunk, wholly and completely, by an iceberg of much larger proportions than the ship itself.

Yet despite the complete "erasure" of the sentence from curricula, scholarship, and teaching materials, students continue to write sentences. And many of the sentences written will, if you allow us some understatement, need more careful attention than they receive. As a result, many writing tutorials attend still to the concern that classroom instruction no longer does: that of the sentence and its clarity, efficiency, and variety.

SENTENCE STYLE AND THE TUTORING OF WRITING

When you work with students on sentence-level concerns, you should be aware that most instructors and readers will consider such matters subordinate to broader concerns of rhetorical appropriateness, claims and evidence, and the development of a strong thesis. This book is arranged to attend to those higher-order concerns first. Yet at the same time, you should be prepared to help any student improve his or her prose sentence style. As you work with the following methods of addressing stylistic concerns, please note that we do not advocate using much in the way of grammatical terminology with students. The methods we describe require only the most rudimentary grammatical knowledge, and we suggest that such terminology generally not be used to describe or categorize errors. Rather, we advocate instead for demonstrating to students when and where the sentence style can be improved; working on a few selected sample sentences in any given paragraph; and demonstrating transferable strategies for revision that students can later employ in other rhetorical situations. As always, patient, focused, engaged dialogue is the key. The methods presented in this chapter range from the relatively straightforward "Who does what?" of Berthoff's

HDWDWW to a slightly more elaborate "Paramedic Method" to a truncated version of Christensen's method of Generative Rhetoric. Each of these methods has a slightly different focus, but all of them can be used to assist student writers with the clarity, efficiency, and variety of their sentence style.

CLARITY: BERTHOFF'S HDWDWW (HOW DOES WHO DO WHAT AND WHY?)

Novice writers do not always realize that well-crafted sentences occur not in a simple flash of inspiration but through a process of careful addition, subtraction, contraction, and reorganization. As Linda Flower (1981) notes, such "writer-based prose" is the hallmark of the inexperienced writer, evidencing a haste to put ideas on paper without rigorous attention to how the prose will be read. Flower's term for the kind of syntactically mature prose composed by experienced writers—"reader-based prose"—instead evidences a more thoughtful process of arranging and rearranging chunks of syntax into purposeful, pleasurable sequences.

When students compose writer-based prose, they may be moving through a developmental stage in which they struggle to articulate well the ideas they are forming about their subjects. Or, in other cases, they may simply be unaware of (or unpracticed with) the kinds of syntactic structures that would allow them to compose more effective, efficient sentences. But in either case, the tutor's role is to help the writer understand both that the sentences need revision and, subsequently, how the writer can conduct those revisions. The best methods for doing so require little in the way of grammatical terminology, and, as mentioned, we caution against using such jargon to describe problems to your students in tutorial sessions. For instance, you might silently diagnose a student's writing as full of syntactic and grammatical flaws: it may be awkward, incomplete, even incomprehensible. But just as it would do little good to say so in so many words, to tell your student that his verbs lack agreement, his modifiers dangle and squint, and his parallelism is inexact will be greeted with at best indifference and at worst a contemptuous silence. Again, your goal is to engage your student in dialogue. So it will make more sense to ask your student a series of commonsensical questions based on Berthoff's HDWDWW heuristic. Such questions can prompt your students to compose more simply structured, direct, declarative sentences.

Who's doing what? The essence of Berthoff's method is encapsulated in this (WDW) part of the question, and it is a question that can be employed in almost every tutorial session addressing sentence-level issues. When you encounter any sentence that lacks a clear agent or a precise verb, ask your student **Who's Doing What?** For instance, if a student writes a sentence like the one that follows, this simple question can motivate a thoughtful revision

---

COMMONSENSE VARIATIONS ON BERTHOFF'S HDWDWW

1. **Who's doing what?**

   Ask this question when the sentence lacks a clear agent or action.

2. **How many actions are there?**

   Ask this question when the sentence includes multiple actions.

3. **How, when, why, or where is the action taking place?**

   Ask this question when the sentence's action is confusing.

4. **Who is saying what about what?**

   Ask this question when a speaker or source's words are not presented clearly.

5. **"What's another word for this?"**

   Ask this question when phrases are inefficient or inexact.

---

that features a clearly identifiable subject and active verb.

> *Looking at the mise en scene, my eyes were drawn to its use of chiaroscuro lighting and cigarette smoke to create swirling pockets of light and shadow that caught every viewer's attention.*

Zoe: I'm wondering who's doing what in this sentence. What's it about, in a word or two?

Serena: The mise en scene? Or my eyes? Or the lighting and smoke? I'm not sure which you mean.

Zoe: That's partly the issue—which of those is most important? Your sentence should have a clear, identifiable subject, and there shouldn't be any confusion like we're having.

Serena: If I had to pick, I guess the mise en scene.

Zoe: Okay, what does it do? Pick a simple, active verb.

Serena: "Uses"?

Zoe: Good. And what does it use?

Serena: Chiaroscuro lighting and cigarette smoke.

Zoe: To ...?

Serena: Okay, so it should read "The mise en scene uses chiaroscuro lighting and cigarette smoke to create swirling pockets of light and shadow that caught every viewer's attention."

Zoe: In part, that's a lot better because it has a clear, simple subject and action. But it's also better because it doesn't try to say what you saw and what everyone else saw at the same time.

In a session like this, Zoe might identify multiple instances where Serena's sentences lack clear agents and active verbs and prompt her with the same "who's doing what" question. After having done so three or four times, Serena should be prompted to identify such sentences and revise them on her own.

How many actions are there? In other instances, a writer may try unsuccessfully to pack two or three separate actions (sometimes ones performed by different agents) into a single sentence. More typically than not, such sentences will be better if the writer makes, and commits to, a choice of a single agent. For instance, in the case of a student who writes a sentence like the one below, identifying the number of agents and actions will help immensely in rebuilding and improving the sentence.

Although he was as fit as any man on the tour, Andre Agassi finally succumbed to a chronic sciatic nerve problem in which he was forced to retire as a result of needing one too many cortisone injections.

Zoe: How many actions are there in this sentence?

Anna: Two? He had a injury and he had to retire?

Zoe: And the injections?

Anna: I guess that's another. Three, then.

Zoe: And what order did they happen in?

Anna: The injury first, then the injections, then the retirement.

Zoe: All right, let's take a look. What did Agassi do, first, second, and then third?

Anna: He was injured, he needed too many injections, he was forced to retire.

Zoe: So let's unpack this: Although he was as fit as any man on the tour, Andre Agassi ... one,

Anna: Fell victim to a chronic sciatic nerve problem ...

Zoe: two ...

Anna: received one too many cortisone injections ...

Zoe: and three ...

Anna: was forced to retire.

Depending upon the session, Zoe might additionally sketch out simple sentence patterns on scratch paper to demonstrate to Anna how she could revise other sentences that intimate multiple actions without making their sequence or importance clear. But in the exchange above, Zoe's focus on asking "How many actions are there?" helps Anna to present her information in a sentence that is logically and syntactically coherent.

How, when, why, or where is the action taking place? If the kernel of Berthoff's HDWDWW method is "Who does what?," then this question can assist with its details. "Who does what?" should yield a subject-verb-object pattern; asking how, when, why, or where the action takes place can help a writer modify that pattern with information that clarifies the action. Consider a sentence like this as our tutor, Zoe, discusses it with the student writer, Alex:

As I was reading this book it is a touching and meaningful story and it makes me realize how much I miss my own family.

Zoe: When is the action occurring in this sentence?

Alex: As I was reading the book? Or no, afterwards, it made me realize how much I missed my family. But I wrote that in present tense.

Zoe: To make it more clear, it's better to pick a clear moment. Did you have that realization as you were reading it, or as you concluded it?

Alex: Both, but if I had to pick, I'd rather say after.

Zoe: Okay. So let's try starting with "the book" as the subject. The book ...

Alex: Made me realize how much I miss my own family.

Zoe: That's much clearer. Now how could you add that it was "touching and meaningful"?

Alex: I could say "The touching and meaningful book made me ..." or "A touching and meaningful story, the book made me ...." Is one of those better than the other?

As Zoe prompts Alex to make more clear when the action of the sentence takes place, notice that Alex's sentence also comes to exhibit a clearer "who-does-what" (subject-verb-object) pattern with "the book made me realize." But asking Alex to choose one moment or the other in which to describe the action forces her to address the inconsistent verb tenses in the existing sentence.

Who is saying what about what? In prose that aims to describe what one or more speakers (or writers) are saying about a concept, novice writers often compose confounding sentences. Such writer-based prose may well result from a lack of experience writing about intellectual ideas. When writers compose sentences like the one below, asking "Who is saying what about what?" may help the writer revise successfully without overlong grammatical explanation.

> *Explaining the principles of the categorical imperative to the reader by stating that one should act only according to that maxim by which you can at the same time will that it would become a universal law is the central purpose of this passage in the text written by Immanuel Kant.*

Zoe: I think I understand what you're saying here, but it's a bit confusing. Who's saying what?

Lynn: Immanuel Kant ... is saying that ... [*reads*] "*one should act only according to that maxim by which you can at the same time will that it would become a universal law.*"

Zoe: Are those his words or have you stated that in your own words?

Lynn: Those are his, that's basically his "categorical imperative."

Zoe: Okay, if you are quoting him directly, enclose that quotation in quotation marks and double-check it for accuracy.

Lynn: Mmm-hmm.

Zoe: Now, here's what some of the rest of the sentence says. "*Explaining the principles of the categorical imperative to the reader by stating that*" ... "*is the central purpose of this passage in the text written by Immanuel Kant.*" How much of this is necessary if you've said that "Kant is saying that ...?"

Lynn: I have to call it the categorical imperative. Otherwise, I don't know if any of it's necessary.

Zoe: Good. So how can you add that?

Lynn: Immanuel Kant's categorical imperative states that "one should act only according to that maxim by which you can at the same time will that it would become a universal law."

As is the case with our other variations on Berthoff's HDWDWW method, asking "Who's saying what about what?" can motivate a clearer, more economical expression of ideas. Novice writers can be especially prone to sentences like Lynn's original above, which, with its tortured syntax and overlong explanation, only creates confusion about "Who's saying what?"

"What's another word for this?" One last benefit of Berthoff's heuristic is that it encourages economy of expression. "Who's doing what?" focuses writers' attention on naming specific nouns and articulating clear actions. In some cases, you might ask a student "What's another word for this?" when you see noticeably inefficient phrasings. Let's return to the dialogue between the student named Serena and our tutor Zoe from a few pages back. You will recall that Serena revised her sentence to articulate more clearly "who's doing what?" Here is how their dialogue might continue from Serena's revision:

> Serena: Okay, so it should read "The mise en scene uses chiaroscuro lighting and cigarette smoke to create swirling pockets of light and shadow that caught every viewer's attention."
>
> Zoe: In part, that's a lot better because it has a clear, simple subject and action. But it's also better because it doesn't try to say what you saw and what everyone else saw at the same time.
>
> Now let me ask you about this phrase: "that caught every viewer's attention." What's another word for this? Is there a single word that would express this idea?
>
> Serena: I don't know. "Eye-catching," maybe.
>
> Zoe: Not bad. Now if you used that, where would it go? In other words, what does that describe.
>
> Serena: The lighting, mostly. How's this: "The mise en scene uses eye-catching chiaroscuro lighting and cigarette smoke to create swirling pockets of light and shadow." Can it just end like that?
>
> Zoe: Sure can.

Berthoff's HDWDWW is powerful not just because it can be used as a generative heuristic but because it can prompt a number of commonsensical questions motivating revisions of awkward sentences. Its kernel—"Who's doing what?"—is the most important of these, but variations on its themes will prove useful, too.

EFFICIENCY: LANHAM'S PARAMEDIC METHOD

In his book *Revising Prose* (1979), rhetorician Richard Lanham describes what he called his "Paramedic Method" (PM) for sentences "that just go on and on, as if they were emerging from a nonstop sausage machine" (p. 9). The shapelessness of sentences that do not present a specific noun and active verb makes them, Lanham says, unreadable, as they cannot be read with any expression or emphasis. Lanham's Paramedic Method has since been employed regularly in writing classrooms and writing centers, in part because it is an efficient method of diagnosing problematic prose, and in equal part because it is every bit as effective in improving it. The Paramedic Method consists of these primary steps:

LANHAM'S PARAMEDIC METHOD

   1. Circle the prepositions.

   2. Circle the "is" forms.

   3. Ask "who is kicking who?"

   4. Put this "kicking" action in a simple (not compound) active verb.

   5. Start fast—no mindless introductions.

---

1. Circle the prepositions. According to Lanham, prose dependent upon strings of prepositional phrases renders a catalog-like monotony. He presents this graphic example of what might appear on the surface to be a perfectly creditable sentence: *Central to our understanding of the character of Lucrece in William Shakespeare's The Rape of Lucrece is the long passage towards the end of the poem devoted to a painting of the fall of Troy* (p. 4). For Lanham, two prepositional phrases in a row "turn on the warning light, three make a problem, and four invite disaster" (p. 5). Circling the prepositions draws attention to them and prompts their remedy if overused. In the example of the sentence above, Lanham illustrates its dependence on strings of prepositional phrases:

Central to our understanding
of the character
of Lucrece
in William Shakespeare's The Rape of Lucrece
is the long passage
towards the end
of the poem devoted
to a painting
of the fall
of Troy.

Lanham's suggested revision, *The Troy poem, described near the poem's end, illuminates Lucrece's character,* eliminates all but one of the prepositional phrases but still accomplishes the same meaning as the original. And it does so in eleven words instead of thirty-five.

Now look at the following sentences. How would you draw a student's attention to the overuse of prepositional phrases in each? How would you suggest potential revisions?

> *One of the many dramatic ironies in the tragedy of* Oedipus the King *by the Greek playwright Sophocles is that only as a result of their many attempts to foil the prophecies of the fates do the predictions of the gods actually become realized for each of the characters, including the protagonist Oedipus.*

> *The proper execution of all the details of the plan should result in no further increases in the funds necessary to expend on the implementation of the projects under the supervision of the various divisions of our organization.*

> *This is in conformity with the policies established in agreements with the representatives of the agencies in the state of Minnesota and at the federal level with contamination oversight responsibilities for the safety of the reservation and of the surrounding area.*

> *A bill that would exclude tax income from the assessed value of new homes from the state education funding formula could mean a loss of revenue for Trempeleau County schools.*

2. Circle the "is" forms. Sentences that depend on the weakest verb in the language project, as Lanham says, "no life, no vigor. They just 'are'" (p. 1). Moreover, they tend, more than others, to generate the strings of prepositional phrases that make rhythm and pattern impossible. Lanham's method asks writers not to eliminate forms of the verb "to be" (*am, is,* *are, was, were, be, being, been*), but to reduce their unnecessary use. Some writers—especially the less experienced and unsure—will write sentences that use no other verb. And many depend entirely too much on unnecessary constructions like "there is" and "there are," when they could instead offer precisely named subjects and active verbs to engage the reader. A sentence like "There was a single flag at half mast silently commemorating his passing" will almost always benefit from a simple revision: excising the "there were" construction to read "A single flag at half mast silently commemorated his passing."

3. Ask "who is kicking who?" Lanham's playful question originates with what he called the disease of the novice writer: unnecessarily complicating sentences with extra verbiage. No one, Lanham contends,

> feels comfortable writing simply "Jim kicks Bill." The system seems to require something like "One can easily see that a kicking situation is taking place between Bill and Jim." Or, "This is the kind of situation in which Jim is a kicker and Bill is a kickee." Jim cannot enjoy kicking Bill; no, for school use, it must be "Kicking Bill is an activity hugely enjoyed by Jim." (1979, p. 1)

Lanham's Paramedic Method suggests that eliminating forms of "to be" and changing unnecessary instances of passive voice (e.g., "the plan was proposed by the Student Senate representative from the junior class" to "the Student Senate representative from the junior class proposed the plan") will remedy most sentences lacking a strong active verb.

4. Put this "kicking" action in a simple (not compound) active verb. Aside from eliminating forms of "to be" and passive constructions, Lanham also recommends "squeezing" compound verbs by reducing them to single words when possible. "Are able to" becomes "can"; "seems to succeed in creating" becomes "creates"; and redundancies like "rushed and hurried" are compressed into a single verb.

5. Start fast—no mindless introductions. The last element of the Paramedic Method is to "amputate" (another of Lanham's playfully active verbs) what he called "mindless introductory phrases." Among these:

- *the fact of the matter is that*
- *it is easy to see that*
- *the manner in which*
- *for all intents and purposes*
- *concerning the matter of*
- *it is crucial/evident/imperative/important that*

Lanham recommends instead that every sentence start by "cutting to the chase," with no needless verbiage prefacing the actual subject of the sentence.

The Paramedic Method is *not* a protocol that must be applied to *all*—or even *most*—sentences. Rather, it serves as a useful guideline for quickly diagnosing and remedying sentences that string together prepositions, depend overly on *is* verbs, avoid active verbs, and delay action with needless verbiage. In our experience, it can be used with at least some success in almost any setting. A writer need not be required to rewrite every sentence of a given piece of discourse to make substantial improvement with this method, either; on the contrary, making demonstrable improvements to even some sentences can yield a significant improvement in the prose style.

In the tutorial session that follows, our tutor, Gina, is working with Jalen, who is considering a career as a nurse. Jalen was able to secure permission to observe an emergency room shift for his "Introduction to Health Professions" course. His instructions for the paper were to describe and narrate the events of the shift he shadowed before speculating on their importance and reflecting on the career choice. Here are the first two paragraphs of Jalen's essay, followed by Gina's introduction and presentation of the Paramedic Method:

> The doors flew open and the young man was rushed and hurried into place. All of the man's recognizable features were disguised by lesions, bruises, and blood. There were bones protruding through his skin on an arm and one leg. His blood was dripping into puddles on the floor and into the hall and in a matter of seconds his chest was sliced wide open by the attending doctor who appeared calm and confident. It was easy to see that for all practical

intents and purposes the doctor and the nurses were all professionals who knew just what to do in a situation like this one.

The young man was losing all his blood and if he was to survive it needed to be stopped. The floor was a pool of blood and there were stained footprints that led in every direction. The bleeding was their number one priority! Once they could stop the bleeding they would be able to let him rest and take care of his other injuries later.

Jalen: So what I tried to do here was to show what that scene was like. But it's so boring. The place was actually pretty exciting—for a minute, it was just like *ER* on TV.

Gina: Is that the impression you were trying to make?

Jalen: Yeah, hectic, fast-paced, even a little scary, but the staff was calm. Here, take a look. [*Jalen reads the two paragraphs above.*]

Gina: Okay. I can see a few things I can help you with. There's an approach called the Paramedic Method. I guess that's appropriate for your subject! Anyway, here's what we do: circle the prepositions and the "is" verbs first. Then we try to look for better subjects and active verbs and get rid of any wordiness. Let's start with the prepositions. Are you good with those?

Jalen: Just circle all of them?

Gina: Yep.

Jalen: [*annotating the first three sentences*] Okay, there's *into, by, through, on, into, on, into, in, of, by.* Wow. That's a lot.

Gina: Well, more than necessary. There's not a rule on this, but two prepositional phrases in a row might be okay, three is probably too many, four is like "don't do it." Do you see some that could be omitted?

Jalen: Sure: "onto the floor" can come out, so can "in a matter of." Are there others?

Gina: Maybe, but let's go on for a second. The next step is to circle the forms of the verb "to be": *is, was, are, were, am,* etc.

Jalen: [*annotating as he goes*] Okay, there's *was rushed and hurried, were disguised, were bones protruding, blood was dripping, was sliced open* ... Oh ... I do this every sentence.

Gina: Yeah, you do, but can you see how you don't need to? For now, just mark the rest and then we'll go on.

Jalen: [*continues to annotate, sighing every time he encounters another instance*] Okay.

Gina: Good, we'll work with some of these. Let's take this sentence as an example: *All of the man's recognizable features were disguised by lesions, bruises, and blood.* My question is this: "who's kicking who?"

Jalen: Huh?

Gina: Sorry. Another what to put it is what's doing what? In other words, what's the sentence about?

Jalen: His features? Or the lesions, bruises, and blood?

Gina: There's two reasons why I think the second answer is better. First is that they do the disguising, right? They're actually doing something. Second is they're more specific and visual than "features," which could be anything. Okay?

Jalen: Okay. So now what?

Gina: What are they doing? Name the simplest, most active verb you can.

Jalen: "Disguised"?

Gina: Great. So what's the sentence?

Jalen: "Lesions, bruises and blood disguised all of his recognizable features." Hey. Not bad.

Gina: Right. Now look at the next sentence: who's kicking who?

Jalen: Bones. *Bones protruded through his skin on an arm and a leg.* [*pauses to look at the next sentence*] *His blood dripped into puddles on the floor and into the hall.*

Gina: That's really good. Keep going.

Jalen: Okay, in the next sentence the doctor's doing the kicking: *In seconds, the attending doctor sliced his chest wide open.*

Gina: Big improvement, don't you think?

Jalen: Is that all there is to it? I can do this.

Gina: One last step, and that's "start fast." Just make sure that your subject is pretty close the start of the sentence. *Bones, blood, doctor*—these all work good. But look at the next sentence.

Jalen: [*reading*] *It was easy to see that for all practical intents and purposes the doctor and the nurses were all professionals who knew just what to do in a situation like this one.*

Gina: Who's kicking who?

Jalen: Well, there's less action here. I'm commenting on the action, not just describing it. But the doctor and nurses are the "who."

Gina: And what do the phrases "it was easy to see that" and "for all practical intents and purposes" do?

Jalen: Ahh, nothing. Get in the way. I hear you. Can I just delete?

Gina: Try it.

Jalen: Yep, better.

Gina: Okay, you're doing great. It's really pretty straightforward. [*Jalen writes notes as Gina dictates.*] Just remember: 1. Circle the prepositions. 2. Circle the "is" forms. 3. Ask "who's kicking who?" 4. Put the kick in a simple active verb. 5. Start fast. Now you don't need to do every sentence, but after you get the hang of it, you can revise a lot of sentences easily and even pretty quickly. If I let you work for a few minutes, do you want to see what you can do with the rest?

Jalen: [*Already at work*] Mm-hmm.

As you can see, Gina works slowly with Jalen to show him each stage of the process separately. But at the same time, doing so allows Jalen ample time to contribute his own findings—simply by being alerted to his reliance on *is* verbs, passive constructions, strings of prepositional phrases, and wordy introductions, Jalen can find ways of improving the sentences. Lanham's Paramedic Method works especially well when the writer's prose suffers from an unnecessary inefficiency or flatness, and it can be used to strong effect even in short sessions concentrating on selected sentences or passages. When Gina returns to assess Jalen's revisions, she can comment on improvements, difficulties, or trouble spots as she sees fit, but as the session concludes, it will be worth her while to reiterate to Jalen the steps in the method and then the strategies for using it. Working his way through every sentence in the essay will be a painstaking task, but it might well be worth Jalen's while, especially if his revision of his first two paragraphs is any indication. Here is the result of Gina's advice and Jalen's revision:

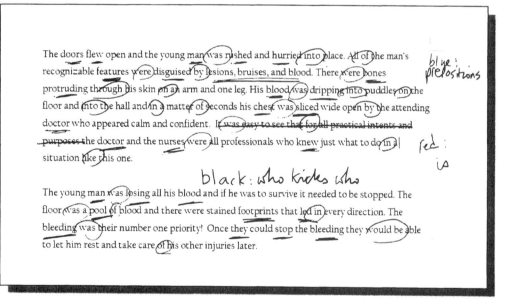

The doors flew open and the young man was hurried into place. Lesions, bruises, and blood disguised all of his recognizable features. Bones protruded through his skin on an arm and one leg. Blood dripped into puddles on the floor and into the hall, and in seconds the calm, confident attending doctor sliced his chest wide open. The doctor and the nurses were all professionals who knew just what to do in a situation like this one.

The puddle of blood became a pool and stained footprints led in every direction. The bleeding—their number one priority—needed to be stopped. Once they could stop the bleeding, the staff would be able to let him rest and take care of his other injuries later.

Lanham's paramedic method is one that many of our tutors have employed in their sessions to good effect. Among its virtues are that it does not rely on any specialized grammatical terminology (i.e. beyond subject, verb, and preposition) and that it is easily summarized, presented, and applied. Writers like Jalen, whose otherwise thoughtful prose is unnecessarily cluttered with inefficiencies and inelegancies, can often learn to apply the method to a small set of three or four sample sentences and then make further revisions on their own. But as is the case with most of the other heuristics we present in this book, the tutor will need to make judicious, informed decisions about when and how to present the method.

VARIETY: CHRISTENSEN'S GENERATIVE RHETORIC

With research that was originally published as a series of articles that later became a monograph and was eventually reworked as a textbook for introductory composition, Francis Christensen articulated what he called "generative rhetoric." Christensen's 1963 article, "A Generative Rhetoric of the Sentence," first put forth his theory that more traditional classroom discussions of the sentence were simple taxonomies, aimed at describing grammatical types of sentences rather than at generating and shaping them. Among the basic assumptions of Christensen's work was that the sentence was the most important element in writing instruction: as a discrete unit one could isolate from larger units of discourse, its grammar could be taught in ways that were truly, as he called it, "generative."

Basing his conclusions on the published fiction and nonfiction prose, Christensen's Generative Rhetoric operated primarily on the principle of *addition*. Students were to compose short "base clauses" (typically consisting of a simple, but active, subject-verb-object structure) and then experiment with "free modifiers" that could either precede the base clause, follow it, or (less frequently) interrupt it. These free modifiers could take different forms—adjective, absolute, or appositive phrases, for instance, all of which we demonstrate below—and they could, furthermore, modify either the base clause or other free modifiers. Christensen's Generative Rhetoric taught students to experiment with different types of free modifiers, located in different positions, formulated in different structures, with the goal of what Christensen called a rich "texture": a sentence style that offered varied combinations of short and long sentences, unmodified and modified base clauses, and different types of modifiers in different positions. (Christensen called prose that was essentially unmodified "bare" and prose that was heavily modified in a Faulkneresque or Joycean style "dense.")

In his textbook *A New Rhetoric*, Christensen led students through a series of exercises in which they would modify simply-structured base clauses. For the sake of illustration, here below are sentences that demonstrate Christensen's pattern of modification. In each, the base clause—that kernel of the sentence containing its main subject and verb—is labeled as level (1), with the subject <u>underlined</u> and the verb <u>double-underlined</u>. A free modifier that modifies the base clause is labeled as level (2); one that modifies a second-level modifier is labeled as level (3); and so on. In Christensen's model, modifiers can continue to modify the base clause or other modifiers indefinitely. And for Christensen, sentences that offered progressively deeper levels of modification were called cumulative sentences. The following sentences were published in an article entitled "Bob Dylan's Blue Highways" in the April 4th, 1991 issue of *Rolling Stone.*

(2) Three CDs,
(2) fifty-eight tracks,
(2) nearly four hours of music,
(1) the first three <u>volumes</u> of The Bootleg Series <u>*stand*</u> *solidly on their own terms as an essential statement of the breadth of Bob Dylan's artistic achievement.*

(1) This <u>collection</u> <u>is</u> obviously not where a newcomer to Dylan—
   (2) whoever such a person might be—
(1) should begin.

(1) These <u>songs</u>—
   (2) outtakes from albums,
   (2) alternative versions of well-known and lesser-known tunes,

(2) the occasional live track,
(2) demos Dylan recorded for his music publisher so his songs could be transcribed and made available to other artists—
(1) <u>are</u> not his greatest hits or his most influential work.

(1) They <u>do not</u> even demonstrate a definite creative progress,
  (2) as do the songs on Biograph,
    (3) despite the absurdly confused chronology of that earlier collection.

  (2) No,
(1) the <u>tracks</u> on The Bootleg Series <u>document</u> *the blue highways of Dylan's imagination,*
  (2) the paths not taken,
  (2) the back roads that sometimes run parallel to and sometimes veer away from the main road—
    (3) songs from a planned live album that got scuttled,
    (3) songs that seemed old-fashioned after fresher impulses gripped Dylan's restless soul,
    (3) songs too similar to or too different from other songs on a particular album,
    (3) sketches that never quite assumed full character.

  (2) With the help of John Bauldie's excellent liner notes—
    (3) detailed without being obsessive,
    (3) interpretive without being bullying,
    (3) appreciative without being fawning—
(1) <u>listeners</u> <u>can get</u> a distinct feel from this set for the kinds of decisions that make a song or shape a career.

As you examine these sentences, please keep in mind that we do not imply that there is anything particularly unusual about them aside from their having been professionally published. Though the article including them appeared a few decades after Christensen's main body of research, they are, like those he studied, from professional writers, and not in any particular way unusual for such. As the author describes the Bob Dylan anthology being reviewed, his rhetorical purpose is both to introduce and describe the contents of that anthology.

> **CHRISTENSEN'S GENERATIVE RHETORIC**
>
> 1. **Mark the end-stop punctuation. ("Connect the dots.")**
> 2. **Mark other punctuation separating free modifiers from base clauses.**
> 3. **Identify short, emphatic, subject-verb-object base clauses.**
> 4. **Connect free modifiers to base clauses: appositive, participial, and absolute phrases.**

From even this cursory review of sentences graphically arranged to demonstrate Christensen's levels of modification, one can see that syntactically mature writing such as this offers free modifiers in a variety of positions (both before and after the base clause) and at a variety of levels. When you work with writers whose prose is less syntactically mature—and you will—you can still nonetheless encourage at least a bit of variety and modification.

Christensen's Generative Rhetoric was proved by experimental research to have a positive effect on the writing of college students (Faigley, 1978), although it should be noted that classroom instructors like those participating in this experiment had had a full semester in which to teach the Christensen method. A tutor, we note, does not. Yet this and other studies demonstrated rather conclusively that Christensen's method can indeed demonstrate to students ways that their prose can present greater variety and maturity. The fact that this and other sentence-level methods are no longer prominent in composition instruction cannot be attributed to any failure on the part of the method itself. In a tutorial setting, Generative Rhetoric has two strong attributes: one, it can be presented in short stages consisting of one or two sessions; and two, it works.

You might choose to rely on the Christensen method when your student writes prose that is unnecessarily bare. Perhaps on occasion you will see sentences that consist only of simple subject-verb-object constructions elaborated with the occasional prepositional phrase. Perhaps you will note a near-complete absence of punctuation that normally sets off free modifiers (commas, dashes). Perhaps just by glancing at the end punctuation of sentences you will observe that every sentence is of similar length: the sentences are all approximately ten to fifteen words long, for example.

To present the principles of Generative Rhetoric to a student in a tutorial setting, we suggest first demonstrating that there is a reason to do so with one of two common methods. First, you can ask the student to mark the ends of sentence boundaries: "connect the dots" is a memorable phrase that can encourage students to circle and note the periods that end each sentence. Second, you can ask the student to circle other uses of punctuation: colons, semicolons, commas, and dashes. In some instances, "connecting the dots" will demonstrate a slavish obeisance to a certain sentence length, and marking the punctuation will demonstrate an avoidance of punctuation other than the period.

In the session that follows, our tutor, Shane, is working with a student in a first-year seminar course, Barry. Barry's seminar is focused on "life stages," and near the end of the course they are concentrating on death and dying. For his assignment, he was asked to analyze "any literary, cinematic, or artistic work students think to be particularly profound in its thematic meaning regarding death and/or dying." Students were additionally required to "discuss the elements of the work along with its meaning or sentiments on the theme." Here is the first paragraph of the essay Barry has brought to his tutorial.

Dylan Thomas was born in Wales in 1914. He was schooled by his father. Dylan Thomas Sr. was Senior English Master at Swansea Grammar School, which Thomas attended. Thomas' father was a quick tempered man who demanded respect from both his students and peers (Ferris 39). The younger Thomas grew up to become a passionate man. He had a propensity for drinking and he was known for his deep baritone voice and popular poetry readings. Thomas' poem "Do not go gentle into that good night" is addressed to his dying father, whom he had much love and respect for. This poem is sometimes referred to as one of the greatest of the twentieth century. The poem is written in the villanelle form. The villanelle is a form that makes use of a very strict rhyme scheme and repetition. A villanelle is required to use a refrain of its first and third lines over and over in its nineteen lines. The villanelle form is typically used for lighter topics. In Thomas's hands the villanelle form is used to speak strongly against the inevitability of death. Vivid imagery is used through figures of speech which address all the senses. In this poem Thomas is urging his father to "rage, rage against the dying of the light." He is telling his father not to submit to death and he is refusing to accept his father's death. "Do not go gentle into that good night" is a poem that demonstrates the grief one feels for a loved one.

Once Shane has, as we've suggested in previous chapters, discerned what he must about the rhetorical situation and the agenda for the session, he can begin assessing the sentence style by directing Barry to read his own work critically.

Shane: The first thing I'm going to ask you to do is to connect the dots—just go through this paragraph and circle each of the periods. Then we'll see what we learn from doing that.

Barry: Okay. [*Barry circles the periods. When he misses a couple, Shane points them out.*] Now what?

Shane: Next I'm going to have you find all the other punctuation. Not quotation marks, but all the commas, and even any dashes, colons, or semicolons. Let's use a different mark for those, maybe just a square around each.

Barry: [*Studies the paragraph.*] I don't see any. Oh wait, here's one. [*Draws a box around the comma following "father."*] Did I miss any others?

Shane: I don't think so. So—from circling the periods, what would you conclude about the length of the sentences?

Barry: Well, they're all about the same length.

Shane: And the other punctuation?

Barry: There isn't any ...

Shane: That's okay — there's not a rule that says you have to use different kinds of punctuation, but the style here could easily use more variety in the length and the structure of the sentences. Any time you see the sentences all the same length and without any punctuation, that means there's work to do connecting and presenting the ideas.

Barry: Do I have to completely rewrite this?

Shane: Well, not necessarily every sentence. I think the ideas and information should be fine, but I can show you how to connect some of the ideas that go together and how to get some more variety into the sentences. When we're done, it should read and sound quite a bit better.

Here are the results of Barry's marking of his text. He has circled each of the periods in the paragraph and noted the lone instance of other punctuation with a check mark. (The slash marks following some of the sentences divide them into topically-related groups, which we will return to later.)

Now that the tutor has demonstrated to Barry the lack of maturity and variety in the paper, the task is to employ Christensen's methods to foster what he called a richer *texture*—that is, again, one where base clauses use different types of modification to achieve greater variety.

Dylan Thomas was born in Wales in 1914. He was schooled by his father. Dylan Thomas Sr. was Senior English Master at Swansea Grammar School, which Thomas attended. Thomas' father was a quick tempered man who demanded respect from both his students and peers (Ferris 39). The younger Thomas grew up to become a passionate man. He had a propensity for drinking and he was known for his deep baritone voice and popular poetry readings. Thomas' poem "Do not go gentle into that good night" is addressed to his dying father, whom he had much love and respect for. This poem is sometimes referred to as one of the greatest of the twentieth century. The poem is written in the villanelle form. The villanelle is a form that makes use of a very strict rhyme scheme and repetition. A villanelle is required to use a refrain of its first and third lines over and over in its nineteen lines. The villanelle form is typically used for lighter topics. In Thomas's hands the villanelle form is used to speak strongly against the inevitability of death. Vivid imagery is used through figures of speech which address all the senses. In this poem Thomas is urging his father to "rage, rage against the dying of the light." He is telling his father not to submit to death and he is refusing to accept his father's death. "Do not go gentle into that good night" is a poem that demonstrates the grief one feels for a loved one.

While Christensen presented his readers with no fewer than eight different kinds of free modifiers, we will simplify by demonstrating just three: **participial phrases**, which often begin with an "-ing" form of a verb; **appositive phrases**, which identify or rename an adjacent noun or pronoun; and **absolute phrases**, which resemble a compete sentence with a missing auxiliary verb. We've selected these three in part because they require precision in using active verbs and descriptive phrasings to present specific information. Each can be used to add description, vary structure, emphasize details, and increase readability. Remember that for writers, the aim is not simply to add modifiers thoughtlessly, but to aim for variety and precision by varying the length, type, and location of modifiers.

Participial phrases: Participial phrases often begin with an "-ing" form of a verb. Like other free modifiers, they can precede the base clause (e.g., example no. 1) or they can follow it (no. 2). Additionally, some can interrupt the base clause (no. 3):

1. *Nudging the shade aside with the rifle barrel, I followed people in my sights as they walked or drove along the street. (Tobias Wolff)*

2. *Quickly he builds a small fire and then skins the rat, shaving off the skin a strip at a time. (Jennifer Toth)*

3. *Professor Kazan, wearing a spotlessly white tropical suit and a wide-brimmed hat, was the first ashore. (Arthur C. Clarke)*

Appositive phrases. Appositive phrases identify or rename an adjacent noun or pronoun. Like all free modifiers, they can precede (e.g., no. 1), follow (no. 2), or interrupt (no. 3) the base clause.

1. *Eddie Driscoll, a wonderfully articulate student ranked number two in the senior class, loved to read and debate and throw out ideas. (H.G. Bissinger)*

2. *It was a helter-skelter stampede, a headlong rush in circles. (Paul Auster)*

3. *A thin, tough, leathery membrane that encases the brain, the dura is dark pink, almost red. (David Noonan)*

Absolute phrases.   Absolute phrases include a subject and a verb but resemble a compete sentence with a missing auxiliary verb. For example, if a sentence were to read *My fright [was] verging on panic,* an absolute phrase would delete the *was* to read *My fright verging on panic.* Since they require a named subject and active verb, and since they delete the auxiliary verb, they lend immediacy and precision to prose style. Like other free modifiers, absolute phrases can precede the base clause or follow it, but their use interrupting the base clause is more rare.

1. *Feet squeaking on the floor, we worked out until I had the moves down cold. (Tobias Wolff)*

2. *"Right or left?" I yell into the darkness, my fright verging on panic. (Jennifer Toth)*

3. *His head is shaved, his eyes and nose taped shut. (David Noonan)*

Before we return to our writer, Barry, and his paper on "Do not go gentle into that good night," let's look at one more set of sentences that illustrate Christensen's principles. The following sentences, from an *Esquire* article by David Noonan entitled "Inside the Brain," employ a number of these kinds of free modifiers. The base clause of each sentence is outlined, with the main subject again underlined and the verb double underlined. Examine the free modifiers carefully, noting Noonan's use of appositive, participial, and absolute phrases.

1. *His head is shaved, his eyes and nose taped shut.*

2. *It is a rare operation, a suboccipital craniectomy, supracerebellar infratentorial approach.*

3. *The only part of him left exposed is the back of his head, which is orange from the sterilizing agent painted on it.*

4. *Then, using powerful plierlike tools called Leksell rongeurs, the doctors bite away at the skull, snapping and crunching bone to turn the four small holes into a single opening about three inches in diameter.*

5. *A thin, tough, leathery membrane that encases the brain, the dura is dark pink, almost red.*

6. *A slight curve creasing its middle,* the dura-sheathed cerebellum looks *oddly like a tiny pair of buttocks.*

7. They start talking to each other, *describing what they both can see, narrating the anatomy.*

8. *Sitting side by side, looking through the scope into the head,* Steinberger and Stein go looking for the tumor.

9. It is a long and tedious process, *working your way into the center of the human brain.*

10. *Laboring hour after hour at the microscope, manipulating their instruments in an area no larger than the inside of a juice can,* neurosurgeons must develop an awesome capacity for sustained concentration.

11. It turns out to be a brainstem glioma, *an invasive intrinsic tumor actually growing up out of the brainstem.*

12. The operation ends six hours after the first incision.

Noonan's aim in writing "Inside the Brain" is to render precisely and vividly the physicality of a brain surgery. Note how he uses **participial phrases** (in sentences 4, 7, 8, 9, and 10) to create a dynamic narrative sequence of events: the surgeons are *snapping, crunching, talking, narrating, working, using, laboring, manipulating.* **Appositive phrases** (in sentences 2 and 5) allow Noonan to introduce new terminology such as the *suboccipital craniectomy* and to describe and define anatomy (the dura is described as *a thin, tough, leathery membrane that encases the brain*). His use of **absolute phrases** (in sentences 1, 6, and 11) allows him to rename subjects and employ active verbs to render the events of the surgery with precise naming and vivid action.

Since Noonan's presentation will be unfamiliar to most lay readers (remember that the piece was published in *Esquire,* not the *Journal of Advanced Neurosurgery*), he is also careful, finally, to arrange his free modifiers so that they do not interrupt what is called the pattern of *given-new* information. The essence of the given-new distinction is that sentences should provide sufficient *given* information for readers to understand their *new* information. Look, for instance, at the sentence which names the tumor. Here, Noonan does not begin with *new* information: the sentence does not open with the words *brainstem glioma*, which would be unfamiliar to readers. Instead, Noonan arranges the sentence so that *given* information is provided first: "*It* [the tumor they have been looking for] *turns out to be a* brainstem glioma." Noonan then uses an appositive phrase to provide sufficient definition for the new term. The given-new distinction is also followed in the sentences that introduce other new concepts: the *suboccipital craniectomy*, the *Leksell rongeurs*, the *dura*, the *cerebellum*—in each instance the new term is preceded by sufficient given information for readers to understand it. The lesson here is that while Christensen's method may seem to imply that sentence components like base clauses and free modifiers can be arranged in any way, writers are still bound to follow the pattern of given-new information to make their prose coherent. Noonan does so here with the care and precision of, well, a surgeon.

Obviously, a writer without Noonan's abilities will not be likely to compose such vivid sentences, but we can learn from his example nonetheless. As we return to the session with our first-year seminar student, Barry, and his tutor, Shane, we will see how the lessons of Christensen's method can be employed to good effect. Given that Barry can now see his tendency to compose sentences of needlessly consistent structure and length, Shane's goal now is to introduce methods of modifying and varying the sentences.

Shane: One way to get a bit more variety into the sentences is to use modifiers. I can show you how to do some. First, let's look for sentences we think we might combine. As I read the paragraph, I want you to tell me where you think the topic is shifting even just a little bit. For example, in the second sentence you shift from Dylan Thomas to his father, and after the fifth sentence, back to Dylan Jr.

Barry: Okay. The next two sentences are about Dylan Jr. as a grown man, and the next three are about this particular poem. After that, let's see: one, two, three, four sentences about the villanelle form—maybe that's too many, but we studied it a lot in high school. And then a couple about the way the villanelle is used here for a serious topic. I guess the last three, then, are basically my thesis.

Shane: Excellent. What we're going to work on is combining each of those groups, if it makes sense to do so, into single sentences that are a little more varied. Of those groups, which seems like it really ought to be grouped into one?

Barry: Maybe all of them, but I probably don't need four on the villanelle form.

Shane: Right. So let's take these to start. There are at least a few ways you can modify simple sentences. [*Takes out a sheet of paper*] One is to use a group of words that renames something in the sentence, like you have right here [*writes as he reads*]: *a form that makes use of a very strict rhyme scheme and repetition.* Without the beginning "a villanelle is," you have a modifying phrase. What can you connect it to?

Barry: Either the sentence before or after.

Shane: Right, though the sentence before may not be necessary. Try connecting to the one after, and then we'll see if we still need the earlier sentence.

Barry: [*Reading*] *A form that makes use of a very strict rhyme scheme and repetition, the villanelle is required to use a refrain of its first and third lines over and over in its nineteen lines.*

Shane: Better?

Barry: Much.

Shane: Okay, that's called an appositive phrase. It's basically a group of words that renames something in the sentence. Two things: when you add it, just make sure it's close to the word it modifies—in this case "villanelle"—and that it's not constructed as a complete sentence. Make sense?

Barry: Makes sense.

Shane: Now let's look at the previous sentence: "The poem is written in the villanelle form." I'm just going to suggest that it's probably not worth a whole sentence to make this simple point, because you've got a lot more to say about it. What if you made it a modifying phrase instead: "written in the villanelle form"? Where could you modify another sentence?

Barry: I suppose where I first introduce it? Maybe here: *Written in the villanelle form, Thomas' poem "Do not go gentle into that good night" is addressed to his dying father, whom he had much love and respect for.* Or here: *Written in the villanelle form, this poem is sometimes referred to as one of the greatest of the twentieth century.*

Shane: Again, good. Either works grammatically. Keep in mind that we're aiming for an economical and varied presentation. So those decisions have to be made in the context of the whole paper. But you get the idea. This kind of phrase is called a "participial," but the main thing to remember is that it begins with an -ing verb and presents an action. It can also come either before or after the main part of the sentence.

Barry: Okay.

Shane: Now let's go on a bit. We found other groups of sentences to work with, too. How would you use either of these kinds of modifiers to group the first two?

The session between Barry and Shane continues in this vein, with Shane helping Barry group and combine sets of sentences. Note that as they work together, Shane attempts to find potential modifying phrases in Barry's text, then prompts him to use those phrases as modifiers of existing sentences. Although he chooses to tell Barry the names of the types of modifiers he is encouraging him to use, he need not do so, nor need he necessarily show Barry more ways to modify the base clauses. For Barry, simply knowing and using the appositive and participial forms will allow him to revise his prose to become more varied, efficient, and mature. As we fast-forward to the end of the session, we see that Barry has now revised his introduction to group each of the sets of sentences he and Shane have marked. Here is his revision:

> Born in Wales in 1914, young Dylan Thomas was schooled by his father, Dylan Thomas Sr., the Senior English Master at Swansea Grammar School, which Thomas attended. Thomas' father was a quick tempered man who demanded respect from both his students and peers (Ferris 39). The younger Thomas grew up to become a passionate man, known for his deep baritone voice and popular poetry readings. Written in the villanelle form, Thomas' poem "Do not go gentle into that good night" is addressed to his dying father, whom he had much love and respect for. A form that makes use of a very strict rhyme scheme and repetition, a villanelle is required to use a refrain of its first and third lines over and over in its nineteen lines and is typically used for lighter topics. But in Thomas's hands, the villanelle form is used to speak strongly against the inevitability of death, with vivid imagery and figurative language. In this poem—sometimes referred to as one of the greatest of the twentieth century—Thomas urges his father to "rage, rage against the dying of the light," telling his father not to submit to death and refusing to accept his father's death. "Do not go gentle into that good night" is a poem that demonstrates the grief one feels for a loved one.

Shane: Okay, tell me about the revisions you made.

Barry: Well, for one, I connected the groups that we talked about. I deleted a bit of information that didn't seem connected to the topic, like his drinking. I moved some parts, like its maybe being one of the greatest of the century, and I set that off with dashes like you said I could.

Shane: Barry, this is really much stronger. You see how the sentences are a lot more varied in length? You can alternate short and long sentences, modified and unmodified ones. Just try to connect the less important information to the base clauses when and where you can. No need to overdo it, but look for strings of short sentences, overly short or simple sentences, and sentences without any punctuation. The revisions don't need to be complicated, they just need to provide some occasional modification using the phrases we talked about.

You will note that while Barry's paper is vastly improved from its prior incarnation, room for still further improvement exists. But simply by pointing out the lack of variety in the length and structure of the sentences, and then by describing and demonstrating two kinds of free modifiers and the ways they can be added to existing sentences, Shane has given Barry what he needs to make dramatic improvements in the prose style. Shane might, as you might in sessions like this, suggest ways that Barry can apply these lessons to the rest of his paper or to other writing situations; he might also suggest that Barry continue working with him in later sessions to learn and practice other strategies for modification.

SUMMARY

While extended focus on the sentence is today rarely a concern of writing instruction, the methods that were developed in earlier decades—Berthoff's HDWDWW, Lanham's Paramedic Method, Christensen's Generative Rhetoric—can all be employed successfully in writing tutorials. To address problematic areas of students' sentence style, we advocate pointing directly to such areas and raising concerns about them rather than using grammatical terminology to name types of errors. If a student's syntax is confusing, ask questions such as "Who's doing what?" or "Who is saying what?" to demonstrate the rhetorical effect of awkward sentences. As your student revises, prompt her towards clear subject-verb-object patterns that address variations on HDWDWW; once these basic patterns are established, they can be more easily and successfully modified. If a student's syntax is overloaded with strings of prepositional phrases or dependent upon forms of *is* verbs, draw attention to them with Lanham's Paramedic Method of circling and highlighting such problems. Once your student has done so, the two of you can employ the "who's kicking who?" and "start fast" revisions. And last, if a student overuses simple, unmodified base-clause sentences without punctuation or free modifiers, you can call attention to such a problem by asking the student to circle the sentence-boundary periods and other punctuation. In these circumstances, a primer on Christensen's Generative Rhetoric, tailored to the student and situation, can present at least a few basic methods for modifying base clauses with participial, appositive, or absolute phrases. This kind of work requires patience and collaboration, but many writers will benefit from close attention to the stylistic concerns these three methods are designed to address.

SUGGESTIONS FOR FURTHER READING

Berthoff, Ann E. (1978). *Forming thinking writing: The composing imagination.* Portsmouth, NH: Heinemann.

Christensen, Francis, and Bonniejean Christensen. (1975). *A new rhetoric.* New York: Harper.

Christensen, Francis. (1963). A generative rhetoric of the sentence. *College Composition and Communication 14,* 155-161.

Connors, Robert. (2000). The erasure of the sentence. *College Composition and Communication 52*(1), 96-128.

Daiker, Donald A., Andrew Kerek, and Max Morenberg. (1978). Sentence combining and syntactic maturity in freshman English. *College Composition and Communication 29,* 36-41.

Dean, Deborah. (2001). Grammar without grammar: Just playing around, writing. *English Journal 91,* 86-89.

Faigley, Lester. (1978). Generative rhetoric as a way of increasing syntactic fluency. *College Composition and Communication 30,* 176-181.

Flower, Linda. (1981.) *Problem-solving strategies for writing.* New York: Harcourt Brace Jovanovich.

Lanham, Richard. (2000). *Revising prose* (4th ed.). Boston: Allyn & Bacon.

Moffett, James. (1968). *Teaching the universe of discourse.* Boston: Houghton Mifflin.

Myers, Sharon. (2003.) Remembering the sentence. *College Composition and Communication 54,* 610-628.

Strong, William. (1985). How sentence-combining works. In Donald A. Daiker, Andrew Kerek, and Max Morenberg (Eds), *Sentence combining: A rhetorical perspective* (pp. 334-350). Carbondale: Southern Illinois University Press.

CASE STUDIES 6.1-6.5

SELECTING AND USING HEURISTICS IN SENTENCE-LEVEL SESSIONS

In each of the following scenarios, we provide brief introductions to the student and the assignment, followed by an excerpt of the student's writing. For each, you should assume that your goal is not to help your student reconsider the argument or approach to the assignment but to assist with sentence-level clarity, efficiency, and variety as necessary. Determine which of the methods presented in this chapter you might employ to tutor the writer towards a more effective sentence style, and demonstrate how you would use these methods in one or two tutorial sessions.

CASE 6.1 : Penny, a nontraditional student recently re-entering college, wrote the following for her nutrition and lifetime wellness course.

> Living in a consumer driven society that stresses a thin body as being the ideal in body shape in order to achieve success and happiness leaves one to question how we arrived at this point in our society today as consumer driven as it is. Recalling the female body being a focal point of society, with such examples as actresses like Marilynne Monroe and the fixation on her legs, Rachel Welsch and her 34-24-34 body shape, game shows with Vanna Whit of *The Wheel of Fortune*, and the slim, sexy women on *The Price Is Right*, the focus was on accentuating the slim beautiful body. Today's icons: Brittney Spears, Linsey Lohan and Jennifer Anston, stress an emphasis on showing more skin along with body piercing and style switching are highlighted topics of this generation of young girls. Today's young women have an emphasis on perfecting the way their body looks whether doing so through dieting, cosmetics, workout, or more difficult and dangerous obsessions with body imaging as a result of their bingeing or even more invasive procedures like plastic surgery.

CASE 6.2: Laylah and Maggie, students in an introductory economics course, wrote the following introduction to a paper that was to introduce, and then analyze, a contemporary economic problem with specific instances and verifiable data.

> Kylee is a junior in college. Most of her tuition is paid for by financial aid. However, books are not included in tuition costs. Kylee comes from a one-parent home. Her mother currently supports two children in college. Kylee pays rent, car payments, and other living expenses, such as food and utilities. Her expenses total $775 per month. As a result, she does not have a lot of extra money to spend on books. Her books for the semester cost $390. In fact, to pay for books this semester, she took out a $200 loan. Even that loan barely covered half of the cost of the books. If she had extra money, Kylee said that she would give more money to charities. Kylee does not complain about the amount of money she needs to spend on books. However, she feels that she could contribute more to society if she could spend less on them.

Since the founding of the first universities in America, books have been the primary source of knowledge for scholars in this country. These books have taught generations of politicians, scientists, doctors, and teachers to understand the world and their field of interest. Now, however, books are becoming less of an aspect in the lives of college students. A poll by the National Association of College Stores estimated that only 42% of students think textbooks are necessary. Twenty percent of students don't bother to get the required texts for their courses (Thomson, A2). More and more students seem to be trying to do without. College bookstores and publishers are having to combat the idea that books are unnecessary. The reason for this has little to do with different teaching methods or newly developed technology. In fact, the lack of books is causing the advent of new teaching methods and new ways of using technology. The real reason for the decreasing importance of textbooks for college students comes down to one word: money. Today's college student can expect to spend as much as $500 per term on textbooks. The money that students spend on textbooks is a dilemma that needs to be addressed.

CASE 6.3: Kunh, a first-year international student taking Intro to Sociology, wrote the following introductory paragraphs to an analysis of Jennifer Toth's book on homelessness, *The Mole People*.

The Mole People is Jennifer Toth's first published non-fiction book. This is a real, touching and meaningful story and it is one of the best stories I have ever read. It is clear, fascinating and I understand it easily. While reading this compassionate and emotional narratives book written by Toth, it makes me shade a drop or two tears. The reasons that make this book so interesting are the compelling story and the author's devoted passion in her researches.

Jennifer Toth is a reporter who works for the *Los Angeles Times* and the *Raleigh News & Observer*. She has written some articles for other magazines and journals such as *International Herald Tribune, Washington Post, Business Week, Asian Wall Street Journal* and, *Max. The Mole People* is her first published book; it is a very successful and compelling book. This book played a role in helping to spur federal funding to help the underground homeless in New York. After this successful story, she continued to write another two books later.

The underground dwellers have established their underground home since a long time ago (before 1980). But, how much attention it gets from the community? And how much concern they get from the people live aboveground? Most of the people will just stay away from those underground dwellers because of the bad images of those dwellers. Nobody wants to know about them and nobody wish to see them around because they are not a "normal human being." But Toth is a kind and devoted reporter, who is willing and love to discover the life of underground homeless people.

CASE 6.4: Dan, a student in first-year composition, read the Tobias Wolff autobiography *This Boy's Life* and composed the essay that begins with these paragraphs. His assignment was to analyze the book's structure and meaning.

We can all remember stories from our past. We all recall the anecdotes and incidents in our lives that stick out in our minds. The are the memories that will stay with us forever. We may be able to recount details of a certain episode from a time in our childhood or our adolescence. We may even be able to describe a memorable instance that formed us into the people we are today. These childhood memories are a part of life. They are shared quite often and with great fervor. I doubt, however, that any of us could communicate our pasts with the same zeal Tobias Wolff shares in his childhood memoir *This Boy's Life*.

This beautifully told account of youth in the western United States is set during the fifties and sixties. The narrative follows Toby, known as Jack to all of his friends, and his mother on a journey of self-discovery. Jack's mother flees her abusive boyfriend in Florida. From there she pursues a life of independence. Jack tags along to Utah and, eventually, Washington. It is there that he spends most of his younger days. Wolff details his youth as a delinquent and a mediocre student through junior high and into high school. Later he falsifies his way into an eastern preparatory school. We follow Jack on a path of misbehavior as he takes up smoking, drinking, swearing, lying, fighting, and many other bad habits. We meet many characters that touched Wolff in his life along the way. We encounter his cruel stepfather and his high school friends and enemies. Jack's life is masterfully woven into a compelling story.

As many autobiographers do, Wolff begins at the beginning, his early childhood. He writes well of his younger years. He does a good job of moving the story along. There are few parts that drag on and none that leave the reader wondering what the point of the incident was. Everything Wolff writes seems to have a point. If that point isn't made right away, it soon comes into play or somehow works its way back into the plot at a later time. This style is intriguing because it makes the book seem more like fiction than an autobiography. David Gates of *Newsweek* mentions this approach in his review. "*This Boy's Life* benefits from a fictionist's technique," writes Gates. "[Wolff] breaks off scenes on emblematic—or simply enigmatic—details or speeches, instead of trudging all the way to the end." This point is well taken. Many autobiographies read as an acute recollection of connecting events. Wolff finds a way to bond the episodes together. This style keeps the narrative moving right along. It is sometimes almost hard to believe the story is non-fiction.

CASE 6.5: Jasmine, a college junior taking an education course called "Foundations of Literacy," has written a report on the decline of reading in America. Her assignment was to present an impartial overview of the research for an audience of interested stakeholders. Below is her introductory paragraph.

It is said that reading in the United States is often touted as being a cause for alarm, and perhaps rightly so. It is obvious that the data is the main reason for the concern. Time and time over the data is saying that Americans are reading less and less. It is important to note that the decline of reading is not limited to just one group of Americans. The decline in reading can be said to cut across every line of education level, gender, and ethnicity. It is easy to see that across the nation Americans are filling their time with activities other than reading. This decline of reading in America across all groups is surprisingly due to a lack of interest and motivation in readers. In fact it is not due to a reported decline in literacy in America which has been shown to be inaccurate. For those people who are studying literacy, English, literature, education, and writing, this decline is doubly troubling because the decline is something that could very well affect his or her future livelihood in the future as he or she undertakes his or her career. The following information should hopefully shed light on the state of reading in America.

CHAPTER SEVEN

GRAMMAR AND USAGE

CHAPTER SEVEN

GRAMMAR AND USAGE

In her improbable bestseller *Eats, Shoots and Leaves: The Zero Tolerance Approach to Punctuation*, author Lynne Truss (2003) writes that grammarians have defined punctuation in a number of ways, including "the basting the holds the fabric of language in shape," and "the traffic signals of language: they tell us to slow down, notice this, take a detour, and stop" (p. 7). Given the present chapter's focus on helping students develop grammatical fluency and accuracy, it is perhaps fitting that Truss's two metaphors—fabric basting and traffic signals—do not mix well with one another. After all, as with these two metaphors, sometimes the grammar in student papers is quite jumbled, a mishmash of partially understood rules and grammatically tangled constructions. To help students find their way through grammar and usage problems, we advocate that you turn to the same dialogic strategies that guide all effective tutoring.

Grammar and usage concerns will likely be a regular part of your writing tutorials. In fact, you will probably seldom tutor *without* encountering at least a few questions about grammar and usage. Sometimes these questions are small, discrete, and simple, as when a writer needs to know about the placement of a particular comma or whether or not a specific pronoun should be singular or plural. At other times, however, you may encounter papers where many of the sentences evidence serious and systematic misunderstandings of grammar and usage, and you may find your ability to address the paper's content sidetracked by the steady stream of surface problems. You may meet students who want tutors to focus only on surface forms—"just check the grammar," they often say—even though the paper needs fairly major content revision as well. Occasionally, you may run across a paper covered in red ink from the student's professor, who has left it up to you as the writing tutor to decipher the comments and explain to the student the particular nature of each grammar or usage problem. You are also likely to meet students who have such a long history of hearing that their writing is grammatically troubled that they will be reluctant to believe that they have any hope of learning how to improve their grammar and usage.

If you are tutoring in a setting where ESL writers are frequent clients, you can count on them having numerous questions about English grammar and usage. Some ESL writers will prove adept at reciting grammatical rules, though they may have less sense of how to apply these rules in their own writing. Other times, papers by ESL writers will evidence patterns of error that may be unknown to you, as when an ESL writer struggles with syntactic rules for word order or correct usage of the definite or indefinite article. Further, ESL writers may come to you with usage questions about which you have never even thought: Why is it correct to write "the Mississippi River" but not "the Lake Superior"? Why is it grammatically incorrect to write "The ceremony was occurred last week"?

To work successfully with students of all ability levels and backgrounds on questions of grammar and usage, you will need a solid understanding of grammatical convention. However, just knowing grammar and usage rules is not enough: you will also need to be able to apply that knowledge using the dialogic strategies presented throughout this book. Fortunately, scholarship in rhetoric and composition has explored many of the causes and consequences of error, providing tutors with the basic premises that can guide effective work with grammar and usage questions. Before getting started, we should say here that the present chapter does not offer step-by-step procedures for solving every conceivable grammar and usage problem. (Such a chapter could easily double the length of this entire book!) Rather, the chapter aims to present practices that can be adapted to nearly all of the grammar and usage concerns you are likely to encounter.

SCHOLARLY PERSPECTIVES ON GRAMMAR AND USAGE

In his article "Grammar, Grammars, and the Teaching of Grammar," Patrick Hartwell (1985) points out that good writers develop skill on two levels: the first involving "the strategies, registers, and procedures of discourse across a range of modes, audiences, contexts, and purposes," and the second the "active manipulation of language with conscious attention to surface form" (p. 125). The first five chapters of this book concern rhetorical facility, flexibility, and accuracy—the first of the two levels Hartwell describes. In the previous chapter and again in this one, we turn our attention to Hartwell's second level, the more particular and local concerns of individual sentences. If tutors are to help writers pay, as Hartwell puts it, "conscious attention to surface form," the first step is to gain critical perspective on the ways that composition studies has productively understood grammar and usage concerns.

Understanding Error in Context

Generally speaking, when most of us think about a grammar or usage error, the connotation of the word is negative. Errors seem to signal a writer's inability to produce text that conforms to the norms of academic English. Beginning with Mina Shaughnessy's (1977) *Errors and Expectations: A Guide for Teachers of Basic Writing*, however, composition scholars have increasingly argued that surface errors are not indications of a lack of intelligence or ability but are instead concrete evidence of a writer's development. For instance, Bartholomae (1980) memorably contended that errors ought to be understood "as stages of learning rather than the failure to learn," with the errors themselves serving "as evidence that . . . writers are using writing as an occasion to learn" (p. 254). Shaughnessy (1977) earlier studied patterns of error in student essays and found that all writing—even texts filled with grammar and usage problems—reveals structured, reasoned, rule-governed behavior. In other words, when students make errors in their writing it is not necessarily because they are randomly guessing at correct forms; rather, they are systematically testing their use of the language, working to bring it closer in line with what they understand to be correct surface forms. Thus, when we find errors in student papers, what we are likely seeing is evidence of a writer's attempt to bring order and cohesion to a syntactical system they have yet to master.

This perspective on error demands a far different response than the one many of us have likely encountered in the past. By the time most of us have completed high school, we have run into at least one teacher who seemingly relished the thought of chastising us for our grammar errors. One of us had a college roommate who received a paper back on which every grammatical misstep and usage problem was circled in dark red ink. The professor's end comment was brusque: "When you stop making so many grammar mistakes, I'll start taking you more seriously."

Judith "Jay" Wootten, now a scholar of composition, tells a story about when as a graduate student she was asked to make a short presentation to members of the English faculty. After Wootten distributed her handout, she immediately "saw thirty hands reach into thirty suit/sport coat pockets, remove thirty red pens, and begin circling typos" (quoted in Haswell and Lu, 2000, p. 62). Some people regard surface error in student writing as indicative of the erosion of standards for the English language. In an email expressing her thoughts on grammar instruction, one of our colleagues half-jokingly expressed this perspective:

> It has become apparent to me that if students are not exposed to grammar, sentence construction, word choice, and punctuation in first-year composition, they may never encounter them. And if we ever live in a society where faulty

parallelism sounds right, and fused sentences litter public discourse, one would do well to stock the cellar, for some rendition of apocalypse can't be far behind.

Though this is hyperbole, knowing that there are professors who view grammar and usage errors in this way certainly raises the stakes of our work with student writers. To be sure, many students are writing for professors who take grammar and usage errors very, very seriously.

And error *is* a serious matter, with serious consequences. In his study of readers' responses to grammar and usage errors, Beason (2001) noted that although not everyone agreed which errors were the most serious, all concurred that when writers make errors, they negatively impact their ethos. For this reason, Beason argues that "[d]efining error as a simply textual matter fails to forefront the 'outside' consequences of error, especially the ways in which readers use errors to make judgments about more than the text itself" (p. 35). If students are to succeed in an environment where their credibility will be judged by their ability to use English correctly, many are going to need assistance to understand the codes and conventions of academic language.

Bartholomae (1985) has argued persuasively that whenever students write within university settings, they must "invent the university by assembling and mimicking its language while finding some compromise between idiosyncrasy, a personal history, on the one hand, and the requirements of conventions, the history of a discipline, on the other" (p. 135). For Bartholomae, it is the tension between "personal history" and "the history of a discipline" that can strain students' ability to "learn to speak our language, to speak as we do, to try on the peculiar ways of knowing, selecting, evaluating, reporting, concluding, and arguing that define the discourse of our community" (p. 135). A part of the process Bartholomae describes is learning to produce prose that is effective, controlled, suasive, and correct in form. And it is precisely the difficulty of this task that will bring many students to a writing center.

As a writing tutor, you certainly will be asked to help students with grammar and usage concerns. Unfortunately, determining *which* areas of grammar and usage will be the *most* deserving of your attention can be difficult. As Williams (1981) has pointed out, when it comes to grammar and usage errors, there is precious little agreement about what constitutes a more or less serious problem. Many student writers have no way of knowing which errors will be forgiven, which errors will sidetrack their message, and which errors, in the words of our colleague, will foretell the apocalypse.

Ultimately, error is just one element of the tutor's work, albeit an important one. In a book-length overview of core issues in composition studies, Joseph Harris (1997) argues that

> Teachers need . . . to respond to what students are trying to say, to the effectiveness of their writing as a whole, and not simply to the presence or absence of local errors in spelling, syntax, or usage. Correctness thus becomes not the single and defining issue in learning how to write but simply one aspect of developing a more general communicative competence. (p. 83)

Student writers, then, are expected to do something for which there is no clear manual and few prescribed steps. And, when we remember that errors are only evidence of students' attempts to write well, it becomes easier both to respect the attempt that led to their formation and to address those errors in productive tutorial dialogue.

Setting the Agenda

It is usually easy to refrain from interfering with a student's ownership of a piece of writing when the issue at hand concerns a larger rhetorical decision about the work. For example, strategies for introducing the topic, ideas about how to develop a particular point, or judgments about the necessity of a given anecdote are typically taken as just that: *strategies* that can be adopted or not. But one of the difficulties of tutoring for grammar and usage is that there *are* definite right answers, and it can sometimes seem like the best or only option you have is to simply provide them. After all, when the matter is as straightforward as the rules for comma usage, tutors can find themselves supplying right answers because they simply do not know what else to do. Tutors may also mistakenly believe that by editing students' papers they are actually teaching students how to avoid errors.

In an article examining teacher comments on student writing, Connors and Lunsford (1993) observed that instructors consistently addressed grammar and usage errors in a similar way, one that "nearly always tended to [use] handbook numbers or the standard set of phatic grunts: 'awk,' 'ww,' 'comma,' etc." (p. 205). The problem, of course, with addressing errors via journalistic editing is that the student never has a good opportunity to understand *why* an error is an error—grammatically and rhetorically—and thus he cannot easily know how to correct the problem in the future.

The temptation to provide students with answers to grammar and usage questions is further increased by the speed with which it can be done. When a tutorial is scheduled for a prescribed period and you recognize that your student's paper contains some sizable content-related problems, it can be hard to justify spending precious minutes on a relatively minor grammatical point or obscure usage rule. It is also not uncommon to be working with a student for whom grammatical accuracy is exceedingly difficult, resulting in a dynamic where the student seemingly has little knowledge on which to call as he tries to answer questions about his grammar and usage, a possibility that can be especially true when working with ESL writers (Harris and Silva, 1993). These scenarios can easily cause tutors to feel as though they have no choice but to resort to editing the student's text—exactly the response that is *least* helpful to the student's long-term development as a writer.

When it comes to tutoring for grammar and usage, then, there really are two main questions: 1) Under what circumstances should you tutor for grammar and usage? 2) Once you decide to address grammar and usage, how should you proceed?

To know *when* to work with students on grammar and usage, tutors can turn to the same agenda-setting process that characterizes all effective tutorial work. After establishing rapport with the student, gaining an understanding of the assignment, and assessing the paper, the tutor will want to negotiate a course of action that is responsive to the document's needs, alert to the student's concerns, and also attentive to the time constraints of the tutorial. Part of this agenda can easily include attention to grammar and usage, prioritized according to its importance in the specific tutorial.

Generally speaking, in most of the agendas tutors negotiate with students, grammar and usage will enter somewhere into the mix of concerns. However, such work seldom tops the list of priorities—unless the student has brought in a polished final draft or a paper on which a professor has directed them to address surface errors. In many cases, we find that tutors do well to address grammar later in the tutorial, focusing especially on those errors that seem to be most widespread, stigmatizing, or distracting, and only on errors that are in passages that are likely to remain in subsequent revisions of the document. After all, it simply is not a good use of time to work through an error in a sentence that will not ultimately remain in the final draft.

One of the likely concerns of new tutors is that they will find themselves working with students whose writing is peppered with grammatical mistakes and usage problems. While you certainly will encounter such papers, you will almost never address every grammar and usage problem in a single tutorial. Rather, as part of the agenda-setting process, tutors can remind students of their allotted time and then get to as much of the work as is feasible, which nearly always includes some time on content and some time on form. The following dialogue illustrates how a tutor, Rupert, works with a student, Avery, to negotiate a tutorial agenda that includes time for grammar and usage concerns.

Rupert: So, what specifically can I help you with?

Avery: Well, on my last paper the professor found errors on every page. She said that my grammar was getting in the way of what I was trying to say.

Rupert: Okay, we can certainly spend some time on grammar and usage. Anything else you'd like me to look at?

Avery: I guess just whether or not the paper makes sense and if I have enough support for my ideas.

Rupert: Why don't you read this aloud while I follow along? This will help me gain a sense of your paper and also help you to reassess the paper's strengths and weaknesses. After you're through, we'll figure out how we want to proceed.

Avery: Sounds good.

[*After Avery reads the paper aloud*]

Rupert: I think this is working pretty well. You do a nice job integrating your outside sources with some of the material you have been reading in your class.

Avery: Good, because that's what we're supposed to do.

Rupert: After hearing you read your paper, I can see a couple areas where we might spend our time today. You were concerned about the grammar and usage, and I did see a number of places where you will want to do some more work. Also, with regard to content, it feels like the second point sort of becomes you just saying what you think without supporting the ideas. I'm wondering if there's a way to ground those ideas in relevant scholarship.

Avery: Yeah, I know. I couldn't figure out how to do that, so I just sort of went with my own ideas.

Rupert: Okay, so we've got grammar and usage concerns throughout the paper, and a major idea that needs development and textual support. Any thoughts on what order to take them in?

Avery: How about grammar and usage first since that's something my professor specifically said I had to improve on?

Rupert: That makes sense. However, I'm actually going to suggest that we start on the content first. We may find that addressing that will greatly alter the sentences in the middle of your paper, meaning that we don't want to spend time working on sentences that ultimately will need to be cut anyway once the content is revised.

Avery: I understand what you're saying.

Rupert: So let's jump right in to that second point and try to talk through what sort of support you need and how you might go about selecting and incorporating it. After that we'll come back to the beginning and try to break the grammar errors down. I do see some patterns in the sentence errors, so we may be able to address a couple different examples of each error. Then, after our appointment, you will hopefully be able to apply what we go over to similar errors elsewhere in the paper.

Avery: That sounds good, but what if I can't find all the others on my own?

Rupert: Well, how about if after you do your best with it you come back by for a second appointment, in that one focusing exclusively on grammar and usage?

Avery: I can definitely do that. This isn't due until next week, so I've got plenty of time to revise after today and then come back for more help.

As Rupert suggests, in order to "fix" all the errors in her paper Avery may need to return for a subsequent appointment. However, as will become clear in the following section, when done well tutoring for correctness can help students like Avery learn to address grammar and usage problems independently.

Approaching Grammar and Usage Through Dialogue

Earlier we posed two questions, the second of which concerned *how* tutors should actually work with students on grammar and usage. The short answer to this question is that tutors can address grammar and usage through the same dialogic questioning strategies they use for other aspects of the tutorial. By asking questions about why a student has written a sentence a particular way, along with what a student knows about the grammar of that sentence, the tutor gathers information about why a student might have made a given grammar error. At times, the tutor might present an actual grammatical rule to the student, following the explanation up with a question about how the student can apply that rule to the sentence under review. Or, depending on the nature of the grammar or usage problem and also the student's conversance with grammatical terminology, the tutor may choose to address grammatical concepts using more everyday language.

While our answer to how we address grammar is rather succinct—we address grammar dialogically—the execution of that answer can be complicated. To demonstrate what we mean by addressing grammar and usage through dialogic question-and-answer, we will consider the following grammatically troubled sentence: "Let's eat grandfather before we go," taken from Teresa Glazier's *The Least You Should Know About English* (1986). As a tutor working with a student who wrote a sentence like this, you may be tempted to simply add the missing commas before and after "grandfather," so that the punctuation of the sentence accurately conveys that the speaker is recommending that she and her grandfather get something to eat before departing (as opposed to the current version, which suggests that the grandfather himself is what is about to be eaten!). While penciling in the commas would produce the intended meaning correctly, the problem is that it would not give the student the opportunity to participate and therein learn something from the process. To see how we can approach the sentence dialogically, we will look at an exchange between a tutor, Robin, and her student, Corinne:

> Robin: I noticed a problem with this next sentence, [*reads*] "Let's eat grandfather before we go."

Corinne: [*Looking at the sentence*] Do I have a typo?

Robin: No. It's that the sentence makes it sound like the grandfather is about to be eaten.

Corinne: Really?

Robin: Yeah, can you see why?

Corinne: I'm not sure I can.

Robin: You're missing some punctuation. Let me read it to you again, only this time, I'll exaggerate the problem. [*Reading quickly*] "Let's-eat-grandfather-before-we-go."

Corinne: I see what you mean. It sounds like the speaker wants to eat his grandpa. That's not good.

Robin: So, if you were reading that sentence aloud, how would you do it to let the listener know that the grandfather was going to be eating something as opposed to being eaten?

Corinne: "Let's eat [*pause*] grandfather [*pause*] before we go."

Robin: Right. Can you think of a way to let a reader know that he or she should pause in the places where you just did?

Corinne: Commas?

Robin: That's right. Commas can signal a place where you want your reader to slow down for just a second before continuing. In this way, they help to prevent the reader from misreading your work.

Corinne: That's easy enough.

Robin: Can you explain the grammar rule here in your own words?

Corinne: Yes. The word "grandfather" has commas around it because I need the reader to stop for a second and realize that the speaker is talking to her grandfather.

While Robin certainly could have just told Corinne where she needed commas, by helping Corinne to come to that understanding on her own, Robin helps Corinne correct the sentence and, more importantly, she increases the likelihood that Corinne will remember the grammatical principle she has just reviewed the next time she writes a similar sentence.

We should say here that not all students have an ear or eye for what sounds or looks correct. So, while it would be nice if, for example, we could address comma usage rules by appealing to students' sense of where a natural pause would occur, this method of placing commas is not one that all students can use, a point that is particularly true for not native-English speakers (Leki, 1992). Further, there are many contexts where the pause that accompanies a comma may be difficult to detect, as in a sentence like "The lecture only lasted for an hour, but Mitch fell asleep anyway." To help students with grammar and usage questions we need to open up lines of questioning that offer and then reinforce the grammatical principles that are behind the correct surface forms.

Approaching grammar and usage dialogically can be slow-going, particularly if the text has a high number of problems. However, keep in mind Stephen North's (1982) advice that as writing tutors it is our job to tutor the *writer* rather than the *paper*. The most responsible way to do so is to slow down and help the writer address the surface features of the text through dialogic question and answer. While some students—both ESL and native-English-speaking—come into writing tutorials expecting us to edit their work, tutors may need to be explicit with regard to letting students know that, in the words of Harris and Silva (1993), they "are supposed to be educators, not personal editors" (p. 531).

Because you cannot ensure that your students' papers will be error-free at the end of the tutorial session, you will want to help students develop some strategies for finding and fixing grammar problems on their own. A simple but effective tactic is to suggest that the student read his paper backwards, one sentence at a time. Because this method breaks up the content of the writing, it has a way of helping the writer focus more carefully on form. In our experience, writers who might read over the same error repeatedly when reading the paper from front to back often have a tendency of catching that error when reading backwards, sentence by sentence.

Mistakes vs. Errors

One important point still needs to be made about the potential causes of grammar and usage problems. Difficulty with grammar and usage can actually come from a variety of sources—poorly or misunderstood rules, ignorance, oversights, and the like. The particular source of a problem can sometimes dictate what the tutor's response should be. A distinction that we have found useful concerns the difference between a grammar or usage *mistake* vs. a grammar or usage *error*. We draw our distinction between mistake and error from the work of applied linguists—scholars who study how languages are taught, learned, processed, and produced.

In studies of Second Language Acquisition (often referred to as SLA), a number of linguists, most famously Corder (1967), have argued that when there are problems with the surface from of a learner's language, what we are really hearing is one of two things: a language mistake or a language error. The difference between the two is simple: a language mistake occurs when a learner knows the rule or correct form, but neglects or forgets to use it because he is busy focusing on some other aspect of communication, likely the content or message he is trying to convey. A language error, however, occurs when the learner produces the incorrect form because he does not know the correct form, as when a non-native English speaker says something like, "How he can know the answer?" rather than "How can he know the answer?" The issue is that such a speaker has not yet mastered the conventions of English question formation. We see this same distinction between mistake and error in the language acquisition of young children as they learn their native language (Lightbown & Spada, 2006).

	MISTAKE	ERROR
Problem	Occurs when learner knows the correct form but does not produce it.	Occurs when learner simply does not know the correct form.
Cause	Learner momentarily forgets correct form because attention is focused elsewhere, e.g., content of message or social dynamic of interaction.	Errors are evidence of a learner's developmental stage, indicating progress in linguistic development.
Correction	The student should be able to self-correct upon identification.	The tutor should use explanation and example to help the student learn the correct form.

It will help if you are attuned to whether your student has a problem in one of her sentences because she made a *mistake* (she knew what the correct form should be but did not produce it, perhaps because what she was trying to say was difficult or complicated, maybe because of a simple oversight) or because she made an *error* (she really did not know how to produce the correct from). While you need not share this distinction with the student, it can give you a sense of what your student knows of grammar and usage rules and allow you to focus your efforts on the errors—those things that the student does not yet know. As for grammar mistakes, these you can usually address simply by drawing the student's attention to the sentences in which they occur.

The logical question, then, concerns how to determine whether you are dealing with a *mistake* or an *error*. Generally speaking, if you see evidence of the correct form produced elsewhere in the paper, you are probably looking at a mistake. The student will usually correct it himself on the spot, or he may assure you that he will take care of it after the tutorial is over. To make a determination regarding whether or not a given grammatical problem is an error, look to see if it occurs multiple times in the paper. If it does, there's a good chance the student does not know the rule. After all, nobody consistently writes sentences with grammar and usage problems on purpose. Perhaps the most reliable way to determine if a specific problem is an error is to isolate the sentence in which it occurs and ask the student if he knows what is wrong with it. If the student can find and articulate the problem, chances are good that you are looking at a grammar mistake and that the solution will therefore be relatively easy. If your student cannot see the problem, you will need to begin working dialogically to help him learn the nature of the error and also some options for addressing it.

STRATEGIES FOR ADDRESSING ERRORS

In the sections that follow we take readers through a brief review of some of the more common grammar and usage problems that surface in writing tutorials. We then demonstrate ways that tutors can lead students towards solutions to their problems. The chapter concludes with a section devoted to learning how to help ESL writers address grammar and usage questions, a job that sometimes is quite unlike helping native-English speakers. Although we cannot anticipate every surface problem that you will encounter in student writing here, we can help you construct a basic approach to tutoring grammar and usage, one that you can adapt to the particularities of the surface problems that you encounter in student papers.

PART 1: PUNCTUATION

To tutor students on grammar and usage effectively, we strongly advise that you familiarize yourself with the rules and conventions of English grammar. You do not need to become a walking grammar handbook, but when you are tutoring you should keep a reliable handbook at your side. You may need to double-check your understanding of a rule or demonstrate it to a student with examples; you may need to check citation forms or document formats. Rather than spout rules at students, a truly dialogic tutor will instead engage writers in discussion, demonstrate conventions and patterns, and confirm students' understanding.

When demonstrating pattern-bound rules and conventions, we advocate for taking time to proceed deliberately. It's worth the effort. For instance, when showing a student how to use a colon or dash, you can offer three or four examples. You might elect to do so with simple pattern sentences, with nonsense sentences, or with examples of the student's own writing. But presenting multiple examples is important: doing so lets the student see that there is a pattern, a principle, governing the error, and not just an isolated, idiosyncratic mistake to be corrected. Following are some brief grammatical reminders about some common grammar and usage problems, accompanied by ideas for how tutors might assist students who have questions.

The comma

The primary purpose of commas is to prevent misreading. Consider, for example, a sentence like "As I was walking the dog started barking." Without a comma after the word "walking," the sentence is unclear because we may initially think that the dog was being walked. Here are some of the contexts in which students frequently have questions.

To list items in a series

Use a comma between all items in a list or series, including the final two.

> *Attending the soccer match were families, business people, dignitaries, and hooligans.*

Though strictly speaking the comma between "dignitaries" and "hooligans" is optional (referred to as a serial comma, it is often omitted in journalism), its inclusion helps to prevent misreading. You may occasionally encounter students who do not know that they need a comma between items in a list, particularly between the last two items. Do not use a comma to join word groups that contain punctuation marks themselves. In these cases, use a semicolon, as in the following example:

> *The committee consisted of three people: Johan, who was new to the company; Thatcher, who would retire within a year or two; and Brenda, about whom I knew very little.*

Because the grammatical rule for items in a series is so straightforward, tutors can usually just inform the student of this rule and then question what items are in the series. As the student identifies each item, the tutor can double-check to make sure that the student knows how to punctuate the list. In our experience, this is usually a simple grammar lesson to teach.

To join two independent clauses with a coordinating conjunction

When a coordinating conjunction—*and, but, or, nor, for, so, yet*—joins two independent clauses, there needs to be a comma before the conjunction, as in the following examples.

> *Experts disagree about the cause, but they seem to concur about the consequences.*

> *Conference attendees can stroll down to the coffee house, or they can catch a bus uptown to an outdoor café.*

One question you (and the students you tutor) may have is what exactly constitutes an independent clause. An independent clause is any group of words that includes a subject and verb and could, if we wanted it to, stand alone as a complete sentence. In our above example, both "Experts disagree about the cause" and "They seem to concur about the consequences" could be sentences all by themselves. However, as explored in chapter six, writers often link short independent clauses together to produce more interesting, more fluid prose.

As will become clear in the dialogue below, there are actually a number of ways that an author might wish to join two independent clauses. A tutor working with a student on this grammatical topic would do well to help the student understand all of the options, as our tutor, Frances, does with Lee, her student, on this sentence: *After three months in France I was ready to return to the United States but I was not looking forward to bidding farewell to my host family in Toulouse.*

Frances: Okay, let's take a look at this sentence. There's a grammar problem with it. Can you see what it is?

Lee: Hmm. I'm not sure I see anything wrong.

Frances: You've got a type of run-on sentence that we'd call a "comma splice." In this case, the problem centers on the word "but."

Lee: Okay.

Frances: To try to help you understand the issue, I'm going to cover up half of the sentence. [*places finger over everything after the word "States"*]. Okay, read what is still visible aloud.

Lee: "After three months in France I was ready to return to the United States."

Frances: Could what you just read stand alone as a complete sentence?

Lee: I think so.

Frances: You're right. Now, I'm going to cover up the first part of the sentence, along with the word "but," and expose the last half of the sentence. Can you read that for me?

Lee: "I was not looking forward to bidding farewell to my host family in Toulouse."

Frances: Could that stand alone as a complete sentence?

Lee: Yes, it could.

Frances: These two halves of the sentence are what we call independent clauses. You know a clause is independent if it can stand by itself as a complete sentence, as both of these can.

Lee: Makes sense so far.

Frances: Good. Now, the problem is that grammatically speaking, we can't join two independent clauses with a single word all by itself.

Lee: You mean like I've done here with "but?"

Frances: Right. That word "but" is what we call a conjunction. "And" and "or" are two other common ones. These are words that actually can join independent clauses, but they can't do it by themselves. They need help from a punctuation mark. Do you have thoughts about what mark that might be?

Lee: A comma?

Frances: Right. A comma. So, can you state back to me the grammar point we've just covered?

Lee: Yeah. If you've got two things that can stand by themselves as complete sentences, if you want to put them in the same sentence you have to use a comma plus a word like "and," "but," or "or."

Frances: That's perfect. And, can you feel how there's just a slight pause there on the comma.

Lee: Yeah, almost like there's a break.

To complete introductory words or phrases

Use a comma after an introductory word or phrase. The purpose of the comma is to signal to the reader that the introductory word or phrase is over and that the rest of the sentence is about to begin.

> *Beyond the farthest reaches of the horizon, a storm was brewing.*
>
> *As any historian will readily acknowledge, the Pilgrims and the Puritans were quite different from one another.*
>
> *Whenever Tennessee and Alabama play each other, most of the people in Knoxville and Tuscaloosa watch the game.*
>
> *Seriously, I wonder whether anyone has ever thought of that.*

To tutor a student who does not follow this convention, the tutor's primary approach is to explain the basic idea of the rule and then question the student about where the introductory words end and the rest of the sentence begins. This can usually be done quickly, as Frances and Lee's continued dialogue indicates:

Frances: In this next sentence, it looks to me like you've got a different sort of error. Go ahead and read it aloud.

Lee: "Although it was difficult to get the words out I knew I would regret it if I didn't tell them how much they meant to me."

Frances: As you read it, does your ear pick out a place where you might pause?

Lee: Not really.

Frances: Okay. As we talked about with the previous sentence, commas often tell the reader to pause. One of the places where we typically look for this pause is after an introductory word or phrase. The pause lets the reader know that the introduction to the sentence is over and that the main part of the sentence is about to start. Here, let's look at the handbook.

Lee: Okay.

Frances: Look at this example here [*points to sentence in the handbook*]. I'll read it out loud and exaggerate the pause: "Between you and me, [*pause*] I don't know why my roommate can't do a few simple dishes."

Lee: Okay, you paused after "me" because that's where the introductory words end and the rest of the sentence begins.

Frances: So, if we transfer that premise to your sentence, where would you add punctuation?

Lee: That's easy. Comma after "out."

Frances: And what rule governs your decision?

Lee: You put a comma after your introduction words so that the reader knows that they are over and that the rest of the sentence is coming.

As is likely evident, the grammar point here is a relatively small and easy one, but by taking the time to help Lee understand it, Frances helps to ensure that Lee will be able to avoid comma errors with introductory words and phrases in the future.

To separate coordinate adjectives

Use a comma to separate two or more adjectives that are working separately to modify the same noun.

> *My employees will be driving a large, dented van.*
> *Serious, mature, smart students are likely to succeed in graduate school.*

The way to determine if adjectives are coordinate is to test to see if they can be linked by "and," as they can in the above sentences. That is, we could rewrite the first sentence to read: "My employees will be driving a large and dented van." If they cannot be linked by "and," the adjectives are what we refer to as cumulative and therefore should not be separated by commas, as in the following example:

> *Five young students showed up late to class.*

It would just not make sense to write "Five and young students..." As a tutor, you can address coordinate adjectives by explaining the rule and asking the student whether or not "and" can be inserted between the adjectives.

To set off a nonrestrictive group of words

Sometimes a sentence in English contains groups of words that modify a noun in a way that is not essential to our understanding of that noun. Consider, for example, the following sentence: "The stockbroker, who has always prided himself on saying what he means, spoke up during the meeting." In this sentence, the relative clause "who has always prided himself on saying what he means" adds extra, non-essential information about the "stockbroker," the noun it modifies. Even without that relative clause, the writer of the sentence appears to believe that the identity of the stockbroker will be clear. We refer to groups of words that merely provide additional, descriptive information about a noun as *nonrestrictive*. Nonrestrictive elements—groups of words that are not essential to our understanding of the identity of the noun they modify—must be set off with commas.

At other times, sentences contain groups of words that are essential to the intended meaning of the noun they modify. If we were to take them out the meaning of the noun would likely be unclear or change completely, as the following sentence exemplifies: "Carol gave her lunch money to the teacher who was wearing red." In this sentence, the relative clause "who was wearing red" is essential because it lets us know which teacher Carol gave her money to. We might imagine a scenario in which there were several teachers present but only one of them was wearing red. The relative clause "who was wearing red" is thus *restrictive* because it limits or restricts the meaning of the word it modifies ("teacher"), letting us know that the specific teacher to whom Carol gave her money was the one that was wearing red.

In writing tutorials, you may work with students who are unsure of the distinction between restrictive/nonrestrictive elements. The following dialogue shows how a tutor, Tashaun, helps his student, Walt, understand the difference between restrictive and nonrestrictive elements.

Tashaun: In terms of content, I think things are working well here. However, I did notice a problem with some of the punctuation.

Walt: Yeah, I always have trouble with that, commas especially.

Tashaun: One of the sentences I'm talking about is this one [reads] "Scholar Lewis Broad who has written extensively about 20th century world politics published the second volume of a two-volume biography on Winston Churchill."

Walt: What's the problem?

Tashaun: That phrase "who has written extensively about 20th century world politics," is it absolutely necessary to the sentence?

Walt: Well, it tells us who Broad is.

Tashaun: That's right. So, it's important. But what's the central idea of the sentence?

Walt: That Broad published the second volume of his two-volume set.

Tashaun: Right. So, that phrase "who has written..." Is it of vital importance to the sentence?

Walt: I guess not. I just included it so people will know a little something about Broad.

Tashaun: Okay, good. Let's just set this aside for a minute and look at two sample sentences. We'll use these to try to illustrate the grammatical point I'm getting at. After I'm done, I'll ask if you can explain how these two sentences are different. [*Writes*]

#1 I bought some shoes that were on sale.

#2 I bought some shoes, which were on sale.

Walt: Well, in the first one, we know that the fact that the shoes were on sale is important. Of all the shoes available, the person bought the ones that were reduced in price.

Tashaun: What about the second sentence?

Walt: The shoes being on sale doesn't really matter all that much. The main thing they want you to know is that they bought some shoes. That they were on sale is just extra information.

Tashaun: Good. You're right. What do you notice about the comma usage in these two sentences?

Walt: The first one, where the information is very important, does not use a comma. In the second one, where the information is just extra, a comma sets it off.

Tashaun: Exactly. If the information is vital the sentence's meaning we can't separate it with a comma. If it's not vital—that is, if it's just extra information—we use commas to separate it.

Walt: That makes sense.

Tashaun: Good. Now, let's go back to your sentence about Lewis Broad. How would you describe the importance of "who has written extensively about 20th century world politics?"

Walt: It's just extra information. So, just like I did with the phrase "which were on sale" in the sample sentence, I need to set it off in commas.

Tashaun: Right. That's it.

As Tashaun works with Walt, one of his strategies is to illustrate the grammatical principle with simple example sentences. This strategy can often work well, particularly because it allows the tutor to help the student understand grammatical concepts inductively. Note too that Tashaun never asks Walt to remember the difference between the terms "restrictive" and "nonrestrictive"; instead, he addresses the difference via judgments about whether or not a given group of words is vital information or merely extra information.

The semicolon

Semicolons can be used in a couple different ways. As shown previously, the semicolon can stands in for the comma if items in a series contain punctuation marks themselves. A more common purpose for a semicolon is to join independent clauses when the writer wishes for the clauses to receive equal emphasis. To illustrate this grammatical rule, we will return to the

dialogue between Lee and Frances, with the two still working on the following sentence:
"After three months in France I was ready to return to the United States but I was not looking forward to bidding farewell to my host family in Toulouse."

Frances: You know, in addition to using a comma and conjunction, you've actually got another option for joining independent clauses. Do you know how to use a semicolon?

Lee: I'm not sure I do. Is that for making lists and things?

Frances: No, that's a colon. A semicolon functions kind of in the same way as a comma plus a conjunction.

Lee: So, are you saying that I could just put a semicolon between "United States" and "I"?

Frances: You could.

Lee: Why would I do that? What's the difference?

Frances: Well, from a grammatical standpoint, the difference is really very small. Part of your decision to use a semicolon to join independent clauses might be for variety's sake, but you really can't use a semicolon very often. If you do it too much they start to feel overused.

Lee: Okay.

Frances: But, the other reason is that the two independent clauses would be ones that share a very close content relationship to one another, so close that you would want to join them together in some way. However, at the same time you would want to ensure that each one received completely equal emphasis. The semicolon helps you do that.

Lee: I think I follow you.

Frances: Here, look, let's try some examples: [Frances writes: (1) *My scholarship covered 50% of my tuition I will owe around $20,000 when I graduate. (2) Tuition is rising fast the amount of government financial aid is decreasing.*] How would you punctuate each of these with a semicolon, and why?

Lee: [points] In the first sentence, here, after "tuition," and in the second, after "fast." In both cases the sentence makes two separate points, but they're roughly equal in importance.

Frances: Okay, good. I know you've got the sentence in your paper correct. Before we move on, can you state in your own words the grammar rule regarding commas and semicolons? Doing so might help it stick with you.

Lee: If you have two clauses that can stand alone as complete sentences, you can join them by using a comma and a conjunction. Or, if you want them to receive the same emphasis as each other, you can join them with just a semicolon and no conjunction.

Frances: Good. You got it.

Frances allows Lee to synthesize information and to articulate what he knows about grammar and usage at key points in the tutorial. Doing so will help Lee increase his grammatical skill set so that he can make better-informed decisions on future writing tasks.

The colon

Colons are used after independent clauses (groups of words that could stand alone as a complete sentence) to prepare the reader for the words that follow the colon. Colons are often used in the following contexts:

A list

The speaker covered three primary topics: the history of U.S. diplomatic relations with China, the reasons for cross-cultural friction between the two nations, and the incentive to forging strong ties between the United States and China.

An appositive

Cubism reached across Europe and can be said to include two major phases: analytic cubism and synthetic cubism.

A quotation

Students should note well Ralph Waldo Emerson's famous maxim: "A foolish consistency is the hobgoblin of little minds."

The most common problem students have with colons is that they often interchange them for semicolons. (Recall during the earlier dialogue between Lee and Frances that semicolons can join two independent clauses, as in the following sentence: "Few sociologists would disagree that poverty has multiple causes; politicians, however, often like to oversimplify the issue in an effort to promote their own agenda.") With this particular problem, tutors can usually take students through a short lesson on the difference between the two punctuation marks—both what they look like and what they do rhetorically—to correct misunderstandings.

As a writing tutor, you will undoubtedly encounter additional questions about punctuation. Often, these will concern question marks, periods, and similarly simple punctuation marks. However, at times you will run across questions that you cannot immediately or easily answer (e.g., a student wondering if he should write 7:00 pm or 7:00 p.m.). In these situations, do not hesitate to use your handbook to show the student how and where to look up the answer. If you ask students to articulate what they understand in their own words before working to apply that understanding to their writing, you will likely find that the majority of punctuation questions are straightforward.

PART 2: CLARITY

Tutorial work often involves a fair amount of attention on students' difficulties with issue of clarity, whether that means tightening sentences that are too wordy, untangling convoluted constructions, revisiting word choice, writing for parallel structure, or fixing dangling or misplaced modifiers. In chapter six, we present strategies to help students improve the overall quality and clarity of their prose. These strategies—especially Berthoff's HDWDWW and Lanham's Paramedic Method—are designed to help students whose prose seems inefficient or inexact. In the sections that follow we introduce some additional clarity problems and suggest strategies for addressing them in a writing tutorial.

Problems with sentence boundaries

Less experienced writers frequently produce writing that does not conform to correct standards for complete sentences. As a tutor, most often this will mean that you will be helping students learn how to spot and eliminate fragments and run-on sentences. The students with whom you work may need a refresher on the meaning of both of these terms as a gateway into learning how to avoid using them in their writing. In what follows, we offer a short review of fragments and run-ons before examining ways that tutors can approach these sentence boundary problems with greater confidence and precision.

Fragments

A fragment is a piece of a sentence that is trying to stand alone as if it were a complete sentence. Sometimes fragments consist of a clause (a subject and a verb), and sometimes they are just a phrase (a group of words that includes either a subject or a verb, but not both). Consider the following examples, each of which contains a fragment in the second half:

The winning team scored three goals in the final period. When the captain truly rose to the occasion.

Gone unchecked, global warming threatens our very existence. Which is why many nations signed the Kyoto Protocol on Climate Change.

The Sociology Department invited a speaker to campus. Who was an expert on teens and drug use.

Many politicians attended the address. Showing their support for the speaker via obligatory applause.

The German army's retreat from the Soviet Union signaled the beginning of the end of the war. The thing that much of the world desperately wanted.

To correct these problems, the fragmented clause or phrase can either be joined to the preceding sentence or turned into a complete sentence by adding the missing elements, as is evident in the following corrections:

The winning team scored three goals in the final period when the captain truly rose to the occasion.

Gone unchecked, global warming threatens our very existence. For this reason, many nations signed the Kyoto Protocol on Climate Change.

The Sociology Department invited a speaker to campus who was an expert on teens and drug use.

Many politicians attended the address and showed their support for the speaker via obligatory applause.

The German army's retreat from the Soviet Union signaled the beginning of the end of the war, which was what much of the world desperately wanted.

When working with students who have problems with sentence fragments, tutors can usually ask the student whether or not the fragmented clause or phrase can stand by itself as a complete sentence. In cases where the student cannot make a determination, the tutor can remind the student that all sentences need both a subject and a verb. Asking the student to pick out the subject and verb is an effective means of correcting fragmented phrases because these contain either a subject or a verb but not both. For fragmented clauses (which can contain a subject and verb), the work can be slightly more difficult. Generally, fragmented clauses begin with words like *after, although, because, before, if, though, unless, when, where, who,* or *which*—words that put the fragmented clause into a subordinate relationship with the preceding sentence. The following dialogue demonstrates how our tutor, Nina, helps a student, Tom, better understand sentence fragments and how to correct them.

Nina: In the next couples of sentence it looks to me like you've got what we'd call a sentence fragment. Would you mind reading them aloud?

Tom: Sure. [*Reads*] "Margaret Atwood explores the consequences of unchecked technological advancement in her novel *Oryx and Crake*. Even if few readers of the text seem to take it as seriously as Atwood intended it."

Nina: Does your ear pick up on the problem?

Tom: I think so, but I'm not sure I can say what it is.

Nina: That second sentence, "Even if few readers..." That's where the problem is. Reading just that part out loud, do you think it feels like a complete sentence?

Tom: [*reads*] "Even if few readers of the text seem to take it as seriously as Atwood intended it." Well, if the first sentence isn't in front of it, it sounds like it's missing something. Like, "Even if what?"

Nina: That's right. So, it feels like a complete sentence only when it gets tacked onto the end of the previous sentence.

Tom: Yeah, that's right. So, I guess maybe I should just put it onto the end of that earlier sentence?

Nina: Yep, you should. Do you know why?

Tom: I'm not sure I do, other than it just sounds better.

Nina: It's true that to some extent you can use your ear to help you with sentence fragments, especially after you read the sentences in isolation. The other thing is that many sentence fragments result from having a fragment that expresses some sort of subordinate relationship to a preceding sentence.

Tom: Subordinate how?

Nina: Grammatically. Here's an example: [*writes*] "I went down to the store. Because I needed bread." That second part, "Because I needed bread" is subordinate to the first. In other words, it needs the first part because it's not grammatically strong enough to be a sentence all by itself.

Tom: I think I see what you mean. So, in my sentence, those words "even if" made what came next subordinate. They needed the first sentence in order to be grammatically correct.

Nina: That's it. Here, the handbook has a list. Words like *after, although, because, before, if, though, unless, when, where, who,* or *which* all set up the same sort of relationship. Be on the lookout for these. If they're by themselves and not part of another sentence, you'll want to check for a sentence fragment.

Once students become aware of the contexts in which sentence fragments are likely—that is, places where there is a subordinate relationship between ideas—it is usually not too difficult to help them see ways that they can combine the fragmented clause with the preceding sentence. Or, if the fragmented clause is rather lengthy, tutors can help students learn to turn it into a complete sentence of its own.

Run-ons

Run-on sentences are incorrectly connected independent clauses. As we will see, there are two mains types of run-ons, though for both types the same four remedies are possible. When writers produce run-ons, they typically have made one of two errors: a fused sentence or a comma splice.

1. **Fused sentence**: a type of run-on in which a writer has joined independent clauses with no punctuation marks whatsoever.

   Physical rehabilitation from knee surgery is harder than most athletes realize they typically push too hard too soon.

   The film's protagonist feels trapped in a world he cannot understand he fails to recognize his own complicity in his continued isolation.

2. **Comma splice**: a second type of run on in which the writer has tried to join two independent clauses with a comma, a mark of punctuation that is not strong enough for this purpose.

   Physical rehabilitation from knee surgery is harder than most athletes realize, they typically push too hard too soon.

   The film's protagonist feels trapped in a world he cannot understand, he fails to recognize his own complicity in his continued isolation.

Comma splices can also be created when the comma that is trying to join independent clauses is next to a word that is not one of our coordinating conjunctions (*and, but, or, nor, for, so, yet*). Most often, when students have this problem it is because they have mistakenly used what we call a conjunctive adverb in place of a coordinating conjunction. (Some common conjunctive adverbs are *therefore, however, consequently, nevertheless, for example, moreover, furthermore, instead, thus, indeed*).

Physical rehabilitation from knee surgery is harder than most athletes realize, thus, they typically push too hard too soon.

The film's protagonist feels trapped in a world he cannot understand, consequently, he fails to recognize his own complicity in his continued isolation.

Regardless of which type of run-on sentence a writer has produced, the options for correction are the same. To correct a run-on sentence, students may:

1. Use a comma plus a coordinating conjunction (see earlier discussion under punctuation);

2. Use a semicolon (see earlier discussion under punctuation);

3. Divide the two independent clauses into two separate sentences; or

4. Rewrite the entire sentence, turning one of the two independent clauses into a dependent, subordinate clause.

Very often, the fourth option is the one that will lead to the most sophisticated, interesting prose, largely because the subordinate clause allows the writer to set two ideas into a more complex relationship with one another. Some of the same strategies discussed previously in our work with correcting sentence fragments are applicable here, as demonstrated in Nina's continued tutoring of Tom.

Nina: Let's take a look at this next sentence. I think we've got a problem here. Would you mind reading it aloud?

Tom: [*reads*] "Many casual readers of Atwood's text likely fail to grasp the novel's significance they view it instead as pleasure reading."

Nina: Okay.

Tom: I don't think I have any fragments in there, do I?

Nina: No, no fragments. You've got something we call a run-on sentence. Any ideas on what might be the problem?

Tom: Well, when I read it aloud just now if felt like I wanted to pause in the middle.

Nina: Where exactly?

Tom: After "significance."

Nina: Good. That's the spot where the sentence has some grammatical trouble. That's where the run-on needs to be addressed. Run-ons on where you've got independent clauses sandwiched together.

Tom: What should I do?

Nina: You've got a few options. You can just put a period right there.

Tom: I think that'd make it sound pretty choppy though.

Nina: You're probably right. It would. This is usually only a good move if the independent clauses are pretty long.

Tom: Okay, so what else?

Nina: You can use a semicolon, but that might create the same problem as using a period. Or, you can use a comma plus conjunction, just like we were talking about earlier when we looked at ways to get rid of sentence fragments.

Tom: Is that what I should do?

Nina: Maybe, but I'm going to suggest one more option. You can also try to rewrite the sentence so that the reader knows how the ideas relate to each other, something the comma plus conjunction doesn't always do. If you can show how the ideas relate, it's a good idea because it lets the reader see more clearly the complexity of your thinking. To get started, let's break the sentence down into its two main parts by drawing lines separating the sentence into two halves.

Tom: Okay. [*divides sentence as follows*] "Many casual readers of Atwood's text likely fail to grasp the novel's significance // they view it instead as pleasure reading."

Nina: What is the most important piece of information here?

Tom: The first part.

Nina: Okay, so what's up with that second part?

Tom: Well, the "pleasure reading" comment kind of just goes along with the first. Like it's giving the reason why people don't grasp the novel's significance. They think it's just a book to read for fun.

Nina: How could you combine that second part to the first in a way that shows that it's explaining the reason for the first idea?

Tom: How about something like "Many casual readers of Atwood's text likely fail to grasp the novel's significance because they view it instead as pleasure reading."

Nina: Right. That word "because" lets you add this, making the second idea work with the first one. Can you see any other options for making the combination?

Tom: Hmmm. "Many casual readers of Atwood's text likely fail to grasp the novel's significance, viewing it instead as pleasure reading."

Nina: What do you think?

Tom: I like the first way because it shows better how the second idea is related to the first. It's the cause. The second one is smooth enough, but I don't like it as well.

Nina: What you've just been working at is getting rid of run-ons by reworking the sentence so that one part depends on the other for it to be grammatical. In this case, "because they view it instead as pleasure reading" needs the first part of the sentence. It can't stand alone grammatically.

Tom: I think I get it.

Nina: What is important is that you know what a run-on is and some of the ways you can fix it. So, can you tell me what a run-on is?

Tom: Maybe. A run-on is where you've got things that could be sentences all by themselves all together in one sentence. But you don't have the right punctuation. It's like they're all just jammed together in one long sentence that doesn't let the reader take a breath.

Nina:	That's good. And what are some ways you can fix them?
Tom:	Divide it into new sentences or use a comma plus and, or, but. Also you can use a semicolon.
Nina:	And the last one?
Tom:	That thing we were just doing. You make one part of the sentence flow from the other. Make it so that it needs the other part to be grammatical.
Nina:	Good. As you work on this, you'll find that there are lots of different ways to do this. Sometimes you'll use a word like "because," as you did here. Or, in other cases that -ing form of the verb—like you tried out earlier—will be just the thing.

Though Nina's work with Tom is likely headed in a good direction, experienced writers will quickly see that there are hundreds of different ways to subordinate information, far more than one can cover in a single tutorial. When addressing run-ons, as a general rule it is effective to try to help the writer understand a few of his options at a time, letting him work through those until he feels confident. Once a writer demonstrates the syntactic and stylistic facility to work with some of the easier fixes for run-on sentences, as a tutor you may want to step in and add some additional options, ones that are more nuanced and interesting.

Parallelism

If two or more ideas in a sentence are parallel to one another, they should be written in a grammatically parallel way. In the following examples, the elements that are (or should be) grammatically parallel are underlined. The grammatically unparallel element is preceded by an asterisk:

Items in a series
- Non-parallel:
  *When sailing in any body of water, one should always have a detailed chart of the waters, a functional radio, a life raft, an emergency kit, and *they can also bring cell phones.*

- Parallel:
  When sailing in any body of water, one should always have a detailed chart of the waters, a functional radio, a life raft, an emergency kit, and a cell phone.

- Non-parallel:

I admire the way you handled the disruptive students, the time you spent answering questions, and *that you set high standards you set for yourself.

- Parallel:

  I admire the way you handled the disruptive students, the time you spent answering questions, and the high standards you set for yourself.

Paired or grouped ideas

- Non-parallel:

  Mark did not know whether to attend the lecture or if *he wanted to accompany his roommate to the basketball game.

- Parallel:

  Mark did not know whether to attend the lecture or to accompany his roommate to the basketball game.

- Non-parallel:

  As a member of the team, Wanda lifted weights, swam laps, attended a yoga class, and *she ate healthy foods.

- Parallel:

  As a member of the team, Wanda lifted weights, swam laps, attended a yoga class, and ate healthy foods.

When ideas are paired or grouped with one another, the writer should strive to articulate those ideas in a grammatically parallel way because this strengthens the connection between those ideas. As a tutor, when you see writing that lacks parallelism, the approach can usually be fairly direct: ask the student to identify the ideas that are parallel or like one another in the sentence. From there, you can prompt the student to choose which mode of grammatical expression they prefer and then to rewrite the non-parallel ideas so that they are grammatically parallel.

Agreement

For writing to be grammatically correct, subjects and verbs and also pronouns and their antecedents must agree with one another. Consider the following examples:

Problems with subject-verb agreement

- Incorrect:

   The students in the crowd roars for the team.

- Correct:

   The students in the crowd roar for the team. (<u>students</u>, not <u>crowd</u>, is the subject of the verb roars; thus, <u>roars</u> should be corrected to <u>roar</u>.)

- Incorrect:

   Increased exposure to radiation and toxic waste carry health risks.

- Correct:

   Increased exposure to radiation and toxic waste carries health risks. (<u>exposure</u>, not <u>radiation and toxic waste</u>, is the subject of the verb; thus, <u>carry</u> should be corrected to carries.)

Problems with pronoun-antecedent agreement

- Incorrect:

   To become a future member of the club, they started doing community service during the summer.

- Correct:

   To become a future member of the club, he started doing community service during the summer.

   To become future members of the club, they started doing community service during the summer. (<u>Member</u> is singular but <u>they</u> is plural, so the two do not agree with one another; one or the other must be changed to correct the agreement error.)

In the following dialogue, the tutor, Brenna, helps Molly address an agreement problem in her writing.

Brenna:	Okay, in this next sentence, you've got what we call an agreement error. Why don't you read it aloud and then tell me if you can spot the problem.
Molly:	[*reads*] "The students and the instructor is responsible for creating a respectful and task-centered learning environment."
Brenna:	What do you think?
Molly:	I'm not sure. It sounded okay when I read it aloud.
Brenna:	Let me ask you this: what is the verb of the sentence?
Molly:	Umm. I think it's "is."
Brenna:	That's right. Now, what's the subject?
Molly:	"Instructor."

Brenna: Is that all?

Molly: Well, maybe "students" is also the subject.

Brenna: That's right. So, you've got a subject—"students and the instructor"—that refers to more than one person. So, we say that your subject is a compound subject, meaning that it's plural.

Molly: I'm with you so far.

Brenna: What about the verb "is"? Is that for a singular subject or a plural subject?

Molly: I get it. "Is" is singular, but my subject is plural.

Brenna: So what should it be?

Molly: "Students and instructor are responsible..."

Brenna: Good. The thing that can be tricky is that the verb must agree with the whole subject, not just the part of the subject that is closest to it.

Students may also write sentences in which the pronoun and its antecedent either do not agree or are otherwise unclear. When the error is an agreement error, the tutor can usually approach the problem in the same way that Brenna does with Molly, asking which is singular and which is plural and then working towards making these two answers match one another. However, when the pronoun reference is simply unclear, the approach can be slightly different:

Brenna: In this next sentence, it's not quite clear what you are referring to. Can you read it aloud?

Molly: [reads] "Students often approach their class work as if this were not the case."

Brenna: What does "this" refer to?

Molly: I guess just that they think the instructor has to control everything.

Brenna: I thought that might be it, but grammatically speaking the sentence doesn't make that clear. I think it'd be stronger if you came right out and said exactly what you mean.

Molly: You mean like, "Students often approach their class work as if they think the instructor has to control the environment."

Brenna: Do you also mean that they think they don't have to do it?

Molly: Yeah.

Brenna: Can you think of a way to say that as well?

Molly: "Students often approach their class work as if they think the instructor alone has to control the environment, leaving them with no responsibility for setting an appropriate class tone."

Brenna: Much better.

In tutoring students on agreement, it is important for tutors to remember that not all students will see clearly what the problem is, let alone how to fix it. In these cases, tutors may need to turn to a sheet of scratch paper and generate some simple examples of the sorts of problems they are seeing in the student's paper. Frequently, when students have an opportunity to work with simple example sentences—as opposed to sentences they have written—it is easier to help them see the grammatical premise behind the problem they are having. Once the students can work with simple sentences, the movement back to the student's prose is sometimes less daunting.

Other Grammar and Usage Problems

This brief catalog of typical problems is less than exhaustive. After all, we have said nothing about slang, parentheses, verb tense, brackets, capitalization, or irregular plural nouns, not to mention *who/whom*, *lie/lay* and a host of other notoriously tricky features of the English language. But regardless of which grammar or usage issue you encounter in a student's paper, your approach will always be essentially the same: to employ dialogic tutoring practices to help the student understand the problem and the options for correction. We stress here that the key is that you allow the student to maintain ownership of the work, with your questions working to nudge the student ever closer to correct form. To do this well, you will need a firm command of grammar and usage rules yourself. After all, if you have to struggle to discern what is grammatical and what is not, it will be nearly impossible for you to help student writers move towards more correct grammar and usage.

One caveat: even if you are confident about your command of the English language, we still recommend all our tutors keep close at hand a reliable grammar and usage handbook. It is not uncommon to run into a question in a writing tutorial that requires consultation of a handbook. There you can expect to find explanations of grammar and usage rules as well as some useful examples. There are also times when you will want to consult that handbook even when you know well what you will find there, simply to model the behavior for your student and demonstrate just how useful the resource can be for any writer.

Grammar and Usage and ESL Writers

Although it is true that ESL writers are in some ways different from their native English-speaking peers, virtually all of the strategies discussed previously in this book are applicable to working with ESL writers. (Before proceeding any further, you may find it useful to review the material on "Working with ESL Writers" in Chapter Three.) And yet, because ESL writers do differ from their native English-speaking counterparts, some special differences arise when helping ESL writers improve their written English grammar and usage.

Prior to addressing these differences, however, it is worth noting that working with ESL writers can be one of the more rewarding aspects of tutorial work. Coming from cultures and backgrounds that are different from native English speaking students, ESL students bring with them perspectives and ideas that are well removed from the mainstream, resulting in written work that is frequently interesting and fresh. For example, imagine a rather generic and overdone argumentative paper topic that asks students to take a stance on an issue like gun control. Most native English speakers tend to respond to that topic using fairly similar sets of cultural information and assumptions. However, possessing different cultural and linguistic backgrounds, ESL students are likely to offer new perspectives, as when a student from southeast Asia brings in aspects of Taoism, Buddhism, or Confucianism to help formulate a position on gun ownership. Or, perhaps a student from a European country where very few people own guns will take a new angle on the topic by juxtaposing attitudes towards gun ownership in their home country with American ideas about guns, using the differences as a way to come at the topic in a different and altogether more interesting way. As a reader of ESL student writing, do not be surprised when you find yourself caught up in what the writing says as this will nearly always result in a tutorial that is more purposeful and enjoyable—both for you and for the student.

Adding to the rewards of working with ESL writers, as Severino (1994) points out (and as we ourselves have noticed), ESL writers' prose can sometimes have an almost poetic quality to it—in part because it works in ways that native speakers may be unaccustomed to seeing. Consider, for instance, the following example sentences by ESL writers:

- *"I can stay in the pool for many hours until my fingers all <u>shrinkle</u>."*

- *"My self-esteem was <u>nibbled by the sense of failure</u> little by little ever since I started to take Rhetoric class. I was afraid."*

- *"The sound of the waves and <u>the wind of the madness ocean</u> made us feel like the voices of unfortunate people yelled out for help before they die."*

- *I am eager to do a certain thing but <u>I am bent on a stick</u> and cannot move."*

- *After my grandma died, my grandpa face <u>never turned bright again</u>."*

- *I had to <u>chase their eyes</u> to understand the quick conversation of my classmates."*
(quoted in Severino, 1994, pp. 22-24)

It is important not to trivialize or romanticize ESL writing simply because on occasion it will demonstrate some of the playful or poetic qualities of the above sentences. Yet, as Severino (1994) suggests, sentences like these do "add richer overtones of meaning and get closer to the truth of what the writers are communicating" (p. 30).

Many ESL students are also highly motivated and will be willing to put in exceptionally long hours on their coursework. For writing tutors, this can mean a steady rotation of ESL writers who will make regular use of tutorial services. And, germane to the present chapter's focus on the surface features of writing, ESL writers often come into their tutorials wanting to focus exclusively on grammar and usage, areas of the language they may struggle to control. However, because the patterns of error evidenced by ESL writers are indeed unfamiliar to most new tutors, writing tutors sometimes feel daunted when it comes to working with ESL students. Consider this opening paragraph from an ESL writer's paper, entitled "Toy Guns are Violent":

> There have been many contradictory arguments about whether children should play with the toy guns or not. Although it might seem that toy guns are just one components of game, actually it can be a socialization with real gun—killer for our little kids. Therefore, for number of reasonable causes we should illegalize toy gun use in the nation.

Although this writer may be having some of the same grammar and usage questions that native English speakers might have, it is also clear that there are some aspects of English that seem to give particular trouble. You will do well to anticipate a certain amount of difficulty when it comes to ESL writers and features of the English language like article usage (*the, a/an*), verb tense, pronoun-antecedent, and idiomatic expression.

As writing tutors ourselves, we have both met ESL writers who made weekly appointments, many of which seemed to involve attention to the same grammar and usage issues that had been addressed in previous tutorials. In our experience, newer tutors sometimes come to view repeated tutorials with the same ESL students as frustrating, usually because the same conversations or types of conversations about English article usage or verb tense will need to be had over and over again. However, the ESL writers with whom we work are being asked to do something that is extraordinarily difficult as they pursue a university degree in a language they do not speak natively. When you tutor the same ESL student for the ninth week in a row, you can rest assured that what this indicates is that *the tutorial work is benefiting the student.* After all, no student would keep coming back if the tutorials were not helpful. Further, you can remind yourself that learning to write well takes a long time and that some of the steps in the process must be made slowly and carefully.

The dialogue that follows demonstrates strategies for addressing ESL writers' grammar and usage concerns. The student, a woman from Japan named Nobumi, is the author of the "Toy Guns are Violent" paper quoted previously. Note the way that the tutor, Ariane, cannot rely on Nobumi's ear to catch the grammar and usage problems; instead, she must call on Nobumi's understanding of English grammar and usage.

> Ariane: Let's take a look at the first paragraph. I think there are some grammar and usage items that we can address.
>
> Nobumi: I am not always sure about these things.
>
> Ariane: It's okay. I know how complicated English can be, even for a native speaker. Why don't you read that first sentence aloud?
>
> Nobumi: [*reads*] "There have been many contradictory arguments about whether children should play with the toy guns or not."

Ariane: Okay, let's look at the article in front of the word "toy." Why did you use "the?"

Nobumi: I don't know.

Ariane: It's okay. English is a tricky language even for native speakers sometimes. Let me ask you this: did you have some specific toy guns in mind or did you mean toy guns in general?

Nobumi: Toy guns in general.

Ariane: Okay. So, to do that, we use either no article at all or a/an. Which of those would seem right?

Nobumi: I can't use "a" because "guns" is plural.

Ariane: Right. So what should you use?

Nobumi: No article.

Ariane: And how do you know?

Nobumi: Because I am not naming specific guns.

Ariane: And because we know that with plural nouns we can't ever use a/an. Now, why don't you read the first half of that next sentence?

Nobumi: [*Reads*] "Although it might seem that toy guns are just one components of game."

Ariane: Do you catch any problem in there?

Nobumi: I can't tell.

Ariane: Is "components" singular or plural?

Nobumi: Plural.

Ariane: Can you use a plural noun with "one." So, "one shoes" or "one books?"

Nobumi: I see. It should be "just one component." Singular.

Ariane: Well, maybe. Is "guns" in that sentence singular or plural?

Nobumi: Plural.

Ariane: So, "guns" plural means that "components" should be what?

Nobumi: Also plural.

Ariane: So what has to happen with "one?"

Nobumi: [*crosses "one" out*]

Ariane: Good. Now, what article would you need before the word "game?"

Nobumi: How can I tell?

Ariane: Do you have a specific game in mind or do you mean "game" in general?

Nobumi: In general.

Ariane: So what should the article be?

Nobumi: "A game." [*first half of sentence now reads "Although it might seem that toy guns are just components of a game"*]

Ariane: Now let's look at the second half. [*reads*] "actually it can be a socialization with real gun—killer for our little kids." What does "it" refer to?

Nobumi: Guns.

Ariane: Guns plural?

Nobumi:	Yes.
Ariane:	So, how could you make that pronoun agree with its plural antecedent?
Nobumi:	"They."
Ariane:	Right. What do you mean by "can be a socialization"?
Nobumi:	I mean that the toy guns can make kids grow accustom to real guns.
Ariane:	You know, I think that's clearer than what you currently have. Do you think you could just use that instead?
Nobumi:	So [*reads*] "Although it might seem that toy guns are just components of a game, actually they can make kids grow accustom to real gun—killer for our little kids."
Ariane:	Good. You're getting there. That word "accustom." Do you notice anything about its form?
Nobumi:	I'm not sure.
Ariane:	Well, you've got the verb "grow" in front of it. So that means that the word that follows is going to need to be an adjective. Can you remember how we usually turn verbs into an adjectives?
Nobumi:	Add "-ed."
Ariane:	That's right. So "grow accustomed." With the phrase "to real gun." Do you only mean one gun?
Nobumi:	I mean all guns.
Ariane:	So singular or plural?
Nobumi:	Plural "guns."
Ariane:	Good. Last question. "killer for our little kids." Is the killing really "for" the kids?
Nobumi:	No. I get confused with the prepositions. I have no idea.
Ariane:	Try "killer *of* our little kids."

As is evident, Ariane and Nobumi's work moves fairly slowly as they pay attention to the minute details of Nobumi's grammar and usage. Ariane, for her part, at times must supply bits of grammatical information to help Nobumi make decisions. And, as happens in their final work on "killer for little kids," at times a tutor may need to step in and provide small pieces of information, to be what we call in earlier chapters a "tour guide" for students whose native language is not English.

Leki (1992) has pointed out that ESL writers may always exhibit a certain amount of "accent" in their writing, even in cases where the ESL writer diligently works to eliminate those features of her writing that mark it as non-native. A writing tutor need not try to eliminate every single grammar and usage problem in papers written by ESL writers. Rather, if you can help the writer isolate and understand some of the problems as well as ways to improve, you will most certainly be acting as a positive force in the ESL writer's development.

SUMMARY

Some of the students you tutor will likely put undue emphasis on perfecting their grammar. However, grammar and usage are but one part of the larger set of rhetorical features that comprise effective writing. And yet, by understanding some of the causes and consequences of students' grammar and usage problems, it becomes easier to see how and why many writers place matters of correctness atop their list of concerns. Frequently, at the outset of your tutorials you will need to help students prioritize grammar and usage concerns. When students come to see that the *way* they say something matters most only once they have attended to *what* they are saying, it is often easier to help them see grammar and usage as one of *many* important features of effective communication—rather than as the single critical variable standing in the way of fluid, successful writing.

When you address grammar and usage in student work, you can turn to the same dialogic techniques that are at the core of all sound tutorial work. Though grammatical questions often do have genuine right answers (as opposed to more subjective judgments, as is the case with many other rhetorical matters), it does not follow that the tutor's job will be to simply provide those answers. This premise is an especially important one to remember when you tutor writers who have little knowledge on which to call when trying to answer your grammar and usage questions. What is often appropriate in such circumstances—whether they involve native-English speakers or L2 writers—is for the tutor to spend some time addressing grammar and usage rules. Sometimes, you will be able to use the student's own text as a forum for teaching grammatical rules; at other times, you might generate examples of your own or turn to a grammar handbook. The salient point is that writers can only make real progress with their writing when they participate actively in the decision-making processes that govern the production effective prose. As you start tutoring, you will develop a sense of how you can adapt the approaches and strategies we recommend to the myriad grammar and usage problems you will encounter in student writing. So long as you keep your focus on the writer—rather than the writing—you can remain confident that your dialogue is leading the student to a more robust understanding of English grammar and usage.

SUGGESTIONS FOR FURTHER READING

Bartholomae, David. (1980). The study of error. *College Composition and Communication,* *31*(3), 253-269.

Bartholomae, David. (1985). Inventing the university. In M. Rose (Ed.), *When a writer can't write* (pp. 134-165). New York: Guilford Press.

Beason, Larry. (2001). Ethos and error: How business people react to errors. *College Composition and Communication, 53*(1), 33-64.

Connors, Robert. J., and Andrea A. Lunsford. (1993). Teachers' rhetorical comments on student papers. *College Composition and Communication, 44*(2), 200-223.

Harris, Joseph. (1997). *A teaching subject: Composition since 1966.* Upper Saddle River, NJ: Prentice Hall.

Harris, Muriel, and Tony Silva. (1993). Tutoring ESL students: Issues and options. *College Composition and Communication, 44*(4), 525-537.

Hartwell, Patrick. (1985). Grammar, grammars, and the teaching of grammar. *College English 47*(2), 105-127.

Leki, Ilona. (1992). *Understanding ESL writers.* Portsmouth, NH: Boynton/Cook.

Severino, Carol. (1994). Inadvertently and intentionally poetic ESL writing. *Journal of Basic Writing, 13*(2), 18-32.

Shaughnessy, Mina. P. (1977). *Errors and expectations: A guide for the teacher of basic writing.* New York: Oxford University Press.

Wall, Susan V., and Glynda A. Hull. (1989). The semantics of error: What do teachers know? In Chris M. Anson (Ed.), *Writing and response: Theory, practice, and research* (pp. 261-292). Urbana, IL: NCTE.

Williams, Joseph M. (1981). The phenomenology of error. *College Composition and Communication, 32*(2), 152-168.

Yule, George. (1998). *Explaining English grammar.* New York: Oxford University Press.

CASE STUDY. 7.1: TROUBLE WITH THE INTRODUCTION

A tutor, Roman, has been working with a student, Vince, on a paper analyzing the stereotypes in television sitcoms for his mass communications class. After twenty minutes of work, the pair has addressed the major rhetorical areas in the paper. In the closing ten minutes of the tutorial, they turn to grammar and usage, in this case correct use of commas and semicolons, something with which Vince is clearly struggling. Read Vince's opening paragraph (in which there are a number of comma and semicolon errors) and then construct a dialogue showing how Roman could approach his work with Vince. Remember that Roman's goal is to help Vince get into a position where he will know how to use commas and semicolons on his own.

The opening paragraph from Vince's paper:

It is a typical evening in the Lopez home; with father George once again barking orders at his family. *George Lopez*, a family comedy in its fourth season of episodes is continuing to lure millions of Americans to their television sets each week, to discover the latest tribulations of the Lopez family. Despite the Lopez family's neat and tidy appearance the relationships and interactions between the family members expose a disturbing trend, in the way minorities are portrayed on television sitcoms.

CASE STUDY. 7.2: WORKING WITH AN ESL WRITER'S OPENING PARAGRAPH

Midway through your shift in the writing center, an ESL writer named Su-Yin enters and asks for some help with a paper she is working on. After interacting with her during the opening minutes of the tutorial, you determine that Su-Yin does not appear to have any trouble understanding you or making herself understood. Su-Yin explains to you that the primary issue she wants help on is her grammar and usage, noting that as a non-native speaker she has persistent trouble making her writing free of distracting errors.

Below is one of the paragraphs from her paper. Construct a dialogue in which you move through the grammar of the paragraph sentence by sentence, keeping in mind that your goal is to let her do as much of the work as possible.

The opening paragraph from Su-Yin's paper:

> A common belief is that raising a federal minimum wage would provided great benefit to those who are the poorest. This theory has unfortunately been proven myth. Instead, higher amount of the money per hour offered entices the people with more advanced skills. Therefore, according to the National Center for Policy Awareness website, the less-skilled job-seekers must measuring up against the greater number of applicants vying for these jobs. So that employers to be more particular in their selections. The notions of leaving a Welfare or Unemployment programs behind for the fair wage could be quickly dashed by a more intensely competitive job market.

CASE STUDY 7.3: AN ESL WRITER IN A NURSING SEMINAR

As you start your shift in the writing center, you note that Gao, an ESL student from China with whom you work on an almost weekly basis, has signed up for an appointment with you. When he arrives, Gao expresses gratitude to you for all the help you provide for him. And, as is his custom, he states that he wants to focus exclusively on grammar. In your past work with Gao, you have found that his writing needs attention to matters beyond his grammar and usage.

For today's tutorial he has brought the opening of a case study he is writing for a nursing seminar entitled "The Patient's Voice: Experiences of Illness." He also has an assignment sheet clearly stating that the opening of the case study must accomplish two objectives: 1) paint a picture of realistic patients seeking help; and 2) frame the set of issues that the case will explore.

Construct a dialogue showing how you would attend to Gao's concerns about grammar and usage as well as your own recognition that the opening paragraph likely needs to do more to meet the assignment's specifications.

The opening paragraph from Gao's case study:

A husband and wife sit in hospital clinic waiting from for eternity. Finally nurse comes out to tell them doctor is ready to see them. In small examination room, a husband holds wife's hand. A doctor explains, "Mammogram shows small mass. We will need to do a biopsy to figure out cancerous or not. If cancerous, radiation should clear it up. You are the healthy woman. I have good chance that it can be isolated." One may only think this the tragic situation.

CASE STUDY. 7.4: BALANCING GRAMMAR AND CONTENT

You are just finishing up a session in the writing center when Ingrid arrives for her 10:00 appointment. You have worked with Ingrid once before and have every reason to believe that the session was a good one. As you conclude your previous appointment, you notice Ingrid is clearly upset, her mouth turned down, her arms crossed, her foot tapping.

As you take a seat, she hands you a graded copy of her last paper—the one you tutored her on. She says that while she knows the ideas in the paper improved as a result of her work with you, her professor appeared to focus only on the grammar, something the two of you didn't have time to address in her previous tutorial. Looking over the paper, you note that her professor circled all of the grammar errors, made no reference to what she had to say, and assigned a grade of C-.

For this tutorial, Ingrid has brought a complete draft of her next paper for this professor. She tells you she wants to focus solely on the grammar since that is what her professor appears to be grading her on. As you read her paper, however, in addition to noticing some grammar and usage problems, you also note some rather sizable rhetorical issues concerning her thesis statement and also her overall level of development. Construct a dialogue in which you negotiate an agenda for the tutorial with Ingrid, paying attention to her anxieties, her professor's apparent expectations, and also your own sense of both the grammatical and rhetorical work that the paper needs.

CASE STUDY 7.5: COLONS AND SEMICOLONS

Dawn, a nontraditional student enrolled in first-year composition, has come to you with a personal narrative written for her class. The paper is due one week from today. After workshopping her draft, Dawn reports that her peers enjoyed the story but told her she was "messed up on" the colons and semicolons.

"I thought I knew what I was doing," she says, "but now that I look at it I have no clue. But I can't get the colons and semicolons straight. So sometimes I just use dashes. When do you use one instead of the other? And when is it best not to use either?"

How would you use the techniques and strategies presented in this chapter to address Dawn's question? (For convenience, we have highlighted and numbered a dozen sentences in her paper for closer examination.)

Horse Sense

It was the day Mom was to come home from the hospital with baby number five. I was thirteen at the time, the oldest, and I was not too happy to have another baby in the house. (1) I was feeling sorry for myself; a new baby would only mean more responsibility for me.

(2) Mom had to spend the last two days recuperating in the hospital: I decided to surprise her by cleaning the house and doing the laundry. I washed the clothes, hanging the bedding on the tipsy old clothesline to dry. Mom loved the smell of the fresh air on her linens. I spent hours scrubbing and polishing. The kitchen always took the longest to clean because it was a very large room where we spent most of our time around the ten foot oak table, eating, playing games, doing homework, or just visiting. (3) The sink where we did the dishes was a dull white metal that had rust spots showing through the latest layer of paint: the few cupboards we had were a wrinkled dark bronze that reminded me of an old piece of leather. The walls and ceiling were painted a shiny, bright white that made the room cheery, even on gray days, and the wood floor was smooth and honey golden from years of footsteps. It was usually spotless, as was the rest of Mom's house.

Dad had been gone a long time to get Mom and the new baby. It seemed to me we lived in the middle of nowhere, thirty miles from the nearest town. But I barely had time to finish making the beds before I heard the car in the driveway. Mom came in carrying what looked like a rolled up blanket and reached out to give me a hug as I met her at the door. Her shiny dark hair smelled like the fresh air of her clean bedding, and her yellow-green eyes, with their perfectly arched eyebrows, sparkled with happiness. (4) Her skin had a healthy, sun-kissed glow; she looked rested and relaxed.

(5) Unfortunately, that image didn't last long; there came a loud squall from the rolled up blanket. I could see Mom's face tighten and I knew she suddenly felt the reality of caring for five children, a husband, a home, and a farm come crashing in on top of her. I knew from past experience this overload would turn her back into a short-tempered, unappeasable parent who constantly complained and criticized. She handed the noisy bundle to me so we

could "get acquainted," while she started the evening meal. "Couldn't someone else in this house see what a mess this silverware drawer is?" she moaned as she gathered the necessary utensils. (6) Disappointment flooded over me—instead of commenting on what I had done, she managed to find something I hadn't done.

Over the next few weeks, Mom left the baby and the supper dishes with me while she helped with the evening milking. I swept the floors, washed and dried the dishes, and managed to keep an eye on my little brother. (7) But it never failed; when Mom came in from the barn, her first comment was always, "Why didn't anyone sweep this floor?" and, despite the fact that I had already swept it once, she would make me sweep it again. One night, when my grandmother was visiting, I decided to let her sweep the floor. Sure enough the minute she walked in the kitchen Mom complained, "This floor is a mess! Sweep it again!" Neither Mom nor Grandma was happy with my little deceit. Mom's sharp remark as she chased me out the door to go horseback riding with my cousin Kathy was, "Get out of here, and for heaven sakes, have more sense than God gave the horse." She was mad at me again, and at that moment, I wondered if I would ever do anything that would make my mom happy.

I loved to ride, and this certainly wasn't a punishment. My cousin's horse was a little mare named Fire. She wasn't what you would call a pretty horse. Her color was somewhere between a speckled brown and gray. But she pranced on her toes, and her dark eyes glowed fire when she saw us coming. (8) She knew me well: we both loved to run. Once I mounted Fire, we took off flying, and instantly, I felt better. The wind blew in my face and took with it all of my self-pity, anger, and frustration. It was perfect therapy. However, in my haste, I neglected to tighten the straps properly. We weren't far from the house when I began to feel the saddle slipping, and before I could get Fire to a halt, I was on the ground in a patch of sandburs. Limping home, while Kathy led my horse, I could feel my skin turning red and itchy with sandbur slivers.

Mom met me at the door, and with a disapproving look, she led me to the bathroom where we spent at least one precious hour of her already overly busy day pulling slivers from my arms, legs, and buttocks. All the while Mom repeatedly reminded me that I indeed did not have the sense God gave the horse.

Mom and I struggled through my teenage years, never giving each other what we needed most--understanding. I felt she was too critical, never giving any positive feedback and very little affection, and I think she felt I was sassy and uncooperative. (9) I couldn't wait to go off to college; when I finally left, I took with me many memories of harsh words and disagreements. Starting a life of my own allowed me leave behind all my feelings of disapproval and of never being quite good enough. I vowed it would be a very long time before I returned, and it was.

Our relationship improved slowly over the years, step by step. I matured, married, and had children of my own which gave me some insight as to why she seemed so overwhelmed. She mellowed as one by one, her children left and with them took their share of her stress.

(10) The other day, as my fourteen-year-old son left with a friend to go horseback riding, I teasingly borrowed my mom's very words—"For heaven sakes, have more sense than God gave the horse." Hours later, he returned with gravel ground into his palms and scrapes and cuts on his head, up his back, and down his arms. I hugged him with tears stuck in my throat and then lead him to the bathroom to spend at least an hour pulling gravel from his messed up hand. (11) I knew he was okay; I couldn't wait to get him cleaned up so that I could telephone my mom and tell her what had happened. (12) I relayed the story to her; I could see her twinkling, yellow-green eyes creasing at the corners, and I could hear her soft chuckle of understanding when she said, "I guess he didn't have the sense God gave the horse."

CASE STUDY 7.6: DIAGNOSING AND ADDRESSING SENTENCE PROBLEMS

Meredith, a student taking Business Communications, has asked for help revising and editing the following memo. What kinds of problems does her writing exhibit? How would you tutor her to compose more effective and correct sentences using the strategies presented in this chapter?

To: Pat Varvick
From: Meredith Meyers
Subject: Brochure Revisions
Date: March 1, 2007

I revised the new brochure and some comments along with it to help you in the future. The revisions and the document is attached.

Most of the revisions were related to point of view and cutting down wordiness. Second person point of view should not be used in the brochure because it is too informal, not consistent, and it leads to confusion. It is important to use concise vocabulary in documents like this because often time's people don't carefully read every word in a brochure, they don't want to have to search for information.

A third problem is that the document design is not coherent. It uses too many different fonts, inconsistent design elements, and the heading of the panel columns is not always parallel. Make sure that you are staying consistent throughout your document, it appears more professional when the reader can see that you have taken the time to stay consistent.

I don't know if you want to make these changes yourself or if revising it is something you want me to do. Overall I think together we made a very well written brochure let me know if you have any other suggestions.

Afterword

In our dealings with students, faculty and administrators, we often encounter one of the more pervasive myths about tutoring writing. Namely, that tutoring writing is a skill reserved for a select few; those who through some combination of aptitude and intelligence simply "get it." Everyone else, or so this myth goes, will be fortunate if they can just get all their commas in the right places. In our experience, however, this myth is just that: a *myth*. While some of the tutors we train certainly do exhibit an almost instinctual ability to master the complexities of dialogic tutoring, many more *make* themselves into effective tutors, working deliberately to develop the interpersonal, rhetorical, and syntactic skill set that all good tutors must possess. And so, in closing, let us emphasize that tutoring writing really is like *any* skill you might choose to develop; the more you practice, the better you will become.

Over the years, it has been extraordinarily gratifying to witness just *how* good many of our tutors have become. In fact, after they leave our program, quite a number of our tutors go on to teach writing—in middle schools, high schools, community education programs, and two- and four-year colleges and universities—in both the United Stated and over seas. Others, meanwhile, put these same skills to use in their careers as editors. Still, others make use of their abilities in corporate settings, lending their expertise to workplace communications; and some put their aptitude to use in writing for public and civic circumstances. All of them, we know, can work from sound theoretical perspectives to make practical decisions as they respond to others' writing.

With this book, we hope we have created opportunities for you to begin or to enhance your development as a tutor. And, whether you picked up the book already knowing a great deal about tutoring, or if you were completely new to the process, we are confident that the strategies, dialogues, and scenarios presented in *Theory and Practice for Writing Tutors* can help you become a more responsive, more rounded, and altogether more effective tutor of writing.

Yet, regardless of how much you knew before undertaking this course of study, your development as a tutor will be most enriching—for you and for the students you tutor—if you consciously seek out opportunities to hone your understandings and abilities. Initially, this continued development may occur as a natural part of your tutorial work. Reflecting on your sessions—either mentally or, perhaps better, in writing—will enable you to more cleanly weigh the decisions you make as you work with writers. Also, we urge you to share with interested colleagues experiences from your tutoring, whether those experiences be meaningful successes or bewildering failures. Frequently, the conversations tutors have with one another lead to a rich and purposeful exchange of ideas that productively informs subsequent tutorials.

Though this probably goes without saying, we would be remiss if we did not acknowledge that you will invariably make mistakes as you tutor. Doing so is, of course, an unavoidable part of any educational endeavor, and we would encourage you to use your mistakes as opportunities to grow your abilities rather than as a reason to run yourself down. After all, tutoring writing is always subject to a dizzying range of variables. No tutor we have ever known—most certainly including the two of us—ever gets *all* those variables lined up properly each and every time. But, all of the many good ones we have known have been self-reflective about their practice, using any mistake as an opportunity to further develop their skills.

As you develop as a tutor, you may want additional resources on the tutoring and teaching of writing. Our "Suggestions for Further Reading" are populated primarily with scholarly articles from the main periodicals in the field, beginning with two professional journals devoted to tutoring; *Writing Center Journal* and *Writing Lab Newsletter*. Dozen of journals publish theoretical and pedagogical articles devoted to writing in general, with some essays specific to tutoring: you might begin with *College Composition and Communication, College English, Journal of Advanced Composition, Written Communication,* and *Teaching English in the Two-Year College*. For scholarship devoted entirely to L2 writing, an excellent place to start is the *Journal of Second Language Writing*. Finally, you might consult the International

Writing Centers Association, or IWCA, a professional organization for writing center administrators and writing tutors of any level. The IWCA encourages scholarship connected to writing-center work and provides a forum for discussing writing center issues, the online version of which can be accessed through the organization's website (www.writingcenters.org). The organization also sponsors professional conferences, including the National Conference on Peer Tutoring in Writing (NCPTW) and the annual IWCA Conference, along with numerous regional conferences.

We end *Theory and Practice for Writing Tutors* by commending you, our readers, for the work you have put into your training. Whether you are an experienced tutor who read this book mainly to confirm much of what you already knew, or a new or developing tutor who diligently worked through the book's case studies and suggested readings, we hope that as you conclude this course of study you have found it to be challenging, informative, and productive. Tutoring writing, particularly when done well, is extraordinarily rewarding work. The environment of the writing tutorial—a student, a text, and a tutor unencumbered by a need to grade or evaluate—really does present some of the purest teaching opportunities either of us has ever known. As you move forward into the many intricacies of this environment, we hope that you will find cause to return to these pages, using them as a resource in your development. But, more than anything else, we hope that you, and all of our readers, find tutoring to be continually challenging, consistently productive, and professionally satisfying.

References

Armstrong, Cherryl. (1986). Reader-based and writer-based perspectives in composition instruction. *Rhetoric Review, 5*(1), 84-89.

Bakhtin, Mikhail M. (1935). *The dialogic imagination: Four essays by M. M. Bakhtin.* (Michael Holquist, Ed., Caryl Emerson and Michael Holquist, Trans.). Austin, TX: University of Texas Press.

Bartholomae, David. (1980). The study of error. *College Composition and Communication, 31*(3), 253-269.

Bartholomae, David. (1985). Inventing the university. In Mike Rose (Ed.), *When a writer can't write* (pp. 134-165). New York: Guilford Press.

Beason, Larry. (2001). Ethos and error: How business people react to errors. *College Composition and Communication, 53*(1), 33-64.

Belenky, Mary Field, Blythe McVicker Clinchy, Nancy Rule Goldberger, and Jill Mattucki Tarule. (1986). *Women's ways of knowing.* New York: Basic Books.

Berkenkotter, Carol. (1981). Understanding a writer's awareness of audience. *College Composition and Communication, 32*, 388-399.

Berlin, James. (1988). Rhetoric and ideology in the writing class. *College English, 50*(5), 477-494.

Berthoff, Ann E. (1978). *Forming thinking writing: The composing imagination.* Portsmouth, NH: Heinemann.

Bishop, Wendy. (1988). Opening lines: Starting the tutoring session. *The Writing Lab Newsletter, 13*(3), 1-4.

Boice, Robert. (1985). Psychotherapies for writing blocks. In Mike Rose (Ed.), *When a writer can't write: Studies in writer's black and other composing-process problems* (pp. 182-218). New York: Guilford.

Bosker, Julie A. (2001). Peer tutoring and Gorgias: Acknowledging aggression in the writing center. *The Writing Center Journal, 21*(2), 21-34.

Bouman, Kurt. (2004). Raising questions about plagiarism. In Shanti Bruce and Ben Rafoth (Eds.), *ESL writers: A guide for writing center tutors* (pp. 105-116). Portsmouth, NH: Boynton/Cook.

Brent, Doug. (1991). Young, Becker and Pike's "Rogerian" rhetoric: A twenty-year reassessment. *College English, 53*, 452-466.

Brooks, Jeff. (1991). Minimalist tutoring: Making the student do all the work. *The Writing Lab Newsletter, 15*(6), 1-4.

Bruffee, Kenneth A. (1973). Collaborative learning: Some practical models. *College English 34*(5), 634-643.

Bruffee, Kenneth A. (1984). Collaborative learning and the 'conversation of mankind.' *College English 46*, 635-652.

Bruffee, Kenneth A. (1986). Social construction, language, and the authority of knowledge: A bibliographical essay. *College English, 48*, 773-790.

Carino, Peter. (1992). What do we talk about when we talk about our metaphors: A cultural critique of clinic, lab, and center. *The Writing Center Journal, 13*, 31-42.

Casanave, Christine Pearson. (2002). *Writing games: Multicultural case studies of academic literacy practices in higher education.* Mahwah, NJ: Lawrence Erlbaum.

Christensen, Francis. (1963). A generative rhetoric of the sentence. *College Composition and Communication, 14*, 155-161.

Christensen, Francis, and Bonniejean Christensen. (1975). *A new rhetoric.* New York: Harper.

Clark, Irene. (1999). Writing centers and plagiarism. In Lise Buranen and Alice M. Roy (Eds.), *Perspectives on plagiarism and intellectual property in a postmodern world* (pp. 155-168). Albany, NY: SUNY Press.

Coleridge, Samuel Taylor. (1985). Kubla Khan. In H. J. Jackson (Ed.), *The Oxford authors: Samuel Taylor Coleridge* (pp. 102-104). New York: Oxford University Press. (Original work published 1798).

Connor, Ulla. (1996). *Contrastive rhetoric: Cross-cultural aspects of second-language writing*. New York: Cambridge University Press.

Connors, Robert J. (1996). Teaching and learning as a man. *College English, 58*(2), 137-57.

Connors, Robert J. (2000). The erasure of the sentence. *College Composition and Communication, 52*(1), 96-128.

Connors, Robert J., and Andrea A. Lunsford. (1993). Teachers' rhetorical comments on student papers. *College Composition and Communication, 44*(2), 200-223.

Cooper, Marilyn. (1994). Really useful knowledge: A cultural studies agenda for writing centers. *The Writing Center Journal, 14,* 97-111.

Corder, Stephen Pit. (1967). The significance of learners' errors. *International Review of Applied Linguistics, 5*(4), 161-170.

Daiker, Donald A., Andrew Kerek, and Max Morenberg. (1978). Sentence combining and syntactic maturity in freshman English. *College Composition and Communication, 29,* 36-41.

Daly, John A. (1985). Writing apprehension. In Mike Rose (Ed.), *When a writer can't write: Studies in writer's black and other composing-process problems* (pp. 43-82). New York: Guilford.

Davis, Kevin M., Nancy Hayward, Kathleen R. Hunter, and David L. Wallace. (1996). The function of talk in the writing conference: A study of tutorial conversation. *The Writing Center Journal, 9,* 45-51.

Dean, Deborah. (2001). Grammar without grammar: Just playing around, writing. *English Journal, 91,* 86-89.

DeCurtis, Anthony. (1991, April 4). Blue highways (Review of Bob Dylan, *The Bootleg Series*). *Rolling Stone,* 53-56.

Devet, Bonnie. F. (2007). "Opening lines: Starting the tutoring session": A synecdochic article from the Writing Lab canon. *The Writing Lab Newsletter, 31*(10), 12-13.

Douglas, Lucille. (1924). Teaching English on the Dalton Plan. *English Journal, 13,* 335-340.

Durkin, Margaret. (1926). The Teaching of English in England under the Dalton Plan. *English Journal, 15*, 256-266.

Ede, Lisa, and Andrea Lunsford. (1984). Audience addressed/audience invoked: The role of audience in composition theory and pedagogy. *College Composition and Communication, 35*, 155-171.

Elbow, Peter. (1987). Closing my eyes as I speak: An argument for ignoring audience. *College English, 49*, 50-69.

Epstein, Edward Jay. (2005). *The big picture: The new logic of money and power in Hollywood*. New York: Random.

Faigley, Lester. (1978). Generative rhetoric as a way of increasing syntactic fluency. *College Composition and Communication, 30*, 176-181.

Flannery, Tim. (2005). *The weather makers: How man is changing the climate and what it means for life on earth*. New York: Atlantic Monthly.

Flower, Linda. (1981). *Problem-solving strategies for writing*. New York: Harcourt Brace Jovanovich.

Flower, Linda, and John R. Hayes. (1980). The cognition of discovery: Defining a rhetorical problem. *College Composition and Communication, 31*(1), 21-32.

Fulkerson, Richard. (1996). *Teaching the argument in writing*. Urbana, IL: NCTE.

Gilligan, Carol. (1982). *In a different voice: Psychological theory and women's development*. Cambridge, MA: Harvard University Press.

Glazier, Teresa Ferster. (1986). *The least you should know about English: Form B* (3rd ed.). New York: Holt, Rinehart and Winston.

Hairston, Maxine. (1976). Carl Rogers' alternative to traditional rhetoric. *College Composition and Communication, 27*, 373-377.

Harris, Joseph. (1997). *A teaching subject: Composition since 1966*. Upper Saddle River, NJ: Prentice Hall.

Harris, Muriel. (1988). Peer tutoring: How tutors learn. *Teaching English in the Two-Year College, 15*(1), 28-33.

Harris, Muriel. (1995). Talking in the middle: Why writers need writing tutors. *College English, 57*, 27-42.

Harris, Muriel, and Tony Silva. (1993). Tutoring ESL students: Issues and options. *College Composition and Communication, 44*(4), 525-537.

Hartwell, Patrick. (1985). Grammar, grammars, and the teaching of grammar. *College English, 47*(2), 105-127.

Haswell, Richard H., and Min-Zhan Lu. (2000). *Comp tales: An introduction to college composition through its stories.* New York: Longman.

Howard, Rebecca Moore. (1995). Plagiarisms, authorships, and the academic death penalty. *College English, 57,* 788-805.

Hymes, Dell. (1986). Models of the interaction of language and social life. In John J. Gumperz and Dell Hymes (Eds.), *Directions in sociolinguistics: The ethnography of communication* (pp. 35-71). Oxford: Basil Blackwell.

Irmscher, William F. (1979). *Teaching expository writing.* New York: Holt, Rinehart & Winston.

Kasden, Lawrence N. (1980). An introduction to basic writing. In Lawrence N. Kasden and Daniel R. Hoeber (Eds.), *Basic writing: Essays for teachers, researchers, administrators* (pp. 1-9). Urbana, IL: NCTE.

Kinneavy, James E. (1969). The basic aims of discourse. *College Composition and Communication, 20*(4), 297-304.

Kinneavy, James E. (1986). *Kairos:* a neglected concept in classical rhetoric. In Jean Dietz Moss (Ed.), *Rhetoric and praxis: The contribution of classical rhetoric to practical reasoning* (pp. 79-105). Washington, DC: Catholic University of America Press.

Kneupper, Charles W. (1978). Teaching argument: An introduction to the Toulmin model. *College Composition and Communication, 29,* 237–241.

Kozol, Jonathan. (1988). *Rachel and her children: Homeless people in America.* New York: Ballantine.

Lamott, Anne. (1994). *Bird by bird: Some instructions on writing and life.* New York: Anchor.

Lanham, Richard. (2000). *Revising prose* (4th ed.). Boston: Allyn & Bacon.

Lassner, Phyllis. (1990). Feminist responses to Rogerian argument. *Rhetoric Review, 8,* 220-232.

LeFevre, Karen Burke. (1987). *Invention as a social act.* Carbondale, IL: Southern Illinois University Press.

Leki, Ilona. (1992). *Understanding ESL writers.* Portsmouth, NH: Boynton/Cook.

Lightbown, Pasty M., and Nina Spada. (2006). *How languages are learned* (3rd ed.). Oxford: Oxford University Press.

Long, Russell C. (1980). Writer-audience relationships: Analysis or invention? *College Composition and Communication, 31,* 221-226.

Lunsford, Andrea A. (1979). Aristotelian vs. Rogerian argument: A reassessment. *College Composition and Communication, 30,* 146-151.

Lunsford, Andrea. A. (1991). Collaboration, control, and the idea of a writing center. *The Writing Center Journal, 12,* 3-10.

MacDonald, Ross B. (1991). An analysis of verbal interactions in college tutorials. *Journal of Developmental Education, 15,* 2-12.

Moffett, James. (1968). *Teaching the universe of discourse.* Boston: Houghton Mifflin.

Moore, Robert H. (1950). The writing clinic and the writing laboratory. *College English, 11,* 388-393.

Mullin, Joan A., and Ray Wallace. (Eds.). (1994). *Intersections: Theory-practice in the writing center.* Urbana, IL: NCTE.

Murphy, Christina. (1989). Freud and the writing center: The psychoanalytics of tutoring well. *The Writing Center Journal, 10*(1), 13-18.

Murphy, Christina. (1991). Writing centers in context: Responding to new educational theory. In Ray Wallace and Jeanne Simpson (Eds.), *The Writing center: New directions* (pp. 276-88). New York: Garland.

Myers, Sharon. (2003). Remembering the sentence. *College Composition and Communication, 54,* 610-628.

Nelson, Jane, and Kathy Evertz. (Eds.). (2001). *The politics of writing centers.* Portsmouth, NH: Boynton/Cook.

Newton, Fred B. (2000). The new student. *About Campus, November-   December,* 8-15.

Noonan, David. (1989). *Neuro: Life on the frontlines of brain surgery and neurological medicine.* New York: Simon & Schuster.

North, Stephen. (1982). Training tutors to talk about writing. *College Composition and Communication, 33*(4), 434-441.

North, Stephen. (1984). The idea of a writing center. *College English, 46,* 433-446.

North, Stephen. (1994). Revisiting "the idea of a writing center." *The Writing Center Journal, 15*(1), 7-19.

Ong, Walter J., S. J. (1975). The writer's audience is always a fiction. *PMLA, 90*(1), 9-21.

Park, Douglas B. (1982). The meanings of "audience." *College Composition and Communication, 44,* 247-257.

Pennycook, Alastair. (1996). Borrowing others' words: Text, ownership, memory, and plagiarism. *TESOL Quarterly, 30*(2), 201-230.

Perry, William G. (1970). *Forms of intellectual and ethical development in the college years.* New York: Holt, Rinehart & Winston.

Reiff, Mary Jo. (1996). Rereading "invoked" and "addressed" readers through a social lens: Towards a recognition of multiple audiences. *JAC Journal of Composition Theory, 16,* 407-424.

Rogers, Carl R. (1961). *On becoming a person.* Boston: Houghton Mifflin.

Rose, Mike. (1984). *Writer's block: The cognitive dimension.* Carbondale, IL: Southern Illinois University Press.

Rose, Mike. (1985). Complexity, rigor, evolving method, and the puzzle of writer's block: Thoughts on composing-process research. In Mike Rose (Ed.), *When a writer can't write: Studies in writer's black and other composing-process problems* (pp. 227-260). New York: Guilford.

Schroeder, Christopher. (1997). Knowledge and power, logic and rhetoric, and other reflections in the Toulmin mirror: A critical consideration of Stephen

Toulmin's contributions to composition. *Journal of Advanced Composition, 17*, 95–107.

Selfe, Cynthia. (1985). An apprehensive writer composes. In Mike Rose (Ed.), *When a writer can't write: Studies in writer's black and other composing-process problems* (pp. 83-95). New York: Guilford.

Severino, Carol. (1994). Inadvertently and intentionally poetic ESL writing. *Journal of Basic Writing, 13*(2), 18-32.

Shamoon, Linda K., and Deborah H. Burns. (1995). A critique of pure tutoring. *The Writing Center Journal, 15(*2), 134-151.

Shaughnessy, Mina P. (1977). *Errors and expectations: A guide for the teacher of basic writing.* New York: Oxford University Press.

Sheridan, Marion C. (1926). An evaluation of the Dalton Plan. *English Journal, 15*(7), 507-514.

Spack, Ruth. (1984). Invention strategies and the ESL college composition student. *TESOL Quarterly, 18*(4), 649-670.

Strong, William. (1985). How sentence-combining works. In Donald A. Daiker, Andrew Kerek, and Max Morenberg (Eds.), *Sentence combining: A rhetorical perspective* (pp. 334-350). Carbondale, IL: Southern Illinois University Press.

Toulmin, Stephen. (1958). *The uses of argument.* New York: Cambridge University Press.

Truss, Lynne. (2003). *Eats, shoots and leaves: The zero tolerance approach to punctuation,* New York: Gotham.

Walker, Carolyn P., and David Elias. (1987). Writing conference talk: Factors associated with high- and low-rated writing conferences. *Research in the Teaching of English, 21*, 266-285.

Wall, Susan V., and Glynda A. Hull. (1989). The semantics of error: What do teachers know? In Chris M. Anson (Ed.), *Writing and response: Theory, practice, and research* (pp. 261-292). Urbana, IL: NCTE.

Williams, Joseph M. (1981). The phenomenology of error. *College Composition and Communication, 32*(2), 152-168.

Wordsworth, William. (1967). Preface to the *Lyrical Ballads*. In Russell Noyes (Ed.), *English Romantic poetry and prose* (pp. 357-367). New York: Oxford University Press. (Original work published 1800).

Young, Richard E., Alton L. Becker, and Kenneth L. Pike. (1970). *Rhetoric: Discovery and change*. New York: Harcourt.

Yule, George. (1998). *Explaining English grammar*. New York: Oxford University Press.